Managing Business and
Service Networks

NETWORK AND SYSTEMS MANAGEMENT

Series Editor: Manu Malek
Lucent Technologies, Bell Laboratories
Holmdel, New Jersey

ACTIVE NETWORKS AND ACTIVE NETWORK
MANAGEMENT: A Proactive Management Framework

Stephen F. Bush and Amit B. Kulkarni

BASIC CONCEPTS FOR MANAGING
TELECOMMUNICATIONS NETWORKS: Copper to Sand to
Glass to Air

Lawrence Bernstein and C. M. Yuhas

COOPERATIVE MANAGEMENT OF ENTERPRISE NETWORKS

Pradeep Ray

MANAGING BUSINESS AND SERVICE NETWORKS

Lundy Lewis

A Continuation Order Plan is available for this series. A continuation order will bring delivery of each new volume immediately upon publication. Volumes are billed only upon actual shipment. For further information please contact the publisher.

Managing Business and Service Networks

Lundy Lewis

KLUWER ACADEMIC/PLENUM PUBLISHERS
New York, Boston, Dordrecht, London, Moscow

Library of Congress Cataloging-in-Publication Data

Lewis, Lundy.
    Managing business and service networks/Lundy Lewis.
        p.   cm.—(Network and systems management)
    Includes bibliographical references and index.
    ISBN 0-306-46559-0
        1. Business networks—Management.   2. Business enterprises—Computer networks.   3.
    Information technology—Management.   4. Computer networks—Management.   I. Title.   II.
    Kluwer Academic/Plenum Publishers network and systems management

    HD69.S8 L495 2001
    658'.0546—dc21

                                                                                    2001022507

ISBN 0-306-46559-0

©2001 Kluwer Academic/Plenum Publishers, New York
233 Spring Street, New York, N.Y. 10013

http://www.wkap.nl/

10   9   8   7   6   5   4   3   2   1

A C.I.P. record for this book is available from the Library of Congress

Printed in the United States of America

For Mom and Dad

Preface

Most everything in our experience requires management in some form or other: our gardens, our automobiles, our minds, our bodies, our love lives, our businesses, our forests, our countries, etc.

Sometimes we don't call it "management" per se. We seldom talk about managing our minds or automobiles. But if we think of management in terms of monitoring, maintaining, and cultivating with respect to some goal, then it makes sense. We certainly monitor an automobile, albeit unconsciously, to make sure that it doesn't exhibit signs of trouble. And we certainly try to cultivate our minds.

This book is about managing networks. That itself is not a new concept. We've been managing the networks that support our telephones for about 100 years, and we've been managing the networks that support our computers for about 20 years.

What *is* new (and what motivated me to write this book) is the following: (i) the enormous advancements in networking technology as we transition from the 20th century to the 21st century, (ii) the increasing dependence of human activities on networking technology, and (iii) the commercialization of services that depend on networking technology (e.g., email and electronic commerce).

A multi-wave optical network is an example of new networking technology for the 21st century. Imagine that you drop a pebble into the edge of a still pool of water and observe the successive waves as they reach the other side. Now imagine that you drop 10 pebbles along the edge of the pool and observe 10 sets of successive crisscrossed waves as they reach the other side. The latter experiment is analogous to multi-wave optical networking, and it affords a tremendous increase in the speed and bulk of the transmission of information.

Now, much in the same way that a garden might become puny if it isn't properly attended to, a network will get puny if it isn't properly managed. And as a garden flourishing in the spring needs extra special attention, networks in the 21st century require extra special management considerations, e.g. managing diverse kinds of interconnected networks in a sort of holistic style, managing the stress placed on networks by increased usage, and plain old monitoring, maintenance, and cultivation. It isn't easy.

That's what this book is about. We discuss good principles and practices in network management, we examine three contemporary case studies, and we prescribe methods and studies for managing 21st century networks.

To the Reader

The book is suitable for several types of readers: network operators, business executives, students, college instructors, developers of networking technology, and researchers and scientists.

Each chapter is followed by a set of exercises and discussion questions. Some questions are intended to induce analytical thinking and speculation, i.e. they don't have clear answers. Others are research questions, i.e. their answers exist but the reader has to delve into the literature to find them. Finally, others are hands-on exercises that require a network, a lab, and a suite of network management tools.

The casual reader may find it useful to simply skim through the exercises. The instructor will probably want to select certain exercises as homework assignments or the basis for a course project.

The hands-on exercises are supported by a popular network management system named Spectrum, offered by Aprisma Management Technologies in the USA. Instructors and researchers are invited to obtain a copy of Spectrum to support those exercises. Qualifications and instructions for doing so are provided in the next section.

Acknowledgements

First acknowledgement goes to Dorothy Minior. She was the first reader of each chapter as the manuscript unfolded. She made sure that the logic and articulation of the concepts in the chapters were in good shape. Thanks Dottie. Thanks for everything.

Several people reviewed the first draft of the manuscript before I sent it to the publisher for an official review. They are Alex Clemm (Cisco Systems), Manu Malek (Lucent Technologies), and Utpal Datta (Nortel Networks). Teresa Cleary, Mahesh Bhatia, Eric Stinson, and Russell Arrowsmith (all at Aprisma Management Technologies) and David St. Onge (Enterprise Management Associates) also reviewed the first draft of the manuscript. All of them gave me useful comments and criticisms that unquestionably improved the book.

Special thanks go to Russell Arrowsmith for making one last pass over the final manuscript. Besides being a first-rate computer scientist, Russ is quite meticulous about grammar and semantics.

There are several other people at Aprisma who helped me find companies for the case study chapters and generally offered encouragement and support while I was writing the book. They are Michael Skubisz, Katrinka McCallum, Chris Crowell, Ted Hebert, Darren Orzechowski, Ed Preston, and Lara Willard. It is rather hard writing a book, but these people helped me to keep going. Thanks to all of you.

I spent a good amount of time working with individuals at the companies represented in the three case study chapters, and I give them a big round of appreciation for their help. They are Frank Toth and Tony Gillespie (Camp LeJeune Marine Corps); Bruce Dyke and Chris Oliver (Vitts Networks); and Chris Caswell and Mark Johnson (North Carolina Network Initiative).

Parts of Chapter 2 were adapted from my previous book. I thank Artech House for giving me permission to use some of that material.

At Kluwer Academic/Plenum Publishers, I thank Tom Cohn, Anna Bozicevic, and Brian Halm. The official reviewers greatly improved the content of the book. Thank you all: Salah Aidarous (NEC America), Gopal Iyengar (Nortel Technologies), Jong-Tae Park (Kyungpook National University, Korea), Reza Peyrovian (AT&T), and Rene Wies (BMW Group).

Finally, I promised to mention the names of my siblings somewhere in the book, and this is probably the best place. I adore my siblings; they are Donna Day, Steve Lewis, and Joey Lewis. While I'm at it, I should mention my Mother and Father: Gladys Lewis and Lundy Lewis. I adore them too.

Getting a Spectrum Academic License

Aprisma Management Technologies offers copies of the Spectrum Management System to support this book and also to support education and research.

There are two kinds of Spectrum licenses that one may obtain towards these ends:

- Spectrum Academic License – intended for college instructors who wish to use Spectrum as a vehicle for teaching, research, or to support their students' graduate projects.

- Spectrum Research License – intended for industry research labs who wish to extend Spectrum into new spaces in collaboration with Aprisma's research department.

The primary qualification for obtaining a Spectrum Academic or Research License is that it not be used for commercial or production purposes.

In addition, Aprisma offers a University Fellowship Program whereby professors and students are given annual stipends to perform innovative research in network management. The Spectrum Academic License is included in the stipend.

Finally, Aprisma offers a cooperative development program in which students integrate part-time work with their normal university studies.

The case study in Chapter 6 is a good example of issuing both academic and research licenses for a project on managing next generation GigaPoP networks. The reader may wish to look over that chapter before making a decision to commit to an agreement with Aprisma.

For further information on these opportunities, the reader should visit Aprisma's web site at www.aprisma.com.

Contents

Part I
Introduction to
Network Management

We begin our book by laying the necessary groundwork for understanding the scope of network management, including discussions on building management systems for different kinds of networks, integrating disparate management systems into a unified whole, and operating disparate networks with a single management system.

The three chapters in Part I discuss the following topics:

* Introduction to the Management of Business and Service Networks
* Architecture and Design of Integrated Management Systems
* Introduction to the Spectrum Management System

Chapter 1 is foundational. The goals of Chapter 1 are (i) to understand the differences between *business* networks and *service provider* networks and (ii) to understand the myriad tasks involved in managing each type of network. The chapter is complemented by a discussion of the evolution of network management in both the data communications space and the telecommunications space. In addition, we discuss existing and emerging standards in network management.

Chapter 2 is likewise foundational. First we look at realistic business requirements for network management. We argue that the rollout of a network management system is much like the rollout of a software system, starting with business requirements, and then moving to analysis, design, implementation, and testing, and then moving back around to re-visit business requirements. Thus we describe the process of software development in general, including common risks to be on guard against and common tactics to mitigate such risks. Finally, we look at common patterns of integrated management in which multiple management systems are combined into a single whole to meet business requirements.

Chapter 3 begins adding substance to the foundational material in Chapters 1 and 2. We describe a classic network management system in the industry: the Spectrum Management System developed by Aprisma Management Technologies in the USA. We discuss the history of Spectrum, showing how it started life as a management system for business enterprise networks in 1990 and matured into a management system for service provider networks in 2000. We show how Spectrum is grounded in object-oriented concepts and we compare its event correlation mechanism with other event correlation mechanisms in the industry.

1 Introduction to the Management of Business and Service Networks

In this first chapter we cover the following topics:

- What are Business and Service Networks?
- What is Network Management?
- What is Integrated Network Management?
- The Evolution of Network Management
- A Guide to Standards in Network Management
- Agenda for the Rest of the Book

First we wish to understand the differences between business networks and service networks (sometimes called enterprise networks and service provider networks). While there is a fair amount of commonality between them, there are special considerations that require alternative management techniques. We will look at examples of each kind of network, including the network of a business enterprise and various examples of networks maintained by service providers in order to support electronic commerce, cable modems, the home, and the office.

Next, we introduce the concepts "network management" and "integrated network management." These terms refer to the monitoring, control, and provisioning of networks with the purpose of keeping them healthy and operational. Consider that other objects in our experience such as the human body, automobiles, assembly lines, and human organizations require monitoring and control to render them healthy and operational throughout their lifetimes. The same is true of networks, and thus network management is an indispensable part of networking and communications in general.

Following this, we look at the history and evolution of network management. First we consider the evolution of the management of data networks, which have been with us for about 25 years. Then we look at the evolution of the management of telecommunications networks, which have been with us for about 100 years. Currently these two domains are beginning to converge, and there is healthy cross-pollination of management methods and techniques in the data and telecommunications communities. The history takes us up to the early 2000s. The story is logical and interesting, and it is

3

important for the reader to understand how we got to where we are and where we're headed.

Next we describe work on the development of network management standards. This work has taken us a long way towards imposing a conceptual structure on the complexity of network management. Thus, it is to our advantage to understand the major themes involved in the standards bodies.

Finally, we describe our agenda for the rest of the book. The first goal of the book is to instill in the reader the necessary conceptual apparatus by which to approach network management challenges. A second goal is to work through some case studies and exercises with a contemporary network management system. A third goal of the book is to uncover areas in network management that are in need of further work and research as we face challenges in networking and network management in the 21st century.

1.1 What are Business and Service Networks?

Consider the following sequence of definitions:

- A *network* is broadly defined as collections of devices and circuits that provide a means for transferring data from one end device to another (e.g. from computer to computer, or from telephone to telephone), where such data transfer is the basis for applications such as telephony, email, video conferencing, manufacturing, inventory, billing, and accounting systems.

- A *business network* is owned by the business enterprise, where the scope of the network is to support the informational and operational requirements of the business such as marketing, sales, accounting, and manufacturing departments, but where the function of the business is to provide some useful commodity for sale to public or private sectors, for example automobiles, pharmaceuticals, and other artifacts.

- A *service network* is owned or leased by a service provider, where the scope of the network is to support communication services for resale to businesses, private end users, and other service providers (e.g. electronic commerce, Internet access, cable modems for the home, banking, tele-medicine, and distance learning), and where the function of a service provider is to provide specialized networking infrastructure, computer systems, business applications, and management methods to support the services.

Thus, the primary difference between business and service networks hinges upon ownership, scope, and function. The scope of a business network is relatively broad because it supports the operation of the business, but the primary function of the business is not to support the network per se. In contrast, the scope of a service network is relatively narrow, and the function of the service provider is to deploy and maintain the network within this narrow scope.

A good example that illustrates the difference between business and service networks is the provision of a web site for electronic commerce. A business might elect to place its web site on a server in its private network. The server and web site become part of a larger business network that additionally supports inventory, accounting, and various other kinds of systems for the sake of the business. That is a business network.

Companies such as Genuity and DIGEX in the USA have networks that host web server farms. The function of these networks is to host servers on which other businesses can place their web sites. We can imagine a large room that contains stacks of networked UNIX and NT servers whose sole purpose is to provide secure web sites that are accessible to consumers around the globe. This is a good example of a service network. Genuity and DIGEX offer a service, web hosting, via their service networks.

On first sight, the distinction might not seem so important. One might be inclined to collapse the two definitions into one, arguing that the business enterprise is in fact a service provider for itself. However, that would be a mistake. There are differences between service and business networks that call for emphasis on different management techniques.

To make this point clear, consider a simple, down-to-earth analogy. If you choose to paint your house (even though you are a not a painter by trade), then inevitable glitches in the paint job are OK. You can live with it. But if you're paying a professional painter to paint the house, then glitches are unacceptable. The glitches call for reparation in some form or other. In sum, the way in which you manage your performance is quite different than the way you manage the professional's performance.

In the same sprit, consider service providers who offer service bundles to the public. It is clear that provisioning, accounting, billing, contractual agreements, and reparation with clients play an important role. But these issues are not as important for businesses that maintain their own networks. Typically, the business wants to know the extent to which departments are utilizing network resources; but contracts and exact billing and accounting are not so important. The business can live with approximations.

Our distinction between business and service networks is useful for the sake of conceptual clarity. Other distinctions are arguable (e.g. enterprise/telecom or data/voice). In practice the distinction might become somewhat blurred. For example, a business might choose to outsource part of its network operation to service providers, but choose to keep other parts under its control. A typical scenario is a business which maintains its network infrastructure and computer systems, but depends upon service provider X for Internet access, service provider Y for maintenance of its web sites for electronic commerce, and service provider Z for specialized applications such as video conferencing.

The goal of this book is to understand the special management requirements for different kinds of networks and the range of services that they support. We hope to instill in the reader known, tried-and-true techniques, and also to provide the conceptual apparatus, experience, and tools by which to approach new kinds of management challenges with confidence. As niches for network usage increase, we can expect challenges in network management to increase proportionally.

1.2 What is Network Management?

A working definition of network management in the early 1990's was this:

> *Network management* is the practice of (i) monitoring and controlling an existing network (i.e. a collection of interconnected routers, hubs, and bridges) so that that the network stays up and running and meets the expectations of network users, (ii) planning for network extensions and modifications in order to meet increasing demands on network operations, and (iii) gracefully incorporating new elements into a network without interfering with existing operations.

This definition is not quite adequate for the 2000's. We tend to say these days that there is more to network management than "network management." To see this, let us offer a new picture of "the network." See Figure 1.1.

First, there is the network infrastructure, by which we mean the *transmission devices* that receive traffic from, and forward traffic to, other transmission devices. Examples of such devices are routers, hubs, switches, access devices for wireless networks, cable modems, and satellite stations.

Second, there are the *transmission media* over which traffic flows. Examples of such media are copper wire, coaxial cable, fiber-optic cable, telephone lines, and airwaves.

Third, there are the *computer systems* that reside on a network, for example desktop computers, workstations, mainframe computers, and laptop computers. We should also include plain old telephones in this category, although many of them aren't composed of computer chips.

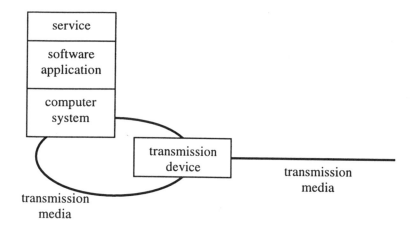

Figure 1.1 The Generic Components of a Network

Fourth, there are the *software applications* that run on the computers, for example document writing applications, database applications, and scientific applications that support mathematical computation and simulations. Note that distributed applications span multiple computer systems that may be distributed over separate networks.

Fifth, and finally, there are various *services* that are supported by software applications. The concept of a service is a recent advancement in our understanding of networking technology. A service is an abstraction, or epi-phenomenon, that arises in virtue of the structure and operation of transmission devices, transmission media, computer systems, and applications. Examples of services are electronic commerce, inter-continental email, and distance learning.

As an aside, we should point out that the term "service" is quite slippery. Some people think of "service" in terms of bandwidth offered by transmission devices and transmission media, while other people think of "service" in terms of how businesses employ distributed applications towards some business goal. The former is network-centric, while the latter is business-centric. Clearly, we are taking the business-centric perspective.

As a further aside, it is interesting to note that some people argue that the human user is a generic component of a network. And if we accept that, we should say also that a business is a component of a network, and perhaps further that a society is part of a network. Those are not such outlandish ideas if we consider that a healthy operation of a network depends upon end users who are trained to use software applications correctly.

This is what we mean when we say that there is more to network management than "network management," i.e. there is more to network management than managing transmission devices, transmission media, and bandwidth. We can modify our definition of network management in the beginning of the section by replacing the term "network" with "transmission device, transmission medium, computer system, software application, and service," although our definition would tend to get a bit sloppy. Nonetheless, this is the notion that we wish to capture in this book, and this leads us straight into the concept of integrated network management.

1.3 What is Integrated Network Management?

If one were to ask the question 'What is Integrated Network Management?' to several network professionals in academia and industry, one would likely get several kinds of answers. That is OK. In this section we describe several senses of the phrase "integrated network management," all of which combine to give us an appreciation of its complexity.

First, there is the sense that we left hanging in the preceding section. That is, network management does not mean management of networking hardware alone. In addition, it means the management of traffic that flows over transmission media, computer systems that reside on the network, software applications that reside on the computer systems, and the services that the applications support.

Second, there is the sense that is described by the acronym FCAPS (fault, configuration, accounting, performance, and security management). FCAPS is the classic model of network management defined by the International Standards Organization, showing the decomposition of network management into five functional areas. The FCAPS model was intended originally for the management of networks. But now, along with our first sense of integrated network management, we see that that the five functional elements of FCAPS also apply to each generic component of a network as well.

Third, there is the sense of integrated management that is described by the Telecommunications Management Network (TMN) model, offered by the International Telecommunications Union. The TMN model considers integrated network management as a three-dimensional space: (i) the partition of management functions into FCAPS as described above, (ii) the partition of network management into layers of abstraction, and (iii) the physical specification by which multiple management systems communicate with each other.

Consider the second dimension: the layers of abstraction. The lowest layer of the abstraction hierarchy consists of "raw" network components (i.e. transmission devices). The second layer looks at individual management techniques for each component (sometimes called element or device management). The third layer considers interdependencies between components, e.g. end-to-end connectivity and flow of traffic over multiple devices. The fourth layer considers management in terms of services that are supported by groups of components, and the fifth layer considers the business processes that are supported by groups of services. We will look at the TMN model more closely in Section 1.5.

Fourth, there is the sense of integrated network management that has resulted from the advent of service providers in the late 1990's and the 2000's. In Section 1.1 we described a typical scenario in which a business elects to maintain its own network infrastructure and computer systems, but depends upon service provider X for Internet access, service provider Y for maintenance of its web sites for electronic commerce, and service provider Z for specialized applications such as video conferencing. Thus, each part of the network is managed by separate parties, and the task is to integrate these separate management responsibilities as if it were a unified whole.

Finally, there is a sense of integrated network management that has resulted from current efforts in integrating services provided by data networks and telecommunications networks. As an extreme example, a proposal for video conferencing is to transmit images over data networks and transmit the voice that goes with images over standard telephone networks. The problem, then, is to synchronize voice and images so that they coincide correctly, and this calls for integrated management of both domains.

Table 1.1 summarizes the different senses of integrated network management. The phrase "integrated network management" is multi-dimensional and multi-faceted. The reader should not be overwhelmed by that observation; rather we wish the reader to be strengthened by an appreciation of the challenges and complexity in managing today's networks and the services they provide.

Table 1.1 Dimensions of Integrated Network Management

Generic components	devices, media, computers, applications, services
Functional areas	fault, configuration, accounting, performance, security
Layers of abstraction	element, network, service, business management
Service networks	network 1, network 2, ... , network n
Voice/data networks	network 1, network 2, ... , network n

1.4 The Evolution of Network Management

Before we begin our story on the evolution of network management, the reader should understand that in the year 2000 the Chief Information Officer (CIO) of a company typically had two separate sub-domains for which to be responsible: the telecommunications domain and the data communications domain.

The telecommunications domain covers services provided by voice networks, and has been with us for about 100 years. The data communications domain covers services provided by data communications networks and the Internet, and has been with us for about 25 years.

Now, with ongoing efforts towards the convergence of voice networks and data networks, that kind of organizational structure is in the midst of change. The two domains can no longer be clearly separated, and that will likely cause headaches for next generation CIOs. It is common practice to transport voice signals over data networks, and also to transport data over voice networks. For example, home computers connect to data networks via modems connected to telephone networks.

USA society has grown accustomed to the high quality of service provided by "Ma Bell." Therefore, as data services begin to interleave with telephone services, people will expect the same quality of service. For example, people will expect a "web tone" when they turn on their computers in the same way that they expect a "dial tone" whenever they pick up a telephone receiver.

It is a well acknowledged fact in the industry that data networks will eventually incorporate all the services offered by the telecom voice networks. Accordingly, service providers are taking steps to migrate their voice networks to data networks.

This section is divided into three parts. First, we discuss the evolution of data communications network management. Second, we discuss the evolution of telecommunications network management. And finally, we discuss the convergence of data and telecommunications networks.

1.4.1 The Evolution of Management Methods for Data Communications Networks

In the 1970's, computer scientists were just beginning to connect computers together via routers and copper wire. To configure a router to behave properly, one had to carry a dumb terminal to the router, plug it into a port on the router, and set configuration variables via a specialized text-based language designed specifically for the router.

That way of doing network management carried us up to the mid-1980's, at which time it was realized that the terminal could reside on the network. Thus one could "mount" the router, or send remote messages to the router in order to configure it.

At about the same time, graphical user interfaces were beginning to replace text-based user interfaces. Thus, one could build a software application that showed an icon that represented the router. The icon could be selected, whereupon a menu showed the operations that could be performed on the router.

By 1990, commercial vendors were beginning to develop network management applications that showed graphical icons representing all the routers, hubs, and bridges involved in one's network. The main products in this space at the turn of the 90's decade were Cabletron's Spectrum, Hewlett Packard's OpenView, IBM's Netview, and Sun's SunNet Manager.

By 1991, traffic management applications had entered the picture. It turned out to be not a hard thing to develop software applications that could read the headers of the packets that flowed through a computer or router without slowing down the transmission of the packet. The packet header contained useful information such as the source of the packet, the destination, the protocol, and the size of the packet. By collecting this information in a table, and with the advancement of computer graphics, software could construct pictures that showed connectivity between computers and the degree of communication among computers per protocol, by line width or line coloring. Good examples in the early 1990's were Silicon Graphics NetVisualizer and Sun's Etherfind.

Thus, in the early 1990's network management and traffic management were well on their way towards commercial viability. However, people began to realize that there was more to network management than that.

By 1992, vendors began to develop software applications that could monitor and control the computer systems that reside on a network. These applications focused on computer system variables such as failed and successful logon attempts, uptime and downtime, CPU usage, disk partition size, and the duration, size, and type of programs that ran on computer systems. The early players in the computer systems management space were Tivoli's TME, Computer Associates' UniCenter, and Calypso's MeistroVision.

By 1994, people began to realize that there is yet more to the story. In addition to computer systems, there exist the software applications that run on the computers. Thus vendors began to build application management systems that monitor and control application variables such as uptime and downtime, CPU usage per application, and the number and duration of client/server connections for distributed applications. An early player in the application management space was BMC's Patrol.

By 1996, an interesting thing had happened to network management. Up until 1996, vendors specialized in network, traffic, computer system, or application management. However, a vendor who specialized in one area of management was criticized by consumers and analysts because the solution was incomplete. As a result, three things happened: (i) Two new terms came into being "enterprise management" and "end-to-end management," (ii) vendors began to concentrate on integrating their products with other products in order to have a complete end-to-end solution for the enterprise, and consequently (iii) vendors introduced Partner Programs.

In 1998, the market changed significantly with the advent of outsourcing network management functions to service providers. Before 1998, networks and the applications that ran on them were owned and maintained primarily by individual businesses. But the effort of managing a network enterprise began to distract the business from its primary goals and functions. Thus, entrepreneurs saw an opportunity to provide specialized services for businesses. Service providers could alleviate the distraction problem by contracting with businesses to do the networking and management work, thereby allowing businesses to concentrate on their special areas of expertise.

Table 1.2 shows how our history of network management in the data communications space is shaping up.

Table 1.2 History of Data Communications Network Management

1975	Device management
1990	Network management
1991	Traffic management
1992	Computer system management
1994	Application management
1996	Enterprise management = network + traffic + computer + application management
1998	Enterprise management = network + traffic + computer + application + service management
2000	Enterprise management = network + traffic + computer + application + service + response time management

To be fair, we should point out that the timeline in Table 1.2 is quite IP-centric and doesn't include the long history of Systems Network Architecture (SNA) networks, developed by IBM in 1974 for IBM mainframe computers. Much of what occurs in the table's timeline in the 1990s was a reality for SNA networks during the 1970s. Before the advent of IP networks, SNA networks were perhaps the most important data networks around. In fact, the concept of service providers for SNA data networks existed back in the 70s.

In the IP world, the change in the marketplace in 1998 led to the introduction of service level agreements (SLAs). Since we now have commercial providers and consumers of networking technology, we also must have contracts between providers and consumers, called SLAs.

SLAs are binding documents that describe the services offered by providers, how the services will be monitored and measured, and the conditions under which the consumer will be billed when services are met or violated. The definition, monitoring, and control of SLAs generally fall under the heading Service Level Management (SLM).

With SLM, however, there arose the problem of how to measure the health of a service. One way to do that is to identify the transmission devices, transmission media, computer systems, and applications upon which a service depends. If that is possible, then one can infer the health of a service by aggregating the healths of the components that render the service possible.

A complementary way to measure the performance of a service is to measure transactional response time. If the service involves a client/server database application, then one can issue periodic artificial transactions to monitor service performance. In similar fashion, response time measurements also apply to ordinary e-mail transactions and e-commerce transactions. By 2000 response time management became an important ingredient in SLM and enterprise management in general.

Interestingly, there is yet more to the story of network management. Thus far we have described the evolution of data communications management. But coincident with that, there has been an important evolution in telecommunications management as well, which we discuss next.

1.4.2 The Evolution of Management Methods for Telecommunications Networks

Our history of telecommunications network management would start properly with Alexander Graham Bell's invention in 1876. However we will cheat just a little and enter its history during the mid-1970's, at about the same time that data networks were getting off the ground. First, consider the architecture of a telephone network circa 1970. See Figure 1.2.

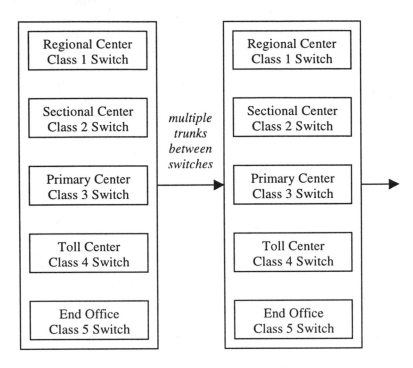

Figure 1.2 Telephone Network Architecture

The generic components of a telephone network are switches and trunks. There are five levels of switches, based loosely on geographical coverage. The Class 5 End Office switch is closest to the subscriber, and it is initially contacted when one makes a phone call from one's home. The Class 4 Toll Center Switch is contacted by a Class 5 switch if the call is not local. The Class 3, Class 2, and Class 1 switches represent primary, sectional, and regional geographic areas respectively, and they can be contacted by equal or lower-level switches depending on traffic demand.

In addition, a telephone network consists of various types of trunks that connect the five levels of switches. If we adhere to the terminology introduced in Section 1.2, we can think of switches as transmission devices, and trunks as transmission media.

Now, given a collection of such switches and trunks, it is easy to imagine a large number of possible routes from a source call to a destination call. Thus, network management in the 1970's meant the monitoring of traffic over trunks and switches and possibly setting up alternative routes or reallocating resources in order to support changing traffic demands. For example, it is well known that a local call might travel a longer distance or travel a more circuitous alternate path if local traffic is congested, without loss of voice clarity.

The management techniques of telecommunications networks from the 1970's to the mid-1990's consisted primarily of monitoring traffic demands, setting up telephone connections accordingly, and correct billing. Thus we see the primary differences between classic telecommunications management and classic data communications management: the former was provisioning/billing-centric with little emphasis on network management, while the latter was network-centric with little emphasis on provisioning and billing. However, that distinction is disappearing in the 2000s. Service provisioning and billing is currently a hot topic in both domains.

The classic telecommunications management functions were achieved largely by developing proprietary communication protocols and management tools. Although the divestiture of the Bell System in 1984 forced the definition of some interface standards among Regional Bell Operating Companies (RBOCs), the networks and management systems were, for all practical purposes, closed systems. However, that introduced the problem of monopoly without competition, which is generally considered a bad thing.

The face of telecommunications network management changed in the mid-1990's when large telephone companies became legally obligated to open up their networks to others as a result of the Telecommunications Act of 1996. That meant that telephone companies had to offer their services to competitors, which in turn meant that they had to publish equipment interfaces at well-defined reference points. Thus, an entrepreneur now had the opportunity of leasing the bandwidth of independent telephone networks in order to provide special services to consumers. In short, the landscape of telecommunications shifted from closed systems to open systems.

It is easy to see, then, that the old way of telecommunications network management was compromised. Since telecommunications networks were opened, there arose the problem of managing two or more separate telecommunications domains because the switches, trunks, communications protocols, and management techniques were largely incompatible.

Fortunately these problems were anticipated. Around 1990 there had begun work on standardization of telecommunication protocols and management methods. This work is still in progress. The main model in the effort is the Telecommunications Management Network (TMN), which we mentioned in Section 1.3.

Note the switch in terms between "telecommunications network management" and "telecommunications management network." TMN implies that management is conceived as a network of integrated sub-management systems, where subsystems exchange information for the sake of keeping the production network healthy and operational (for example via the Transaction Language 1 (TL1) protocol). We will look at the TMN model and other standards a bit more closely in Section 1.5.

Table 1.3 summarizes the history of telecommunications network management.

Table 1.3 History of Telecommunications Network Management

1975	Closed networks with proprietary management methods
1990	Standardization work in anticipation of open systems
1996	Open systems, service providers begin to emerge
2000	Standards begin to be applied in the field

However, it was not anticipated that data and telecom networks would begin to interleave, or that data would evolve such that it could begin to accommodate services provided by traditional telecom networks. That adds additional complexity to the problem of integrated management.

1.4.3 The Evolution of Management Methods for Integrated Data and Telecommunications Networks

This section is rather easy to write because the management of integrated data and telecommunications networks is in its infancy. Some good news is that there is a healthy cross-pollination of management methods between the data and telecommunications communities.

Many of the concepts and methods in the TMN model are carrying over to the data network. A good example is the simple notion of a management network and the notion of layers of abstraction between network objects and business processes. The reverse is also true. A good example is the trend to manage telephone switches via the Simple Network Management Protocol (SNMP, see Section 1.5).

Figure 1.3 shows a data service and a voice service d, v (say email and ordinary telephony) that simultaneously traverse a telecommunications network and a data network. Suppose the telecommunications network is managed by a service provider with system A and the data network is managed by a service provider with system B. Assume that systems A and B incorporate diverse management methods and techniques.

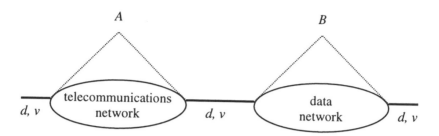

Figure 1.3 Services d, v Traversing Telecommunications and Data Networks

At least two problems arise in this kind of situation. First, the overall view of quality of service (QoS) of d,v from one end to the other is hard to achieve. A might have a narrow definition of QoS with respect to the telecommunications network, while B might have a different definition with respect to the data network. At the writing of this book, researchers are in the midst of trying to figure out how to translate QoS definitions across different network technologies, thereby achieving an overall, integrated view of QoS for d, v type services.

Second, consider d, v type services from the user's point of view. Whom does the user call when his service is degraded? The immediate answer is that he calls his service provider; he isn't aware that two networks influence his QoS. But that raises an obvious problem: the cause of poor QoS might not lie in his service provider's domain. Therefore, the important question is whether the management methods of A and B are integrated in some fashion.

Consider the following: Figure 1.4 shows a higher-level service provider with system C whose scope encompasses both A and B. But let us ask: What is the nature of C?

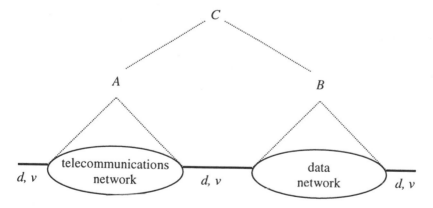

Figure 1.4 A Higher-Level Management System C

C's responsibility is to monitor both network domains and correlate management information from each. Logically, there are three ways that can happen. Figure 1.5 shows three possible scenarios: (i) C collects select management information from A and B, (ii) C is actually A, where B forwards select information to A, and (iii) C is actually B, where A forwards select information to B.

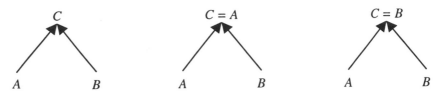

Figure 1.5 Three Approaches to Integration of Disparate Management Systems

With the first approach, the sole job of C is to correlate select information from A and B. But with the latter two approaches, the primary management system has to perform its usual duties of monitoring and controlling its particular domain, and additionally correlate information that issues from its peer management system.

Each approach is a reasonable way to look at things. But there are hidden issues that cause headaches. It is likely that the syntax and semantics of messages that issue from each management system are incommensurable. With either approach one has to worry about message parsing and working out ambiguities and vagueness in terms. That is much like an English speaker and a Portuguese speaker trying to carry on an intelligent conversation.

An obvious solution to this problem comes to mind. Simply: Let's set down a standard that all systems must adhere to. Then the problem goes away. That is the ultimate goal of standards bodies. The Common Information Model (CIM) is a good example of such a solution. However, there are problems there as well, including problems having to do with politics and the continual evolution of networking hardware in both domains.

Nonetheless, there has been good progress in the standards bodies, and that combined with the "necessity of invention" in the field renders it possible to design and implement reasonably good integrated network management solutions today. That is what our case studies are about.

1.5 A Guide to Standards in Network Management

Today's business and service networks are complex. The current state of any particular network more than likely evolved piecemeal and thus includes heterogeneous kinds of components from multiple vendors and various kinds of management techniques. To make matters worse, management techniques vary over countries and in districts within countries.

In a few cases this state of affairs has resulted in a management nightmare. In other cases the result is piecemeal management, in which narrowly focused management solutions co-exist but do not cooperate with each other. The best case, however, is integrated management, in which these management techniques cooperate in a standardized enterprise management scheme.

The ultimate goal of international standards bodies is to provide a uniform framework and methodology for network management practices, including organizational structure, management functions, communication mechanisms, and information models. We present a short guide to standards work in integrated management below. The exposition is logical, rather than chronological. It shows how the various standards are interrelated. See the Further Studies section at the end of the chapter for more detail.

1.5.1 FCAPS

We mentioned FCAPS in Section 1.3 as the second sense of the phrase "integrated network management." FCAPS is considered the "traditional" decomposition of network management into interdependent functional areas.

- *Fault management* includes trouble management, which looks after corrective actions for service, fault recovery, and proactive maintenance and provides capabilities for self-healing. Trouble management correlates alarms to services and resources, initiates tests, performs diagnostics to isolate faults to a replaceable component, triggers service restoral, and performs activities necessary to repair the diagnosed fault. Proactive maintenance responds to near-fault conditions that degrade system reliability and may eventually result in an impact on services. It performs routine maintenance activities on a scheduled basis and initiates tests to detect or correct problems before service troubles are reported.

- *Configuration management* includes timely deployment of resources to satisfy the expected service demands, and the assignment of services and features to end-users. It identifies, exercises control over, collects data from, and provides data to the network for the purpose of preparing for, initializing, starting, and providing for the operation and termination of services. It deals with logical, service, or custom networks such as the toll network, local public switched telephone network, and private networks.

- *Accounting management* processes and manipulates service and resource utilization records and generates customer billing reports for services rendered. It establishes charges and identifies costs for the use of services and resources in the network.

- *Performance management* addresses processes that ensure the most efficient utilization of network resources and their ability to meet user service-level objectives. It evaluates and reports on the behavior of network resources and ensures the peak performance and delivery of each voice, data, or video service.

- *Security management* controls access to and protects both the network and network management systems against intentional or accidental abuse, unauthorized access, and communication loss. Flexibility methods are built into security mechanisms to accommodate ranges and inquiry privileges that result from the variety of access modes by operations systems, service provider groups, and customers.

FCAPS has evolved considerably during the 90's decade, although the major themes remained intact. For example, people have pointed out other functional domains in network management that aren't covered explicitly in basic FCAPS, including network planning, workflow management, and network procurement, cost and accounting.

An important area that isn't covered in FCAPS is the alignment of networking technology with the goals of the business. Heretofore it has been somewhat difficult to understand how expenditures on networking technology and management systems contribute to the income of business. A different way to state the problem is that there is a communication barrier between business overseers and network overseers.

A current theme in network management holds that the concept of *service* is the common ground and intermediate link between business concerns and networking concerns. By mapping networking components to services, and mapping services to business processes, one can begin to understand the cost/benefit ratio of network expenses.

Finally, some of the traditional areas in FCAPS have branched out into other important areas. Performance management has issued areas such as quality of service management and service level management. Fault management has issued the important area of event correlation, whereby events from multiple management systems are compared and correlated in order to isolate a cause of a fault in an integrated, heterogeneous network. And configuration management has evolved into automated service provisioning.

We saw in Section 1.3 that FCAPS is one of three dimensions in the TMN model. Let us proceed now to discuss TMN in more detail.

1.5.2 The Five-Layer Telecommunications Management Network (TMN) Model

A conceptual model of integrated management in terms of layers of abstraction is shown in Figure 1.6. The model is provided by the International Telecommunications Union – Telecommunications (ITU-T) and is called the Telecommunications Management Network (TMN). TMN has received general acceptance in both standards communities and industry.

The TMN model is partitioned into five layers: the element layer, the element management layer, the network management layer, the service management layer, and the business management layer. Each layer, going from bottom to top, represents a transformation of technical detail to more business-oriented information.

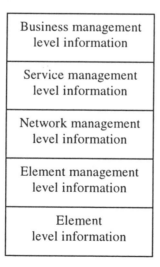

Figure 1.6 The TMN Layers of Abstraction

- The business layer is concerned with the overall management of the telecom carrier business. It covers aspects relating to business processes and strategic business planning. Further, it seeks to capture information to determine whether business objectives and policies are being met.

- The service management layer is concerned with the management of services provided by a service provider to a customer or to another service provider. Examples of such services include billing, order processing, and trouble ticket handling.

- The network management layer is concerned with a network with multiple elements. As such it supports network monitoring and remote configuration. In addition, this layer supports issues such as bandwidth control, performance, quality of service, end-to-end flow control, and network congestion control.

- The element management layer is concerned with the management of individual network elements, for example switches, routers, bridges, and transmission facilities.

- The element layer refers to bare elements that are to be managed.

The salient points regarding the TMN model are these:

1. The TMN is itself a network that monitors and controls another network.

2. The TMN may be separate from or share facilities with the network it controls.

3. Every piecemeal management system is meant to be part of an interconnected hierarchy (i.e. the TMN), able to give up its specialized management information to other systems and to ask for specialized management information from other systems.

4. Each layer in the TMN model is an abstraction over the level beneath it. Tasks at the higher layers are those that need a more abstract view of the network resources and those at the lower levels require a less abstract, more detailed view.

5. TMN defines standards for interoperability with graphical user interfaces such as X windows, interoperability with telecommunications network elements, and importantly, interoperability of TMN functions on different layers or within a layer.

6. The major telecom operators favor the TMN model, and its use in the management of telecommunications systems is well understood.

7. The TMN model includes the service and business/enterprise layers, and at the writing of this book, the implementations of those layers are evolving. However, fielded implementations of the model are limited to the network management layer and element management layer.

Regarding point 7, we should note that there are fielded implementations that have accomplished integration beyond the element management layer and network management layer, however much of the componentry is custom-developed.

Although many vendors are supplying point solutions to fit within the TMN hierarchy, none have successfully embraced both the horizontal and vertical dimensions. For example, the company OSI (USA) offers pieces that cover a large part of the TMN model but they are not all compliant regarding interoperability with pieces provided by other vendors.

1.5.3 The Telecommunications Information Networking Architecture (TINA)

Bellcore (now Telcordia Technologies) initiated the TINA Consortium. TINA is designed to tackle the issues in service management. Recall that TMN included this area, although most work on TMN has focused on the challenges in the layers beneath the service management layer.

Figure 1.7 shows a comparison of the TMN model and the TINA model. Particularly, note that the TMN network management layer and element layer collapse into a general resource layer. This is because TINA is designed specifically with the goals of service management in mind, abstracting away from network details.

A key concept in TINA is the notion of distributed processing and negotiation among a number of agents in order to realize a service. For example, consider the management of the services offered by a futuristic full service network (FSN).

The goal of the FSN is to provide a single platform that combines video, voice, and data. The FSN will provide a diverse and useful range of services to the customer. Examples of such services are email, interactive TV, teleworking, distributed games, video telephony, remote wardens, and access to online public access catalogs. Generally, we refer to such a range of services that combine video, voice, and data as multi-media services.

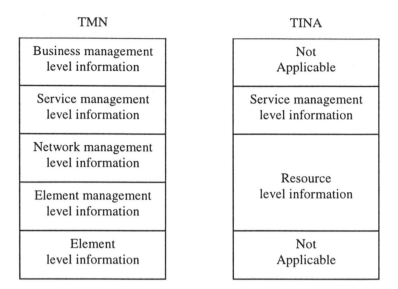

Figure 1.7 Comparison of TMN and TINA Management Layers

The subscriber should be able to choose a service, pay for the service online, and then receive the service soon after. The platform takes care of all the technical details of the resources required to deliver and maintain the service during its lifetime. Figure 1.8 shows a collection of agents that might be required to handle this scenario.

The interface agent is the medium through which the consumer interacts with the rest of the system. The handset and a TV screen might provide this function. The profile agent holds information about the consumer such as personal preferences and credit rating. Thus the selection of some particular service would have to be approved by the profile agent before further processing can happen.

Assuming that the service is approved, then the session agent is granted permission to take over. The session agent confers with the resource agent who initializes and maintains resources for the session. The session agent then delivers the service, and is in continuous correspondence with all other agents with the goal of maintaining the service during the session.

This high-level description of the service management scenario sounds appealing, but working out details such as interface protocols and sequencing semantics has proved to be a formidable task. However, it is tasks such as these that the TINA consortium has undertaken. Understandably, the TINA model has not yet received the general acceptance and popularity enjoyed by the basic TMN model.

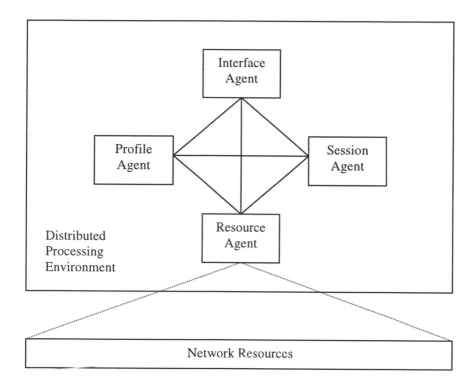

Figure 1.8 Service Management via Distributed Processing

1.5.4 SNMP, CMIP, and CORBA

Let us refer back to the TMN model in Figure 1.6. Clearly, there is a need for communication between each layer of the TMN model in order to realize comprehensive integrated management. And if we consider the TINA model, we see that there is a need for communication among agents in one particular layer -- the service layer.

The challenge for standards bodies is to specify a standard language by which agents in an integrated management platform communicate, whether they be in a manager-object relationship (i.e. layer N to layer N −1 relationship) or a peer-to-peer relationship (i.e. layer N to layer N relationship).

In this section we briefly discuss SNMP, CMIP, and CORBA. We should also mention TL1, but we'll leave that as an exercise.

The Simple Network Management Protocol (SNMP), produced by the Internet community, is the de facto standard for element management and network management. The great majority of industry products in the data communications world depend upon SNMP to communicate with the network elements.

The structure of SNMP includes two primary components: (i) a structure for organizing information in management information bases (MIBs) and (ii) a query protocol to access these databases. If a vendor produces a product, be it a transmission device or an application, and includes an internet-compliant MIB with the product, then the product can be managed by anyone who knows about the query protocol. The protocol primitives are Get, Set, Get-Next, and Trap.

SNMP is quite simple, which has contributed to its success. However, its simplicity has also resulted in some limitations:

- The MIB structure is defined at design time, and thus it is difficult to re-engineer the MIB in the field if one needs additional data that was not part of the original design.
- The MIB structure does not include provisions to represent relations among a collection of managed entities.
- SNMP does not support aggregated retrieval facilities, nor does it support facilities to filter retrieved data.

The Common Management Information Protocol (CMIP) developed by OSI also has two components like SNMP: a management information tree (MIT) and a query protocol to retrieve information from the MIT (Create, Delete, Get, Set, Action, Event-report).

In general, the CMIP model is substantially more complex than SNMP, but there is more you can do with it in terms of management. Thus there is a trade-off: SNMP is simple to implement and has low overhead in terms of computing resources, but lacks expressive power; while CMIP enjoys expressive power, but is relatively hard to implement and has high overhead. Neither model provides good facilities to support agents in a distributed processing environment.

The Common Object Request Broker Architecture (CORBA), defined by the Object Modeling Group, provides a computing environment to support multiple collaborating managers. It borrows the concept of a "software object bus" from the software engineering community, with particular application to the interoperability of disparate managers of networking equipment.

The CORBA standard is made up of the following:

- An Interface Definition Language (IDL) to define the external behavior of managers.
- Specifications for building manager-to-manager requests dynamically.

- An interface repository which contains descriptions of all manager interfaces in use in a given system.

CORBA is expected to be adopted by the TINA consortium. Note that while CORBA provides the computing environment for distributed processing, it does not provide a specification for some particular set of managers and manager interfaces that are required to support a specific task. These are specifications that remain to be defined.

Figure 1.9 is a summary picture that shows (i) the primitive commands between an SNMP manager and an SNMP agent, (ii) the primitive commands between a CMIP manager and a CMIP agent, and (iii) the communications between SNMP and CMIP managers via CORBA IDLs. Note that SNMP and CMIP manager-to-agent primitives are pre-defined, but CORBA manager-to-manager communications are dynamically defined and published for anyone who wishes to use them.

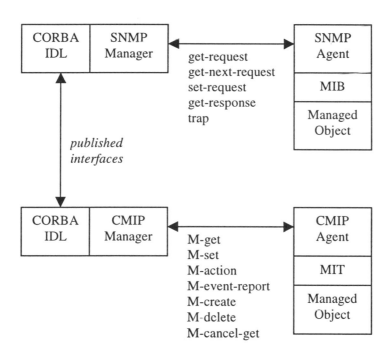

Figure 1.9 A Summary Picture of SNMP, CMIP, and CORBA

An important question in the industry today is how these different methods and techniques will fit together. For example, one possible scenario is shown in Figure 1.10, in which SNMP is used for element management and network management, and TINA/CORBA is used for service and business management. The gateway between the service layer and the network layer is SNMP-based. But this is little more than speculation. Some working prototypes use SNMP throughout.

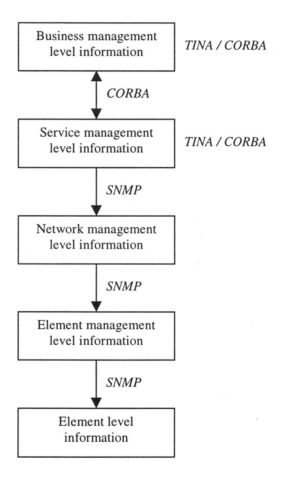

Figure 1.10 A Possible Configuration for Integrated Management

1.6 Agenda for the Rest of the Book

Our book is divided into three parts. Part I is introductory. Part II examines case studies in network management. And Part III proposes directions for further work in network management.

In Chapter 2, we discuss issues regarding the architecture and design of integrated network management solutions. Our premise is that integrated network management is much like the practice of software engineering (SE). In SE courses, one learns about the different phases of producing a software product:

Phase 1: Understand the initial requirements of a software product from a user's perspective.

Phase 2: Derive a conceptual architecture from user requirements.

Phase 3: Derive a physical architecture from the conceptual architecture.

Phase 4: Implement the physical architecture.

Phase 5: Test the implementation.

Phase 6: Deploy the implementation and get user feedback.

Phase 7: Start at Phase 1 again, replacing the word "initial" with "subsequent."

These are simple guidelines, albeit hard to follow in practice. The software product in our domain is a network management system. However, given that a theme that runs through our book is integrated network management, we will see that network management systems will require an integration of several individual management systems, e.g. device, transmission media, computer system, application, or service management systems.

In Chapter 3, we describe the Spectrum Management System developed by Aprisma Management Technologies. Spectrum is just one example of network management system, and it is a candidate implementation vehicle when one enters Phase 3 of the SE process. We discuss the architecture of Spectrum and its history. We describe how Spectrum is used to monitor and control physical and logical constructs in business and service domains, including components that belong in the tele-communications space and the data communications space. In addition, we describe methods for integrating Spectrum with other specialized management applications.

Chapters 1 and 2 will have instilled in the reader the conceptual apparatus by which to approach network management challenges. Chapter 3 will have described a popular management system by which to implement network management solutions.

Chapters 4 through 6 in Part II are discussions of particular kinds of networks and their management challenges. Each chapter focuses on the following themes:

- Definition of the Domain
- Management Challenges
- A Case Study
- Management Architecture, Implementation, and Deployment
- Successes and Challenges for Future Work

In Chapter 4, the domain under consideration is a micro city network. In Chapter 5, the domain is a service provider network. And in Chapter 6, the domain is an Internet2 GigaPoP network.

Other kinds of networks are surely forthcoming as networking technology and usage gain momentum in the 2000's. The goal of the chapters in Part II is to lay groundwork, both conceptual and experiential, by which to approach new challenges in the 2000's.

In Chapter 7 we take a close look at what network operators actually do in the field, and we also take a look at the sorts of things that researchers in network management are thinking about. Also, we discuss the problem of combining research and practice in network management.

Finally, in Chapter 8 we step back and take a look at the broader picture of network management. We look at the space of networking technologies, propose a universal *conceptual* network management system, discuss the challenges of building such a universal management system, and finally propose directions for further work in network management.

Chapter Summary

In this chapter we distinguished between business networks and service networks. The distinction hinges upon ownership, scope, and function. Typically, business networks are owned by a company and are used to support the informational requirements of the company's operation. In contrast, service networks are owned or leased by a service provider and are used to offer some specialized service to a company, for example Internet access, electronic commerce, and other specialized services.

Next we discussed the multiple aspects of "network management" and "integrated network management." We argued that integrated network management connotes the integration of the management of (i) multiple generic components in a network, (ii) the five sub-management functional areas of FCAPS, (iii) multiple layers of abstraction described in the TNM model, (iv) independently-owned service provider networks, and (v) data networks and telecommunications networks.

We discussed the evolution of network management from a data communications perspective and from a telecommunications perspective. We entered the history in the 1970's, and argued that there is now a healthy discourse between the data and telecommunications communities regarding methods and techniques in network management.

We described some work in the standards bodies, including FCAPS, TMN, TINA, SNMP, CMIP, and CORBA. This work has taken us a long way towards the design and implementation of intercommunication methods among disparate management systems.

Finally, we outlined the agenda for the rest of the book. In Chapter 2 we will look at design and implementation techniques for integrated network management. In Chapter 3 we describe Spectrum, which we will use as our implementation vehicle in the case studies in Chapters 4 through 6. Chapters 4 through 6 describe case studies in the management of three rather disparate kinds of networks – micro city networks, service provider networks, and Internet2 GigaPoP networks. Chapters 7 and 8 conclude the book with discussions of successes, anomalies, and directions for further work and research in network management.

Exercises and Discussion Questions

1. In Section 1.2 we described five generic components of networks. Is our categorization complete? Are there other generic components that should be included? Should we consider the human user as a component of the network?

2. Consider a transmission device. Is a transmission device better defined as a software application that runs on a computer system?

3. Questions 1 and 2 have to do with the ontology of networks. What is ontology? Why is it important?

4. Suppose you cannot access your email. You call the help desk. A troubleshooter comes over and finds that the wall port was faulty. Discuss this episode with respect to five senses of integrated network management we described in Section 1.3.

5. What is TL1? What is the relation between TL1 and SNMP, CMIP, and CORBA? Why is TL1 attractive? How does it fit in with our discussion

of the history and evolution of management methods for telecommunications networks?

6. Since FCAPS was introduced formally by OSI, the definitions have been expanded, and other functional areas have been introduced. Write an essay that defines a modern-day version of FCAPS. Are there other areas not included in FCAPS? Propose a new acronym that denotes a modern-day version of FCAPS.

7. Below are some important topics in network management.
    Policy-based management
    Web-based management
    Quality of Service (QoS) management
    Response time management
    Service level management
    Event correlation
    Pick one of these topics and write an essay that includes answers to the following questions:
    What is the problem that motivates the topic?
    How does the topic solve the problem?
    What standards (if any) address the topic?
    What commercial products exist that address the topic?

8. The term QoS means several different things depending upon context. Search the literature and write an essay on its different meanings.

9. Write an essay on the history of the Internet. Include a section on Internet2. What are the anticipated advantages of Internet2? What is the current state of Internet2?

10. Write an essay that describes the differences between SNMPv1, SNMPv2, and SNMPv3. What is the relation between IPv6 and SNMP?

Further Studies

A very good textbook on Network Management is Subramanian's *Network Management: Principles and Practice*. The book provides (i) an overview of data communications, telecommunications, and management methods, (ii) SNMP, Broadband, and TMN Management, and (iii) management tools, systems, and applications. One of the systems described is Spectrum, which we will use as our implementation vehicle in later chapters.

A classic book on telecommunications network management is Aidarous and Plevyak's edited volume *Telecommunications Network Management into the 21st Century*. The discussion of FCAPS in Section 1.5 was derived from this book, although one will find numerous discussions of FCAPS in the literature.

Two other good books on telecommunications management are Bernstein and Yuhas' *Basic Concepts for Managing Telecommunications Networks* and Raman's *Fundamentals of Telecommunications Network Management*. The latter book focuses directly on the TMN model.

The student of network management should be familiar with the major conferences on network management, including the International Symposium on Integrated Network Management (ISINM, renamed simply Integrated Management (IM) in 1999) and Network Operations and Management Symposium (NOMS). The proceedings of these conferences are first rate, and the student should have access to that material.

There are many conferences on networking and communications in general, and most of these conferences have special sections on issues in network management. In addition, there are symposia and workshops on special topics in network management that are announced in IEEE Network Magazine and IEEE Communications Magazine.

The serious student should study the web site of the IEEE Communications Society (www.comsoc.org). It contains links to other important web sites, and these to yet others, and so on.

The premier journal on network management is the Journal of Network and Systems Management (JNSM). For example, JNSM has a special issue dealing with TMN (March 1995) and a special issue on TINA (December 1997). The JNSM web site is www.cstp.umkc/jnsm.

References

Aidarous, S. and T. Plevyak (editors). *Telecommunications Network Management into the 21st Century*. IEEE Press. 1994.

Bernstein, L. and C. M. Yuhas. *Basic Concepts for Managing Telecommunications Networks*. Kluwer Academic/Plenum Publishers. 1999.

Raman, L. G. *Fundamentals of Telecommunications Network Management*. IEEE Press. 1999.

Subramanian, M. *Network Management: Principles and Practice*. Addison-Wesley. 2000.

2 Architecture and Design of Integrated Management Systems

In this chapter we first describe principles in the architecture and design of management systems in general. It is well known that knowledge of sound methodological principles goes a long way towards increasing the chance of building a system that really works in the field.

We discuss the following topics in this chapter:

- Requirements for Integrated Management Systems
- Integrated Management is like Software Engineering
- Architecture and Design of Software Systems
- Patterns of Integrated Management
- Implementation Challenges

First we look at some common arguments for integrated management that one often hears from customers in the field -- from both enterprise customers and service providers. These arguments can be construed as business requirements, from which we are to design and implement satisfactory solutions.

Second, we argue that the construction of integrated management systems is much like the construction of software systems in general. In the software engineering community, software development always starts with a sound understanding of business requirements, including an understanding of risks and pitfalls in software development. After that, we proceed to develop an architecture, a design, an implementation, and test procedures. The same is true for constructing integrated management systems.

Next, we study good practices in developing architectures and designs in software engineering so that we can apply that knowledge to the construction of integrated management systems. We will describe the object-oriented software engineering methodology in some detail.

Finally we discuss a variety of patterns in integrated management systems, including the transfer of topology information, the exchange of events and alarms, and the integration of management systems with help desks. These patterns can be considered as a sort of conceptual toolbox with which to approach integrated management challenges. We assume that there exist adequate management systems and tools for individual tasks; we are concerned about how to integrate them together into a whole (as opposed to building a whole system from scratch).

2.1 Requirements for Integrated Management Systems

This section is a survey of requirements for developing integrated management systems. It demonstrates sentiments that are often espoused by industry analysts or informed, well-educated executives that oversee the operations of large business and service networks. It is not a complete survey, but it is a good representation of what one will hear from consumers.

A designer or developer should learn how to read and comprehend such requirements. Importantly, one should understand that the final, deployed management system must answer the sentiments of the executive who laid down the requirements in the first place. It is a common phenomenon that system developers lose track of business requirements as they get involved in the engineering intricacies of system development. We wish to avoid that; otherwise our efforts might be for naught.

2.1.1 Multi-Domain Management

Computer networks are widely used to provide increased computing power, sharing of resources, and communication between users. Networks may include a number of computer devices within a room, building, or site that are connected by high-speed local data links such as token ring, Ethernet, SONET, and ATM switch fabrics.

Local area networks (LAN's) in different locations may be interconnected by packet switches, microwave links, and satellite links to form a wide area network (WAN). A network may include several hundred or more connected devices, distributed across several geographical locations and belonging to several organizations.

Many existing networks are so large that a network administrator will partition the network into multiple domains for ease of management. There are various types of domains. One example is based on geographical location. For example, a company may operate a network that covers two domains A and B, where A and B are identified with two separate cities such as Chicago and New York.

Another domain type is based on organization or departments, e.g., accounting, engineering, sales, support, and marketing. The company may have a computer network spanning multiple organizations and multiple geographical locations, but there may not be a one-to-one mapping of organizations to geographical locations. Thus, two separate organizations may both share network resources within first and second geographical locations. For purposes of network accounting (e.g., to allocate network charges to the appropriate organization) or for other reasons, it may be advantageous to consider the network resources of the first organization as being a separate domain from the network resources of the second organization.

A third example of a domain type is a grouping based upon functional characteristics of network resources. For example, one functional domain may consist of a collection of network resources that support computer-aided design. Another functional domain may consist of network resources that support financial analysis, where such resources are especially adapted to provide financial data. The network resources of these two domains may be distributed across several geographical locations and several organizations of the company.

Additional examples of communication network domains also exist, and a single company or organization may have domains that fall into several categories.

The examples above have to do with one company owning and managing its own network. Similar situations exist for any entity that manages and/or owns a network, for example a service provider that offers network services to several companies.

In the operation and maintenance of computer networks a number of issues arise, including traffic overload on parts of the network, optimum placement and interconnection of network resources, security, and isolation of network faults. These issues become increasingly complex and difficult to manage as the network becomes larger and more complex. For example, if a network device is not sending messages, it may be difficult to determine whether the fault is in the device itself, a communication link, or an intermediate network device between the sending and receiving devices.

Network management systems are intended to resolve such issues. Older management systems typically operated by collecting large volumes of information that required evaluation by a human network administrator. More recent network management systems mimic the knowledge of the networking expert such that common problems of a single domain (i.e., a portion of the network under common management) can be detected, isolated and repaired, either automatically or under expert supervision.

The newer management systems typically include a graphical representation of that portion of the network being monitored by the system. Alarms are generated to inform an administrator that an event has occurred that requires attention. Since a large network may have many such events occurring simultaneously, some network management systems provide event filtering and correlation (i.e., only certain events, or collections of event, generate an alarm).

However, in each instance the existing network management system manages only a single domain. For example, a company having a network consisting of several domains will typically purchase one copy of a network management system for each domain. Each copy of the network management system may be referred to as an instance.

Thus, in the functional domain example described above, a first instance of a network management system may manage the computer-aided design domain, while a second instance of a network management system may manage the financial analysis domain. Each instance of the network management system receives information only from the resources of a single respective domain, and generates alarms that are specific only to the single respective domain. Such alarms may be referred to as *intra*-domain alarms.

Because each instance of a network management system manages only one domain, there is currently no diagnosis or management that takes into account the relationships among multiple domains. Since domains may be interconnected, an intra-domain alarm might be generated for a first domain, even though the event or fault that is causing the intra-domain alarm may be contained within the network resources of a different domain.

For example, domain A in a network may include a router that forwards network traffic to a resource in domain B. If a router in A fails or begins to degrade, the performance of domain B may appear sluggish (e.g., excessive delays or low throughput), even though the network resources within B are operating correctly. This sluggishness may cause an alarm to be generated from the instance of the network management system that manages B. However, the system that manages B doesn't know about the alarm detected by the system that manages A, and thus might make an incorrect diagnosis.

We require, then, an inter-domain alarm manager that provides alarm correlation among a plurality of domains. See Figure 2.1. Individual network management systems each monitor a single respective domain of the network and provide intra-domain alarms indicative of status specific to the single respective domain (the upward-pointing arrows).

The inter-domain alarm manager receives the intra-domain alarms, and correlates them to provide inter-domain alarms as well as responses in the form of corrective actions (the downward-pointing arrows). The inter-domain manager thus provides a high level of correlation and response for the entire network while each single-domain network management system provides a lower level of correlation and response for an individual domain of the network.

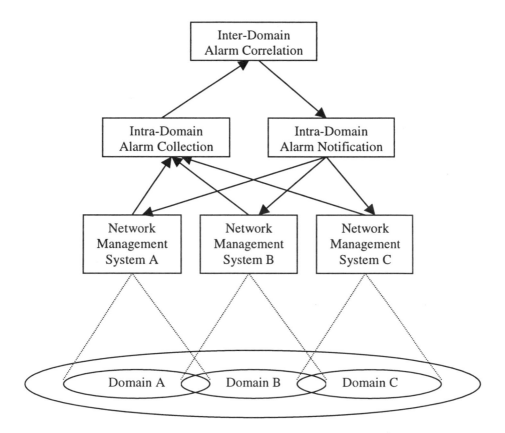

Figure 2.1 A Multi-Domain Management System

By providing two levels of correlation, one at the network management system level (within a domain), and a second at the alarm manager level (across multiple domains), an improvement in scalability is provided that is not possible with prior systems.

2.1.2 Resolving Network Faults

All networks experience faults during network operation. Faults may include a failure of hardware portions of the network such as workstations and peripheral devices or a failure of software portions of the network such as software application programs and data management programs.

In small stable homogeneous communications networks (i.e., those in which all of the equipment is provided by the same vendor and the network configuration does not change), management and repair of network faults is relatively straightforward. However, as a network becomes increasingly large and heterogeneous (i.e., those in which different types of equipment are connected together over large areas, such as an entire country), fault management becomes more difficult.

One of the ways to improve fault management in large networks is to use a trouble ticketing system. This system provides a number of tools that can be used by network users, administrators, and repair and maintenance personnel. The basic data structure, a "trouble ticket," has a number of fields in which a user can enter data describing the parameters of an observed network fault. A trouble ticket filled out by a user may then be transmitted by, for example, an electronic mail system to maintenance and repair personnel.

Note that a trouble ticketing system is different than an alarm management system. An alarm management system analyzes events that occur within the network, while a trouble ticketing system first collects problematic symptoms as perceived by users and then passes the ticket through the hands of repairpersons and testers.

A trouble ticket describing a current network fault that needs to be acted on is called an "outstanding trouble ticket". When the network fault has been corrected, the solution to the problem, typically called a "resolution" is entered into an appropriate data field in the trouble ticket. When a network fault has been resolved, the trouble ticket is closed.

The system provides for storage of completed trouble tickets in a database and thus a library of such tickets is created, allowing users, administrators, and maintenance and repair personnel to refer to these stored completed trouble tickets for assistance in determining solutions to new network faults.

The trouble ticketing system thus provides a convenient, structured way of managing fault resolutions and for storing solutions to network faults in a manner that allows this stored body of knowledge to be accessed and applied to outstanding network faults.

A structured trouble-ticketing system, however, does not provide a complete solution to the fault management problem. For time-critical network services, the downtime that elapses from the observation of a network fault, the submission of a trouble ticket, to the completion of the trouble ticket can be expensive.

Downtime can be reduced by providing a communication link between a network fault detection system and a trouble ticketing system. The communication link allows fault information collected by the fault detection system to be transmitted to the trouble-ticketing system in the form of an automatically generated and filled out trouble ticket. The trouble ticketing system then manages maintenance and repair in the normal manner to resolve the outstanding trouble ticket.

We require, then, an integration between a network management system and trouble-ticketing system, as shown in Figure 2.2.The advantage of such an integration is that network faults may be detected, forwarded to the trouble ticket system, and repaired by maintenance personnel before the end-user begins to observe the effects of the fault.

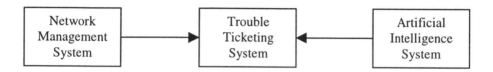

Figure 2.2 An Integrated Fault Management System

Although this solution allows trouble tickets to reach the fault management system and appropriate maintenance and repair personnel more quickly, it does not reduce the time necessary to resolve an outstanding fault. A maintenance and repair person is still required to research and resolve the outstanding fault. This is not only time-consuming, but expensive as well.

To reduce the time in which faults are resolved, artificial intelligence (AI) systems may be used to assist in resolving the outstanding trouble ticket. Thus, as shown in Figure 2.2, we also require an integration between the trouble-ticketing system and an AI system that helps the administrator determine causes and repair procedures for network faults.

2.1.3 Network Simulation

Network simulation systems are often used to help network designers make decisions about reconfiguring or extending networks with new equipment and applications. In this way, the simulation expert is able to verify the behavior of a network before actually making the changes.

In order to accurately simulate the behavior of a live network, accurate network topology information must be provided to the network simulation tool. Currently, the simulation tools require a user to manually construct models of the network and models of traffic profiles per application. Typically, that is done by hand with a special-purpose graphics package.

Clearly, the manual method is time-consuming and error-prone. The user must have a conception of the model, or else consult other engineers, before building the model for the simulation tool. Consumption of time and error may result from the conceptualization process and in the manual entering of the network model.

A more time-efficient and accurate means for providing topology and traffic information of a live network to the network simulator is highly desirable. Since many network management systems discover the topology of a network via auto-discovery techniques, that would be a good source for accurate simulation data. Further, since a traffic monitoring application can construct patterns of traffic per application, that would be a good source for accurate traffic profiles.

We require, then, an integration among network, traffic, and simulation applications in which topology and traffic profiles are collected, formatted, and forwarded to the simulation application. Figure 2.3 shows the basic structure of such an integrated system.

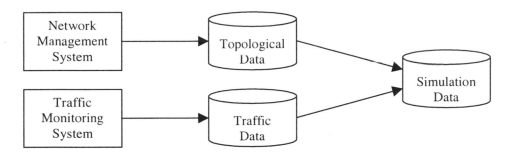

Figure 2.3 An Integrated System in Support of Simulation Studies

2.1.4 Integrated IP and Telephony Management

There are a variety of service offerings and applications hosted by combined Internet Protocol (IP) and telephony networks. The network is becoming increasingly complex, with the need for interoperable multi-vendor equipment. The need is arising for a single network management system to oversee all the disparate parts of the IP and telephony infrastructure.

The mapping of business requirements to network requirements will shape the success of next-generation converged networks. The urgency for such a platform is growing with the emergence of integrated voice and data technologies such as Voice over IP (VoIP).

Clients who are looking to deploy VoIP technologies, IP-based telephone switches (e.g. PBXs), and other voice and data convergence technologies need a means for managing the network infrastructure. They also require integrated software solutions that will provide them with the information for calculating the Total Cost of Ownership of this converged network, thereby bridging the gap between business requirements and network requirements.

Service providers such as telecommunications carriers (including incumbent local exchange carriers and competitive local exchange carriers), Internet service providers, national service providers, inter-exchange carriers, cable operators, and IT outsourcers are looking for new areas for generating additional revenue. The largest potential is for a single voice and data service offering.

However, one of the anticipated problems most commonly associated with the advent of converged voice and data networks is that of developing a single platform for end-to-end management that allows traditional FCAPS management in addition to dynamic service provisioning, monitoring, and accounting.

We require, then, a platform that (i) spans across converged networks, (ii) includes traditional FCAPS management, and (iii) allows service definition, provisioning, monitoring, and accounting. Figure 2.4 shows the basic structure of such an integrated system.

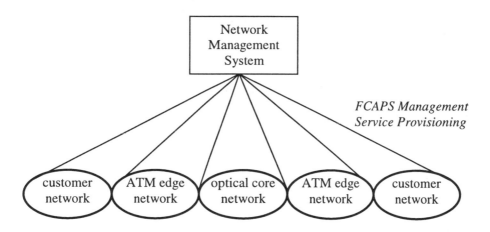

Figure 2.4 Integrated Management over Multiple Networking Technologies

As an example of the challenges in developing such a platform, consider telephony PBX management. Currently there are no SNMP management standards for PBXs, and hardware vendors are offering different levels of SNMP support. The typical approach to managing this type of hardware is to offer basic SNMP management, and to complement that with a means to invoke a proprietary PBX element manager from the primary SNMP platform.

While this solution may work for the short term, clearly it is rather inelegant. We require a solution that provides standards-based management of both IP and telephony equipment from a single management system.

2.1.5 Service Level Agreements

Consider the following sequence of definitions.

1. *Business processes* (BPs) refer to the unique ways in which a company coordinates and organizes work activities, information, and knowledge to produce a valuable commodity. For example, an investment firm might depend on its web servers and network infrastructure to allow customers to trade stocks with their web browsers. The BP, then, can be labeled "Web-based stock trading."

2. A *service* is any component, application, or medium upon which the BP depends. Typically, a BP will depend upon a collection of services. Consider the simple BP in Figure 2.5 in which web server S in LAN2 serves clients C1, C2, C3, and C4 in LAN 1, clients C5, C6, and C7 in LAN2, and a host of server hits over the internet connection. Thus, the BP is a function of at least seven services: LAN1, LAN2, the web server, the Internet connection, the Backbone, router R1, and router R2.

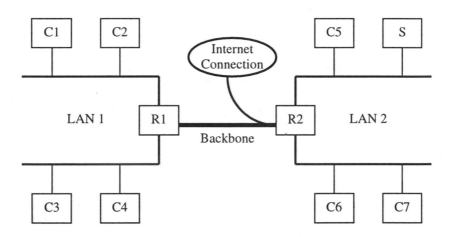

Figure 2.5 A Simple Business Process with Supporting Services

3. A *service parameter* is a measurable quantity that is an index into the health of a service. For example, at the application level, service parameters include reliability, response time (a.k.a. latency), and jitter (where jitter is defined as the variation over response time). At the network medium level, service parameters include bandwidth, load, and bytes in/out.

4. A *service level* is some mark by which to qualify acceptability of a service parameter. The simplest kind of marking is binary. For example, we may say that the backbone performance in Figure 2.2 is acceptable only if its throughput during normal business hours is never more than 40% of total available bandwidth.

5. A *Service Level Agreement* (SLA, a.k.a. Document of Understanding) is a contract between a supplier and a consumer showing the BP, the supporting services, service parameters, acceptable/unacceptable service levels, liabilities on the part of a supplier and the consumer, and actions to be taken in specific circumstances.

6. A *Service Level Report* (SLR) is a document that shows the SLA and a mark showing the actual value of a service parameter over some period of time.

7. *Service Level Management* (SLM) refers to the process of (i) identifying services, service parameters, service levels, (ii) negotiating and articulating an SLA, (3) deploying agents to monitor and control service parameters, and (4) producing SLRs.

Let us assume that the provider understands the consumer's BPs and underlying services, and is in the midst of selecting service parameters and management tools for SLM monitoring.

The concept of "Monitor Agent" is a good way to think about methods of monitoring the service parameters. Monitor agents generally fall into the following categories:

1. *Network Agents* have a focused view of the connection nodes in the network infrastructure, for example bridges, hubs, and routers. Service parameters typically include port-level statistics.

2. *Traffic Agents* have a focused view of the traffic that flows over transmission media in the network infrastructure. Examples of service

parameters include bytes over source/destination pairs and protocol categories thereof.

3. *System Agents* have a focused view of the computer systems that reside on the network. Typically, these agents reside on the system, read the system log files, and perform system queries to gather statistics. Service parameters include CPU usage, disk partition capacities, and login records.

4. *Application Agents* have a focused view of business applications that are distributed over networks and computers. These agents also reside on the system that hosts the application. Some applications offer agents that provide indices into their own performance levels. Service parameters include thread distribution, CPU usage per application, and file/disk capacity per application.

5. *Special-Purpose Agents* can be built to monitor parameters that are not covered by any of the above. A good example is an agent whose purpose is to issue a synthetic query from point A to point B and (optionally) back to point A to measure reliability and response time of an application. Note that the synthetic query is representative of authentic application queries. An example is an e-commerce agent that monitors the reliability and response time of web page retrievals from some geographical domain to a web server farm in a second geographical domain.

6. *Enterprise Agents* have a wide-angle view of the network infrastructure, including connection nodes, systems, and applications that make up the network. These agents are also cognizant of relations among the components at various levels of abstraction, and are able to reason about events that issue from multiple enterprise components. This is called *event correlation* or *alarm roll-up*. Service parameters that are accessible by enterprise agents are numerous, including router and hub statistics, ATM services, frame relay services, and link bandwidth usage.

Clearly, SLM systems will involve multiple agents of different types in some combination of the above. Thus we require an integrated platform that (i) allows monitoring of select elements in the network, (ii) maps performance data of select elements into a service model, and (iii) generates reports on the performance of the service. Figure 2.6 shows an example of such an integrated system.

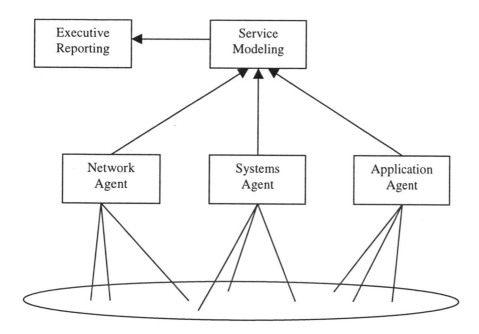

Figure 2.6 Integration in Support of End-to-End Service Level Agreements

2.2 Integrated Management is like Software Engineering

The examples above give us of a taste of the kinds of requirements that are common in the industry. Let us now talk about how to go about building systems to satisfy such requirements.

The construction of integrated management systems is much like the construction of software in general. In software engineering (SE) courses, one learns about the different phases of producing a software product:

Phase 1: Understand the initial requirements of a software product from user and business perspectives.

Phase 2: Derive a conceptual architecture from user and business requirements.

Phase 3: Derive a physical architecture from the conceptual architecture.

Phase 4: Implement the physical architecture.

Phase 5: Test the implementation.

Phase 6: Deploy the implementation and get user feedback.

Phase 7: Return to Phase 1, replacing the word "initial" with "subsequent."

These are simple guidelines, albeit hard to follow in practice. A common pitfall is that not enough emphasis is placed on Phase 1 – understanding requirements from user and business perspectives. Engineers tend to proceed too quickly to Phase 4, and what sometimes happens is that the final product is not quite what the business or user wanted. A related pitfall is that the business perspective is considered without due consideration to the user, and the risk is that users tend not to use the software. The goal of SE methodology is to mitigate risks such as those.

Let us take a closer look at the magnitude of the risks in SE projects. In the United States in 1995, $250 billion was spent on approximately 175,000 software projects. Of that, an estimated $59 billion was spent on cost overruns and another $81 billion was spent on canceled software projects.

These facts suggest that about 25% of SE projects cost more than the original estimated cost and that another 30% end in failure. If we assume that SE projects and integrated management projects share the same risks, then we have about a 45% chance of carrying an integrated management program to completion within budget and according to plan.

Why is it that less than half of SE projects complete within budget? A related 1995 study examined opinions of SE project managers in the United States, Finland, and Hong Kong and produced the following general consensus of answers to this question. The answers are listed in order of decreasing importance:

1. Lack of top management commitment to the project
2. Failure to gain user commitment
3. Misunderstanding the requirements
4. Lack of adequate user involvement
5. Failure to manage end user expectations
6. Changing scope/objectives
7. Lack of required knowledge/skills in the project personnel
8. Lack of frozen requirements
9. Introduction of new technology
10. Insufficient/inappropriate staffing
11. Conflict between user departments

An examination of this list reveals that the lack of user involvement is the primary factor that causes an unsuccessful SE program (2, 4, 5, and 11). A related factor is the lack of a firm establishment and understanding of user requirements (3, 6, and 8).

It is reasonable to group these two factors into one simple, overarching principle: *Get users involved and establish firm requirements up front.* Besides that general admonishment, it is clear that one has to have top management commitment (1) and to have appropriate staffing and technology (7, 9, and 10).

A separate 1995 study of SE projects in England examined the opinions of SE managers who had experienced so-called runaway projects – i.e. those projects that threatened to spiral out of control. When asked what they have done in the past to try to gain control of runaway projects, the consensus was this:

1. Extend the schedule (85%)
2. Incorporate better project management procedures (54%)
3. Add more people (53%)
4. Add more funds (43%)
5. Put pressure on suppliers by withholding payment (38%)
6. Reduce project scope (28%)
7. Get outside help (27%)
8. Introduce better development methodologies (25%)
9. Put pressure on suppliers by threat of litigation (20%)
10. Introduce new technology (13%)
11. Abandon the project (9%)

Interestingly, when the same companies were asked what they intend to do in the future to thwart potential runaway projects, the general consensus was:

1. Improve project management (86%)
2. Perform better feasibility studies (84%)
3. Incorporate more user involvement (68%)
4. Incorporate more external advice (56%)

We should consider the findings in these empirical studies as sobering facts. We run similar risks when constructing management systems for business and service networks. It is to our advantage, then, to grasp good principles in SE methodology at the outset and make use of them as we construct integrated management systems. In the next section we do just that.

Before we start, there is some encouraging news. The main difference between large SE projects and integrated management projects is the amount of code that we write. In SE projects one typically writes a very large amount of code during the implementation phase. In integrated management projects, however, the code that we write is usually restricted to integration code, i.e. the code that provides the glue among agents and management systems in the overall system.

In a few cases, an integrated management system can be constructed without writing any code. For example, some systems provide mechanisms for simply launching one application from another, where integration particulars are guided by a GUI. The code is written automatically.

2.3 Architecture and Design of Software Systems

Figure 2.7 shows a prominent SE methodology called object-oriented software engineering (OOSE). It is part of the Unified Modeling Language (UML) approach to software engineering. We will work through the OOSE methodology slowly and conscientiously.

First we assume that we have an understanding of the user and business requirements of a network management system. The requirements should include (i) a description of the nature of the business, (ii) reasons for developing a management solution, (iii) how the management system will be used, and (iv) how the management system supports the goals of the business.

Importantly, the requirements should not include technical detail. They should be written purely from a business perspective. We saw some examples of requirements in Section 2.1, and we will see some more in our case studies in Part II.

2.3.1 The Use Case Model

The first step in OOSE is to translate the original requirements into a Use Case Model. This model is a very simple picture, much like the drawing of a five-year old. It consists of just two kinds of constructs: actors and use cases.

Figure 2.7 shows three use cases A, B, and C. In general, the set of use cases spans the entire functionality space that is to be covered by a management system. Issues such as performance and reliability are typically considered after the functionality of a system is well understood. We'll see an example shortly.

An actor represents a user of the system, whereas a use case is a simple phrase that describes what the system will do for the actor. In addition, the Use Case Model is accompanied by short, clear text that explains the role of each actor and a walk-through of what happens during each use case.

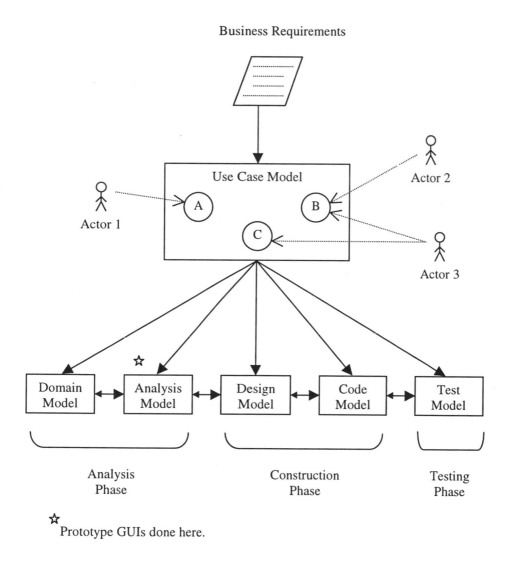

Figure 2.7 Object Oriented Software Engineering

The most important feature of the Use Case Model is that it is the common understanding between the users of a system and the developers of a system. It is a well-known fact that users and developers employ different languages and have different conceptual interpretations of what a system is supposed to do. This is one of the primary problems in SE project development: What comes out at the end is not what users wanted in the beginning. The prominence of the Use Case Model in OOSE methodology goes a long way towards alleviating this problem.

For example, Figure 2.8 shows a candidate Use Case Model that answers the requirements for Service Level Agreements in Section 2.1.5. There are two actors and six use cases. The supplier and consumer of services are expected to use the management system in the same way; thus a single actor represents both of them. A second actor, the system administrator, configures and monitors the overall system.

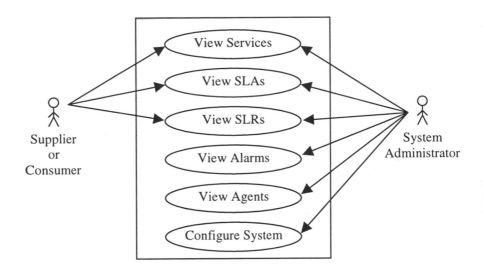

Figure 2.8 Sample SLA Use Case Model

After the Use Case Model is agreed upon, developers proceed to what they do best. Five models of the system are built in increments: the domain, analysis, design, code, and test models. Each model is derived from the Use Case Model and the model immediately preceding it. For example, in Figure 2.7 the Analysis Model is derived from the Use Case Model and the Domain Model, as shown by the two arrows leading into the Analysis Model.

Below we describe the five models. However, we refer the reader to the Further Studies Section for a source that continues the SLA example.

2.3.2 The Domain Model

The Domain Model is a preliminary sketch of the objects that are involved in the system, including objects that are within the SE system and the objects outside the system. For network management systems, typically the objects that are outside the system are transmission devices, transmission media, computer systems, and applications running on the systems.

The objects within the system, however, include (i) interfaces with outside objects, (ii) interfaces between multiple management systems, and (iii) objects in management software that reason about the state of the network, offer reports of network state, and issue control instructions.

2.3.3 The Analysis Model

The Analysis Model is a step towards the identification of a collection of objects that will offer each use case in the Use Case Model. There are three categories of objects: interface objects, entity objects, and control objects.

- Interface objects are the means by which the system connects with the objects outside the domain. The classic example of an interface object is graphical user interface (GUI), where the external object is just the user at a terminal. Other examples include a command line interface into the system, or a database interface.

- Entity objects exist for the sole function of holding data. For example, during runtime an entity object may instruct a database interface object to fetch and return a pre-specified chunk of data from a database (which is outside the system).

- Control objects exist to process data. We may consider control objects as algorithms that take data as input, perform some function over the data, and return a value. For example, a control object may be instructed to perform a trend analysis on data handed to it by an entity object.

A general rule of thumb is to never have a particular kind of object performing functions that rightly belong to another kind of object. For example we don't want to have interface objects processing data, nor do we want entity objects displaying data. But this is a rule of thumb. Sometimes it makes sense to combine the duties of two objects into a hybrid object.

The time is ripe at this juncture to explain the arrow that connects the Domain Model to the Analysis Model in Figure 2.7. The arrow is a double-barbed arrow, where the right-end barb is bigger than the left-end barb. This means that we want to carry as much information as possible from the Domain Model to the Analysis Model, although we allow some backtracking and perhaps a minimal amount of back-and-forth play between them.

For example, our development of the Analysis Model might uncover some objects that were overlooked in the Domain Model, or it might cause us to re-think the boundary that separates system objects from non-system objects. It is entirely acceptable if Analysis Model influences the Domain Model, although if we have done a good job developing the latter, the influence will be minimal. This point holds true as we move through each model in the methodology, as Figure 2.7 shows.

2.3.4 The Design Model

Recall that the Analysis Model is conceived without regard to implementation constraints or available tools. We consider the Analysis Model as an approximation of the ideal system and assume that we will have all the tools we need when we go about implementing it.

When we construct the Design Model we face reality. We try to find tools, commercial or otherwise, that fit the structure of the Analysis Model. Also, we have to pay attention to performance and usability issues. There are two reasons for taking this approach:

- In making the move from the Analysis Model to the Design Model we retain the maximal amount of structure of the ideal system.

- What's left over serves as (i) a guide for further research and development for academic/industry labs and (ii) a guide for product requirements to be considered by commercial vendors and integrators.

2.3.5 The Code Model

The Code Model is simply the code itself. We noted earlier that the code in integrated management systems usually involves integration code. Fortunately for us we don't have to worry too much about developing software systems from scratch. Rather, we have to worry about how existing software systems work with each other to realize the Design Model and, by implication, the Analysis Model and Use Case Model.

2.3.6 The Test Model

Like all other models, the Test Model is derived from the Use Case Model and the model that precedes it, in this case the Code Model. Unit testing will have been done while constructing the Code Model. Importantly, the walk-through of each use case in the original Use Case model is mapped directly to the Test Model. This insures that what the system does at the end of the methodology is what was planned for at the beginning of the methodology.

2.3.7 Other Important Considerations

Refer back to the big picture of OOSE in Figure 2.7. Thus far we have covered everything in the methodology except one important feature: when to start developing prototype GUIs.

It is common in SE projects to develop a prototype GUI straight from the original user requirements. Sometimes the GUI is constructed with pencil and paper. Other times it is constructed quickly with GUI development environments such as Visual Basic. In either case, what is expected to take place behind the GUI is imagined or staged.

The OOSE Methodology advises that this is a bad idea. What happens is that the prototype GUI begins to influence what the system is suppose to do, when we really want our understanding of what the system is supposed to do to influence the prototype GUI. Further, we begin to understand what the system is supposed to do somewhere around the beginning of the Analysis Model. The star in Figure 2.7 shows this. The general advice of the OOSE Methodology is to simply think about the system for a while before constructing prototype GUIs, i.e. somewhere in the Analysis Phase.

We can apply this piece of advice also to building any kind of prototype, e.g. prototyping an integration of two management tools. In general, building a prototype before the requirements are understood may have significant impact on the total cost of product development. Additional costs and frustration often arise in having to re-engineer a product to meet the requirements that were not understood the first time around.

2.3.8 Summary of OOSE Methodology

The overall picture in Figure 2.7 is a good summary of OOSE. The main points of the methodology that we should keep in mind as we develop integrated management systems are these:

- Our ultimate goal is to avoid the kinds of risks that were discussed at the beginning of this section, the main one being to avoid a divergence from user specifications during development.

- The Use Case Model is a good way to express a common understanding between users and developers (or integrators) of network management systems.

- Developers and integrators should be careful not to stray from the original Use Case Model. As each incremental model is developed, the Use Case Model should be observed.

- During the Analysis Phase, in which we build the Domain and Analysis Models, implementation details should not bog down developers or integrators.

- Although it is not likely that we will have a perfect transformation from the Analysis Model to the Design Model, we retain as much of the ideal structure as possible and have a good indication of further work to do.

- One should not be premature in building prototype GUIs. GUI prototypes should be developed and demonstrated to end-users during the analysis phase. Further, keep in mind that many good software projects have failed because of the lack of acceptance by users, although the use cases did indeed cover the functionality of the system.

2.4 Patterns of Integrated Management

In this section we examine some common patterns in integrated management. The discussion should be considered as a conceptual toolbox that can be used during the Analysis Phase of OOSE methodology. Note that in this section we don't worry about the physical mechanisms by which to implement the patterns. We will see plenty examples of that in later chapters.

The list is fairly exhaustive, although other integration patterns may emerge as we uncover new requirements for managing networks.

2.4.1 Event-Driven Integration

Event-driven integration is the passing of events from one management application to another. An event is a text string that denotes information about a component that is being managed. Classic kinds of events are powering up a computer, powering down a computer, or a successful or failed log on attempt. These kinds of events, and many others, can be forwarded to other management applications for further processing.

Figure 2.9 shows patterns of event-driven integration. Management application 1 (MA-1) is responsible for monitoring a particular domain of a network and MA-2 is responsible for monitoring another domain. We use the term "domain" loosely. For example MA-1 and MA-2 could be responsible for two geographical domains. On the other hand, MA-1 could be responsible for all transmission devices in a particular domain, whereas MA-2 is responsible for all computer systems in the same domain.

MA-3 is an optional MA that is once removed from the network. It is sometimes called a manager of managers (MOM). That is, MA-3 doesn't monitor anything. Rather MA-3 simply receives events from multiple management applications in order to perform event correlation, consolidated event displays, reporting, trouble shooting, or other specialized management functions.

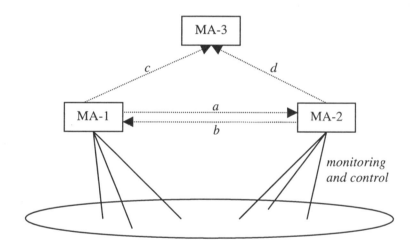

Figure 2.9 Generic Event-Driven Integration

The arrows *a*, *b*, *c*, and *d* in Figure 2.9 represent the source and destination of event passing. These arrows demonstrate the range of possibilities. In the example above where MA-3 is a MOM, events are passed along arrows *c* and *d*. We will see some examples later in this section in which it makes sense to pass information along arrows *a* and *b*. For the moment, the reader is invited to think about cases in which it makes sense to do that.

2.4.2 Alarm-Driven Integration

The pattern of alarm-driven integration is the same as event-driven integration in Figure 2.9, with the exception of the definitions of "event" and "alarm." Many management applications have mechanisms that provide event-correlation over their particular areas of interest, i.e. a method of inferring an alarm from a stream or collection of events. The content of an alarm, then, represents a consolidation of events into one over arching alarm.

The classic example of event correlation is when an event that denotes the failure of a transmission device A on the edge of a network causes hundreds of other events that denote failure of devices downstream from A. An event-correlation method would suppress the hundreds of events and raise the one event as an alarm. Other event correlation scenarios are numerous, and we will see many of them in later chapters.

The advantage of alarm-driven correlation is that the MA may pass a few alarms to a peer application rather than a large number of events. Thus, the job of alarm-correlation of the receiving application may be considerably easier. For example, if in Figure 2.9 there were half a dozen MA's passing streams of events to MA-3, then it is very likely that MA-3 would exhibit poor performance. But if the half dozen MA's were each performing event correlation and passing a few select alarms to MA-3, then MA-3's job is less difficult.

2.4.3 Manual Event/Alarm Integration

An obvious variation on event/alarm-driven integration is to put the decision of event/alarm passing into the hands of an administrator. To do this, one places a button or pull-down menu on an alarm or a device icon upon which an alarm occurs. The button collects information surrounding the alarm, including IP address, alarm status, connectivity, or various other parameters, and that information is forwarded to another application on demand by clicking the button or selecting the menu item.

2.4.4 Collaboration-Driven Integration

We can think of events and alarms as simple informative statements. MA-1 wishes to inform MA-3 of an alarm. Now, however, let us think in terms of MA-1 asking a question of a peer application, the answer to which would determine the behavior of MA-1. We call that a collaboration between MA-1 and MA-2.

Consider an example. In Figure 2.9 suppose that MA-1 is a network MA and MA-2 is a computer system MA. Further suppose that the sole function of MA-1 is to monitor network infrastructure while the function of MA-2 is to monitor the computer systems that are hosted by the network infrastructure. Consider the same example above in which a failed router causes apparent failure of computer systems downstream from the router. In that case, MA-2 might raise an alarm for each computer system. However, if MA-2 were smart enough to send a message to MA-1 asking about any network alarms that might be the cause of apparent computer failures, MA-2 might reason that it should suppress its alarms.

That is an example of collaboration-driven integration via arrows a and b in Figure 2.9, where a constitutes a question and b constitutes an answer. Also, it is a good example of event correlation distributed over multiple management systems, rather than being carried out by a single management system.

Other scenarios in which collaboration among MAs would be useful should come mind. Consider a software distribution MA. If such an application were instructed to do a software upgrade for hundreds of computer systems, it would be a good idea to ask questions of network and computer MAs first to be reasonably sure that the task would complete successfully. Or, if a network MA observed that a transmission device is failing or about to fail, it would be a good idea to send a message to the software distribution MA saying "Just in case you're in the midst of a software distribution task, it would be a good idea for you to suspend it until I send a message telling you otherwise."

2.4.5 Help Desk Integration

Most all integrated management solutions require integration between a management system and a help desk. The help desk is the call center where users report application problems. Many of the problems will be user-error problems or have to do with application malfunctioning.

However, if an application is distributed over a network (e.g. a client/server application), then a user's problem may have to with network or computer malfunctions. Clearly, it is useful for a troubleshooter to have knowledge of existing network or computer malfunctions when trying to diagnose a user's complaint. If a troubleshooter receives a call about application A, which resides on computer C, which is hosted by network N, then one of the things the troubleshooter can do is check on current alarms having to do with C and N.

Help desk integration is a straightforward example of event or alarm-driven integration as discussed above. The idea is to transform network and computer systems alarms into trouble tickets, in the same way that help desk operators transform emails or telephone calls into trouble tickets. In Figure 2.9, then, we may consider MA-3 as a help desk system, where MA-1 is a network management application and MA-2 is a computer management application.

2.4.6 View Integration

Consider Figure 2.9 again. Suppose we have a management system such that MA-3 receives alarms from other lower-level MA's in MOM fashion. Suppose the function of MA-3 is to list all alarms in a central GUI. Now, the lower-level MA's will have other relevant information regarding the alarm, for example information regarding the configuration, performance, and connectivity of the device on which the alarm occurred. Thus, an administrator sitting at the console of MA-3 may find it helpful to obtain other information regarding the alarm.

A way to do that is to invoke views from lower-level management applications. This is sometimes called "launching-in-state" or view integration. In integrated management solutions, alarm-driven integration and view integration typically go hand in hand. We will see some concrete examples in later chapters.

2.4.7 Database Integration

Most management applications store information in a database regarding their managed objects. This is sometimes called historical information. It may be used for generating reports or uncovering trends in network usage.

Now, given that most business and service networks have separate MAs that cover different aspects of their operation, it follows that there will likely be a number of different historical databases. Further, there may be instances in which it is required that select information in the databases be consolidated. Figure 2.10 shows general patterns of database integration.

Figure 2.10 is rather complex. But remember that the figure shows the range of possibilities. It will never be the case that historical information is passed along all arrows a to h simultaneously.

One possible kind of database integration is that MA-1 and MA-2 bypass their respective databases entirely and elect to forward their information to db-3 via g and h. A second kind of integration is that portions of db-1 and db-2 are entered into db-3 via *c* and *d* for a specialized reporting application MA-3. A third kind of integration is that select portions of MA-1's database is entered into MA-2's database via *a*. And yet another kind of integration, not shown in the figure, is that a web-based application reaches out to fetch select data from multiple databases in order to generate cross-domain reports.

As an example, consider a network simulation system. As discussed earlier, most simulation systems require one to construct network topology and traffic profiles manually through a GUI. However, the manual method can be tedious and error-prone.

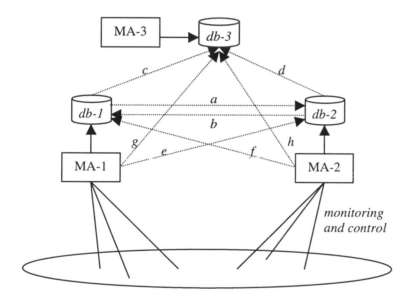

Figure 2.10 Patterns of Database Integration

On the other hand, consider that a network management application can construct a model of network topology autonomously with a network discovery tool. For example, the tool can be given a list or range of IP addresses, whereupon it simply walks down the list, pinging the address and listening for a response. More sophisticated discovery tools discover port-level connectivity as well, while others build up a representation of network topology in terms of a pre-defined language. We'll see an example of such a language in the next chapter. The important point for this discussion is that there exists a database that holds an accurate representation of network devices, relations among devices, and connectivity.

Next, consider that a traffic monitoring tool can be used to construct traffic profiles over a given period of time. The tool reads the headers of packets as they flow over a medium, aggregating variables such as load per application between two separate devices or two separate domains. Thus there exists a database that holds a more-or-less accurate representation of traffic patterns in one's actual network.

It would make sense to pass accurate topology information and traffic profiles to the simulation database. With this baseline, simulation experts can proceed to study what-if scenarios by altering the topology or traffic loads. This is a good example of database integration along arrows *c* and *d*, where MA-1 is a network management application, MA-2 is a traffic management application, and MA-3 is a network simulation application.

Other kinds of database integration should come to mind depending upon the business requirements.

2.5 Implementation Challenges

During the analysis phase of OOSE, we argued that integrated management architectures should be conceived without regard to implementation details. The integration patterns discussed above do just that. We haven't said anything about particular management products or the means by which information is passed from one to the other.

During the construction phase, when we transform an analysis model into a design and implementation model, complications certainly will arise. Common problems include integrations with mandated or legacy MAs, communication mechanisms, formatting problems, data synchronization among disparate management systems, and naming problems.

Consider the pattern of help desk integration combined with view integration. Assume that a company has mandated X as their network MA and Y as their help desk MA. Assume further that these applications currently work in standalone mode, although it is acknowledged that an operational and business advantage would be gained if they were integrated as described above. That is, we wish that alarms detected by X were passed to Y, and we want a mechanism in Y by which to invoke detailed views in X on demand. How do we achieve that?

It is very likely that the format of alarms sent from X will be different from the format that Y expects to receive them. Thus, parsing has to be done before the alarm is forwarded, or else after the alarm is received. That is not an insurmountable problem, but one has to pay heed to the semantics of the alarm text on both ends. As in natural languages and human communication, terms can have different meanings and sometimes two different terms have the same meaning.

That is what we mean by the naming problem. Often two MA's will have different names for the same device. If the help desk contains an inventory database and the network MA passes an alarm to the help desk, then clearly the network MA needs to know the naming conventions in the inventory database. Further, if the help desk operator wishes to invoke a particular view of a component in the network MA, then the help desk needs to know the naming conventions of the network MA.

Typically, at least in the data communications domain, the IP Address or MAC address is shared by both MAs. Many integrations require a look-up table that correlates different naming conventions. A row in the table might have the form:

IP Address	MAC Address	Name-1	Name-2

Essentially, an MA asks the question "What do you call this thing I call X?"

Finally, the physical communication problem arises when we enter the design and implementation phase. Help desk applications can have a number of ways by which to receive messages from external sources, for example emails, remote procedural calls, SNMP traps, CMIP traps, or CORBA IDLs. Another popular way is that the help desk application periodically looks in a file to see if alarms from external sources have been placed there.

Whatever the means of receiving alarms, the network MA is constrained to use that means. For example, the network MA might have to embed alarm information in an SNMP wrapper and then forward it to the help desk as an SNMP trap. Alternatively, the network management MA may execute a remote function on the computer that hosts the help desk, where the arguments of the function contain particulars about the alarm.

These problems are design and implementation problems. We have used help desk integration as an example, but they apply to all the integration patterns discussed above. The world would be a good place indeed if all vendors in telecommunications and data communications domains used identical formatting, naming, and communication conventions. That, of course, is the ultimate goal of standards bodies, but we are a rather far way from that state of affairs. Nonetheless, as system engineers with practical problems to solve in the field, we do what we can with what we've got, so to speak, making use of accepted standards where possible.

Importantly, such design problems should not be considered during the analysis phase of OOSE. The Analysis model should be derived from the Use Case model, which in turn is derived from business requirements. That way, one knows what the ideal integrated management system should look like from a conceptual point of view. Thus, when the model is transformed into the design model, one retains the best features of the ideal system and what's left over serves as a guide for further research and development. That is a good strategy by which to carry out integrated management programs.

Chapter Summary

In this chapter we looked at issues surrounding the architecture and design of integrated management systems. Importantly, we explored these issues without regard to technical, implementation-specific detail. The reason is that we wish to have a good understanding of what an ideal management system would look like before considering how to implement it. The advantage of this is that we can transform the maximum structure of the ideal system into a working system, and what's left over may be handed over to research labs as a guide for further work.

First we presented some examples of common requirements for integrated management systems: multi-domain management, fault management, network simulation, integration with the help desk, integrated IP and telephony management, and service level management.

From such business requirements we are expected to develop a corresponding management system, and that calls for an understanding of sound methodological principles. We argued that the development of integrated management systems is similar to the development of software systems in general. Thus we presented a prominent methodology called object-oriented software engineering. We will make use of the methodology in the remainder of the book.

Finally, we listed some common patterns that one will find in integrated management systems. We saw that some of the patterns answer some of the business requirements listed at the beginning of the chapter. In general, these patterns should be considered as a sort of conceptual toolbox with which to approach management challenges in the field. We will refer to these patterns during the remainder of the book.

In short, this chapter has provided us with important groundwork for the rest of the book, as well as important groundwork for developing integrated management systems for business and service networks in the field.

Exercises and Discussion Questions

1. Develop a Use Case Model for the section Resolving Network Faults. Discuss the model with your peers.

2. Develop a Use Case Model for the section Network Simulation and discuss it with your peers.

3. Develop a Use Case Model for the section Integrated IP and Telephony Management and discuss it with your peers.

4. Evaluate and criticize the SLA Use Case Model in Figure 2.8.

5. This is a research exercise. You are charged to write an additional piece for Section 2.1 entitled Management by Policy. What is Management by Policy? What business requirements call for it? Does it require an integrated management solution? Write a short essay that answers these questions.

6. Exercises 6 through 9 represent toy hands-on exercises, but they require a fair amount of work. They will give you an appreciation of the difficulties in building integrated management systems. Consider Microsoft Access as a trouble ticketing system, whereby end users enter complaints into the system via email. Set up a ticket database in Access and implement the means by which it receives emails from end-users.

7. If you have access to some network management application, try to set it up such that an event automatically sends an email to Access in the form of a trouble ticket.

8. Set up the management application in accordance with the Manual Event/Alarm Integration pattern in Section 2.4.3.

9. Integrate Access and the management application in accordance with the View Integration pattern in Section 2.4.6.

10. If you have installed the Spectrum Management System, repeat Question #7. (Hint: see the Spectrum AlarmNotifier Manual).

Further Studies

Our discussion of risks in software development is based on Keil et al's paper "A Framework for Identifying Software Project Risks" and Glass's paper "Short-Term and Long-Term Remedies for Runaway Projects."
  Our study of the Object Oriented Software engineering is based on Jacobson et al's book *Object-Oriented Software Engineering: A Use Case*

Driven Approach. Jacobson is a prominent name in the OOSE community, but there are others: Booch, Rumbaugh, Coad, Yourdan, Shlaer, Mellor, Martin, Odell, Coleman, de Champeaux, Henderson-Selers, Wirfs-Brock, and Edwards.

Jacobson, Booch, and Rumbaugh have combined the best features of their respective methodologies into the Unified Modeling Language (UML). Three books on UML (jointly authored by Jacobson, Booch, and Rumbaugh) are listed in the References.

A book that continues the SLA example in Section 2.3 is Lewis' *Service Level Management for Enterprise Networks*.

A good book that complements this chapter is Hegering and Abeck's *Integrated Network and Systems Management*. Also, see Ghetie's *Network and Systems Management Platforms*. The latter book compares several commercial management platforms along multiple dimensions, including the platforms' mechanisms by which to integrate with other systems.

Some parts of this chapter were adapted from the Spectrum Guide to Integrated Applications manual, posted on www.aprisma.com. That manual describes generic integration patterns, mechanisms in Spectrum by which to implement the patterns, and case studies of integrated management systems.

References

Booch, G., J. Rumbaugh, and I. Jacobson. *The Unified Modeling Language User Guide*. Addison-Wesley. 1999.

Ghetie, J. *Network and Systems Management Platforms*. Kluwer Academic Publishers. 1997.

Glass, R. "Short-Term and Long-Term Remedies for Runaway Projects" in *Communications of the ACM*. July 1998/Vol. 41, No. 7.

Hegering, H. and S. Abeck. *Integrated Network and Systems Management*. Addison-Wesley. 1994.

Jacobson, I., M. Christerson, P. Jonsson, and G. Overgaard. *Object-Oriented Software Engineering: A Use Case Driven Approach*. Addison-Wesley. 1995[1992].

Jacobson, I., G. Booch, and J. Rumbaugh. *The Unified Software Development Process*. Addison-Wesley. 1999.

Keil, M., P. Cule, K. Lyytinen, and R. Schmidt. "A Framework for Identifying Software Project Risks" in *Communications of the ACM*. November 1998/Vol. 41, No. 11.

Lewis, L. *Service Level Management for Enterprise Networks*. Artech House. 1999.

Rumbaugh, J., I. Jacobson, and G. Booch. *The Unified Modeling Language Reference Manual*. Addison-Wesley. 1999.

3 Introduction to the Spectrum Management System

In Chapter 2 we examined (i) sample requirements for integrated management systems, (ii) a methodology for developing management systems, and (iii) common patterns in integrated management. In this chapter we discuss a particular management system that is based on the principles in the preceding chapter, viz. the Spectrum Management System developed by Aprisma Management Technologies. There are plenty others; thus the reader should consider our discussion of Spectrum as a representative example.

We discuss the following topics in this chapter:

- History of Spectrum
- The Spectrum Perspective on Network Management
- Event Correlation in Spectrum and Other Applications
- Integrating Management Applications with Spectrum

First we describe Spectrum's history, starting in 1990. We will see that Spectrum began life as a multi-vendor "network" management system for data communications networks, but has matured over the years into a system for managing service networks and multi-domain networks, including facilities for service level management, integrated data/telephony management, and business process management.

Second, we describe Spectrum's object-oriented perspective on network management. We discuss the way in which Spectrum represents multi-vendor network components and show how the initial 1990 architecture set the stage for an evolution towards managing business and service networks of the 2000s.

Third, we discuss monitoring, reasoning, and control of networks. Early management systems included monitoring only, and reasoning and control were performed by network administrators. The hallmark of "reasoning" in a network management system is event correlation. Thus, we describe Spectrum's event correlation mechanism and compare it with other management systems.

Finally, we look at methods for integrating other management applications with Spectrum. We will go into a fair amount of technical detail, following the requirements and patterns that were presented in Chapter 2. The discussion will prepare us for the Case Studies in Part II.

3.1 History of Spectrum

Spectrum, built by Aprisma Management Technologies, is one of two leading network management systems in the industry. It belongs in the same category as Hewlett Packard's *OpenView*.

The goal of these systems is to take a network-centric view of network management, as opposed to an element-centric view. Both systems allow representation and management of multi-vendor network devices in a single system. However, the primary difference between the two is that OpenView offers skeletal, no-frills representations of devices. If one wants to perform special-purpose management functions on a device, one simply launches the vendor's element management application from OpenView.

In Spectrum, the goal is to eliminate the launching of multiple element managers. That means that Spectrum architects have to duplicate the basic management functions of vendors' devices, and add value on top of that with mechanisms for event correlation, multi-domain management, service level management, and applications/systems management.

Both Spectrum and OpenView have evolved considerably since their inception in the late 1980s. Here, we focus on the history of Spectrum. Literature on the history of OpenView is provided in the References section.

3.1.1 Spectrum in the 2000s

The description of Spectrum in 2000 can be stated as follows:

Spectrum (2000) is a management system that monitors and controls business processes, services, applications, transmission devices, computer systems, and traffic in small to very large multi-vendor networked domains, including business enterprises, service provider networks, and combined data/telephony networks; and provides the means to:

- Discover the components of the networked domain,
- Represent the relations among components in a centralized or distributed data repository,
- Collect performance data over time (i.e. historical data) in an archive data repository,

- Perform traditional fault, configuration, accounting, performance, and security (FCAPS) management,
- Perform TMN-style management, including element, network, service, and business management.
- Reason about the state of the networked domain (a.k.a. event correlation),
- Provide reports on the state of the networked domain,
- Demonstrate the connection between the networked domain and business operations (a.k.a. network/business alignment),
- Integrate with complementary management systems,
- Manage the networked domain with a web browser.

Figure 3.1 is a sample Spectrum view that shows the decomposition of a service into network components. The icon labels are probably difficult to read because the graphic was reduced for this book, so we will explain the picture below.

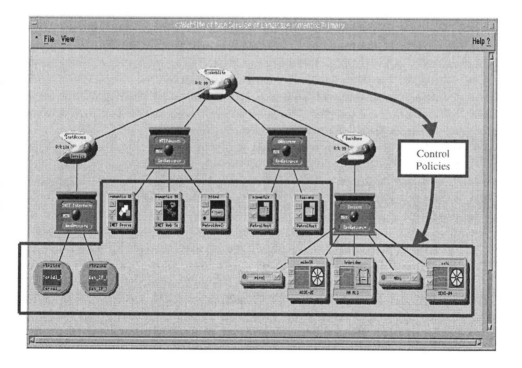

Figure 3.1 Sample Spectrum View Showing Services and Network Components

The icons that look like pac-men represent services. The topmost service is named IcsWebSite. (ICS is a software/services company in Germany.) The icons on the second tier show the decomposition of IcsWebSite into four components: two other services named InetAccess and Backbone. The two icons in the middle of the second tier look like safes. The safes represent logical categories of components upon which the topmost service depends. In this case they are named HTTPdaemon and WWWserver.

We then show how a service is logically decomposed into some subset of low-level network components, including networks, hardware, applications, and computer systems. To make that clear, we have drawn a border around those low-level components. The low-level items are monitored by Spectrum such that their individual performances are integrated to show the performance of the topmost service.

A business executive would probably be interested only in performance views and service level reports regarding the topmost IcsWebSite service. In this way, the executive may get insight into the relation between network behavior and the operation of the business without having to know the technical details of network operation. On the other hand, networking technologists would be interested in FCAPS-style management of the lower-level network components.

We have also taken liberty to insert a Control Policies box in the picture (hand-drawn). The work on policy-based control is in the research stage, but it is gaining momentum in the industry. The idea is that the creation and provisioning of a service will be associated with a set of policies that govern low-level network components. An example is "policy-based routing" where the addition or deletion of a service regulates the possible traffic patterns in a network. We will see an example of that in Chapter 8.

Figure 3.1 illustrates some of the capabilities of Spectrum in 2000, and we will see plenty more in our Case Study chapters. However, Spectrum began life in 1990 with more modest goals, although in 1990 those goals were considered rather ambitious.

3.1.2 Spectrum in 1990

The description of Spectrum in 1990 was this:

Spectrum (1990) is a management system that monitors and controls transmission devices in small to medium multi-vendor business enterprises; and provides the means to:

- Discover the transmission devices in the networked domain,

- Represent the relations among devices in a centralized data repository,
- Collect performance data over time (i.e. historical data) in an archive data repository,
- Perform fault, configuration, and performance (FCP) management,
- Reason about the state of the networked domain (a.k.a. event correlation),
- Provide reports on the state of the networked domain.

The difference between Spectrum (1990) and Spectrum (2000) is the following: In 1990 Spectrum managed multi-vendor devices of data communications networks only (for example the network components enclosed in the border in Figure 3.1). The ideas of managing computer systems, applications, services, business processes, multi-domain networks, service provider networks, management by policy, and combined data and telecommunications networks were things of the future. Further, the idea of integrated management was a foreign concept in 1990.

3.1.3 Historical Foundations

Spectrum emerged in 1990 in the following way. By 1988 Cabletron Systems had become a major provider of network hardware, but there were other providers -- Cisco Systems, Bay Networks, Synoptics, and 3COM. It was clear to all hardware manufacturers in 1988 that a necessary requirement for selling networking hardware was to offer some way to manage it.

When Cabletron's architects began thinking about network management in 1988, they made an important decision: The network management system should not only manage Cabletron devices; it should also manage other popular devices from Cisco, Bay, and 3COM. Since the Simple Management Network Protocol (SNMP) and Management Information Bases (MIBs) showed promise as de facto standards, and since other devices could be managed in the same way as Cabletron devices, the architects decided to build a multi-vendor network management system.

Further, they saw the need for event correlation and fault isolation in management systems. For example a router could fail, thereby causing apparent failures of all routers and devices connected to it, regardless of the vendor that manufactured it. There was a need, then, to build a system that could isolate faults in a network, distinguish real failures from apparent failures, and suppress alarms that have to do with apparent failures.

To implement the multi-vendor management idea, the architects designed a system based on the general object-oriented paradigm, where hardware devices were conceived as objects. In this way, they could develop a generic object that represents a router, and then instantiate the generic router with Cabletron, Cisco, Bay, or 3COM routers. Each specific router would inherit the characteristics of a generic router but additionally include special features of the vendor-specific router.

To implement event correlation and fault isolation over multi-vendor networks, the architects borrowed a method from the artificial intelligence community called model-based reasoning. This method was developed at the Massachusetts Institute of Technology in the mid-1980s. We will describe how it works in Section 3.3.2.

Those were fortunate design decisions made in 1988. Multi-vendor management, object orientation, and event correlation via model-based reasoning are now considered the state of the science in network management.

However, Spectrum's multi-vendor management paradigm went fairly unnoticed for the first half of the 90s decade. The reason is that Cabletron was considered primarily a manufacturer of networking hardware. Most people assumed that Cabletron's Spectrum would manage only Cabletron gear, in classic element management style.

A consequence of this state of affairs was that hardware vendors such as Cisco, Bay, and 3COM were somewhat skeptical about cooperating with Spectrum architects during the 1990s. Although their MIBs were in the public domain, and thus Spectrum architects could demonstrate the management of their hardware, there remained the lingering, natural suspicion that something was not right. Why would Cabletron's Spectrum want to management their hardware, when the main business of Cabletron was to sell Cabletron hardware?

The reason is that Spectrum architects were following a management-focused track that was gaining momentum during the 90s. They were concerned primarily with the management of networks and all their facets, from low-level component management to higher-level business process management. While the management of Cabletron gear was certainly important, and while Cabletron exploited Spectrum's capabilities when marketing Cabletron hardware, the Spectrum architects were following the track of network management in general.

In this regard the reader should review the Evolution of Network Management in Section 1.4 of Chapter 1. That is the track that Spectrum architects followed during the 1990s, starting with plain "network" management in 1990 and evolving to the management of services offered by combined data and telecommunications networks in 2000.

In 1999 it became clear to Cabletron that network management had become a discipline in its own right and could be pursued independently of hardware. Thus, a second important decision was made at Cabletron, namely to separate the Spectrum network management division from the hardware division.

Thus the Spectrum organization was spun off into a separate company named Aprisma Management Technologies. Thanks to that decision, Spectrum is now rightly considered as an open, vendor-independent management system, and Aprisma architects can continue following and contributing to the evolution of network management.

In the following sections we go into more detail regarding Spectrum's architecture, how it is used to manage business and service networks, and how it can be extended to accommodate the management requirements of 21st century networks.

3.1.4 Spectrum's Architecture

The Spectrum Management System is based on a distributed client/server architecture, as shown in Figure 3.2. The Spectrum servers, called SpectroSERVERS (SSs), monitor and control devices in individual network domains. The Spectrum clients, called SpectroGRAPHS (SGs), may attach to any SS to graphically present the state of that SS's domain, including topological information, event and alarm information, and configuration information.

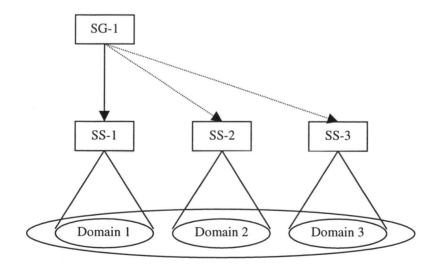

Figure 3.2 Spectrum's Distributed Client/Server Architecture

The SGs are examples of interface objects, while the SSs are examples of hybrid interface/control objects (see Section 2.3.3). The SGs are the interfaces to the network administrators, but the SGs do not have direct access to network components. The SSs provide the interfaces and communication links to the network components, but they are not responsible for displaying data. They pass data to the SGs for display.

Let us pause briefly to discuss the technical aspects of the communications among SGs and SSs. The SS is a computer process (i.e. a running program) that responds to remote SG requests. The SS can get the requested information from its database or directly from a managed node via SNMP or some other device management protocol. However, the SG doesn't know how the information is retrieved; it knows only how to request information from the SS. For example, the SG can request the SS to send unsolicited messages about the changing status of a managed node.

SGs communicate with SSs through the SS Application Programming Interface (SSAPI). There are two modes of communication through the SSAPI. The *synchronous* mode causes the SG to pause execution until the response to a request has been returned, at which point the SG continues. The *asynchronous* mode works with a callback routine. The SG initiates a request and returns to what it was doing. When the SS has the reply ready, the SG receives a call from the SS indicating that the response can be retrieved.

Now, from the perspective of the network operator in the field, that is all transparent. The operator simply perceives that all networking domains and the devices within the domains can be viewed from a single SG. If SG-1 in Figure 3.2 is in communication to SS-1, but one wishes to monitor and control the domain covered by SS-2, then one can click on an icon in SG-1 that represents SS-2. Figure 3.2 shows a primary client/server communication between SG-1 and SS-1. Virtual communications between SG-1 and the other SSs are indicated by dotted lines.

3.2 The Spectrum Perspective on Network Management

The first important design decision made by Spectrum architects was to adopt the object-oriented paradigm (OOP) for network management. Therefore, let us explain OOP as it relates to network management.

3.2.1 Physical Entities and Logical Entities are Objects

First let us distinguish between physical entities and logical entities. A physical entity is something that a management system can talk to via SNMP or some other management protocol. A logical entity, on the other hand, is a mental construct and therefore cannot be talked to, properly speaking.

A "domain" is a good example of a logical entity. A management system doesn't talk to a domain; rather, it talks to the physical entities that comprise the domain. An "email service" is another example of a logical entity. A management system doesn't talk to an email service; rather, it talks to the physical entities upon which the email service depends.

(As an aside, the author has often wondered how the phrase "logical entity" came to refer to such mental constructs as domains and services. A better phrase would have been "fictional entity." However, "logical" has caught on in the industry, so we'll stick with that.)

Now, an object in OOP is a software representation of any physical or logical entity. In Spectrum one can model any network component, including physical and logical entities, as objects. Referring back to Figure 3.1, the topmost IcsWebSite icon represents a service, which is a logical entity. The icons within the border at the bottom of the figure are representations of physical entities.

Objects have descriptions, behaviors, and relations to other objects. For example, in the same way that people have descriptions such as a name, a unique ID number, height, and myriad other attributes, network objects have descriptions such as name, IP address, vendor, type, MIB attributes, and so on.

In the same way that people exhibit behaviors when asked to do so, network objects exhibit behaviors when asked to do so, e.g. change your name from X to Y, give me statistics for MIB variable Z from time t_1 to t_n, and send events of type T to management application MA-1. In Figure 3.1, for example, the bottommost physical entities exhibit the behavior of passing performance data upward to logical entities that they compose.

Finally, in the same way that people are described in terms of their relations to other people, network objects are described in terms of their relations to other objects. Classic examples are that ports 1 to 12 reside on Router R1, ports 13 to 24 reside on router R2, port 5 is connected to port 20, and so forth. In Figure 3.1, the IcsWebSite object is related to the objects InetAccess and Backbone via the relation "is composed of."

In Spectrum one can model any physical or logical entity, including ports, transmission media, protocols, routers, hubs, switches, users, domains, buildings, organizational units, services, business processes, and so on.

One often hears that OOP takes an anthropomorphic view of the domain it represents, where "anthropomorphism" refers to the ascription of human emotions and characteristics to non-human entities. Although it's a stretch to say that network objects have feelings like humans, we can indeed structure their descriptions, behaviors, and relations in the same way that we structure human descriptions, behaviors, and relations.

3.2.2 Other Concepts in the Object-Oriented Paradigm

There are a few other concepts in OOP that we should cover in order to describe Spectrum internals: encapsulation, classes, inheritance, class hierarchies, and collaboration.

Encapsulation in OOP means "information hiding." If one were to look at an object from the outside, one would see only its interface. Its interface is a list of messages that can be sent to it. Messages can be questions about its description and relations to other objects, or they can be requests to perform some kind of behavior. Now, exactly how the object responds to the question is hidden from the object that sends the message. The sending object knows only about the form of messages it can send, and the format of the message it will get in return.

Recall that an object is a reflection in software of the actual or logical entity it represents. Now, a *class* is an object template, not an object as such. However, we get the object proper when we instantiate the template. In Spectrum, when we instantiate a template we have to provide a name, IP Address, MAC Address, or some other unique identifier depending on naming conventions. The object template has to communicate with the real object in order to collect initial data by which to flesh out the object.

When one instantiates a class to make an object, the object at once exhibits the generic description, behaviors, and relations of the class. Further, when the object begins communicating with its real-world counterpart, it will add device-specific information. In addition, one can construct a class that *inherits* descriptions and behaviors from other classes via an "is a kind of" relation. That is called a *class hierarchy*. An example is below.

Spectrum is equipped with a set of class hierarchies that cover most types of physical and logical entities. Figure 3.3 shows a small portion of it. For example, a Hub is a kind of Device, which is a kind of EntityType.

The best case scenario is that one runs the Spectrum Auto-Discovery, whereupon Spectrum internals develop a virtual network model by matching templates with the real-world objects it discovers.

Sometimes, however, one will run across a network component for which there is not an explicit template. Such an object shows up as a Unknown Device object. In that case, an administrator may search through class hierarchies looking for a class that is sufficiently similar to the unknown device, and derive a new class from that class. It is this feature that allows Spectrum to be extendable into new network management domains.

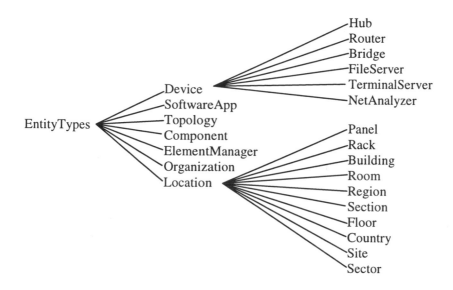

Figure 3.3 Spectrum Model Type Hierarchy (partial)

A *collaboration* between two objects means that the objects send messages to each other for some purpose. In network management systems, collaborations among objects are the means by which to realize event correlation, fault isolation, and other management functions. We will look at event correlation in Spectrum and compare it with other approaches to event correlation in the next section. Now, however, we wish to say a word about Spectrum terminology.

3.2.3 Spectrum Terminology

Spectrum employs the object-oriented perspective of network management. However, the Spectrum brand name for this perspective is *Inductive Modeling Technology*. Further, a class in OOP is called a *model-type* in Spectrum, a class hierarchy is called a *model-type hierarchy*, an object is called a *model*, class inheritance is called a *model-type derivation*, and a collaboration among objects is called *model based reasoning*. Table 3.1 shows the comparison of OOP terminology and Spectrum terminology.

When we talk about Spectrum in later chapters, we use Spectrum terminology. The reader should keep in mind, however, that these terms are grounded in the general object-oriented framework.

Table 3.1 Comparison of OOP Terms and Spectrum Terms

In OOP	In Spectrum
OOP	Inductive Modeling Technology
Class	Model-type
Class Hierarchy	Model-type Hierarchy
Class Inheritance	Model-type Derivation
Object	Model
Object Collaboration	Model Based Reasoning

3.3 Event Correlation in Spectrum and Other Applications

Event correlation and fault isolation have become issues of paramount importance in network management, especially with the advent of multi-domain networks and combined data and telecommunications networks.

Event correlation can be defined loosely as the process of making sense of a very large number of events, where "making sense" entails throwing some of them away, observing cause-and-effect relations between others, inferring an alarm from a set of related events, or identifying the culprit event in a misbehaving enterprise. Figure 3.4 illustrates this idea.

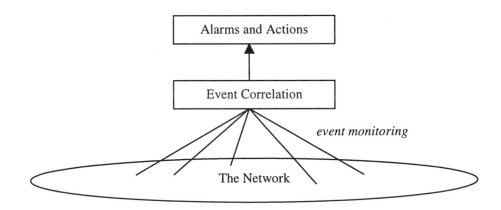

Figure 3.4 Event Correlation over the Network

The event correlation task is somewhat analogous to the interaction between the brain and the five senses (another example of anthropomorphism). The senses deliver a very large number of impressions to the brain. However, our brain has evolved such that we ignore the great majority of these signals. Further, our brain has the capacity to interpret our impressions. For example, we may infer the simple idea of "impending trouble" based on our surroundings.

In this section we look at five approaches to the event correlation task and corresponding management applications in the industry:

- Rule-based reasoning (Tivoli's TME, RiverSoft's OpenRiver)
- Model-based reasoning (Aprisma's Spectrum)
- State transition graphs (SeaGates's NerveCenter)
- Codebooks (SMARTS' InCharge)
- Case-based reasoning (Aprisma's SpectroRx)

3.3.1 Rule-Based Reasoning

A common approach to the event correlation task is to represent knowledge and expertise in a rule-based reasoning (RBR) system (a.k.a. expert systems, production systems, or blackboard systems). See Figure 3.5. An RBR system consists of three basic parts:

- A Working Memory
- A Rule Base
- A Reasoning Algorithm

The working memory consists of facts. The rule base represents knowledge about what other facts to infer, or what actions to take, given the particular facts in working memory. The reasoning algorithm is the mechanism that actually makes the inference.

The best way to think about the operation of the reasoning algorithm is to recall the classic *Modus Ponens* inference rule in elementary logic:

A	*A fact in working memory*
If A then B	*A rule in the rule base*
Therefore, B	*An inference made by a reasoning algorithm*

In this simple example, since the antecedent *A* of the rule *If A then B* matches fact *A* in the working memory, we say that the rule fires and the directive *B* is executed.

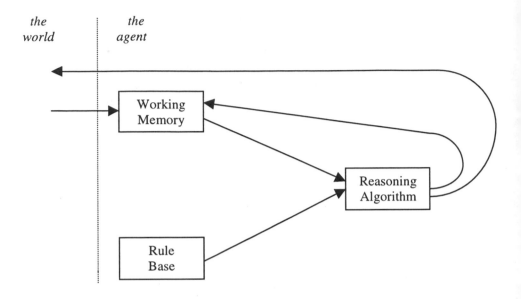

Figure 3.5 The Basic Structure of RBR Systems

Note that B can be several kinds of directive:

- Add a new fact to working memory.
- Perform a test on some part of the enterprise and add the result to working memory.
- Query a database and add the result to working memory.
- Query an agent and add the result to working memory.
- Execute a control command on some enterprise component (e.g. re-configure a router, or prohibit a certain class of traffic over a link).
- Issue an alarm via some alarm notification medium.

For example:

Rule 1: *if*   load(N1, t1) = high *and*
                packet_loss(N1, t1) = high *and*
                connection_failure(C3, S, t1) = true *and*
                connection_failure(C4, S, t1) = true
         then add_to_memory(problem(t1) = traffic congestion)

Rule 2: *if*   problem(t1) = traffic congestion
         then add_to_memory(Show traffic from t1–10 to t1)

Regardless of the particular directive, after the reasoning algorithm makes a first pass over the working memory and the rule base, the working memory becomes enlarged with new facts. The enlargement might be a result of the directives, or it might be a result of the monitoring agents entering new events in working memory over time. In either case, on the second pass there might be other rules that fire and offer new directives and therefore new facts, and so on for each subsequent pass.

At this juncture we should be able to appreciate the sort of complexity entailed by representing knowledge with RBR systems. The good news is that rules are rather intuitive, as is the basic operation of an RBR system. But the bad news is that it is non-trivial to come up with a correct set of rules that behave in the way that we conceptualize them. This problem shows up especially when subsequent passes over the memory and rule base issue unplanned directives, or seem to be going nowhere, or when the control algorithm gets caught in a non-ending loop.

The general consensus in the industry regarding the use of RBR systems is this:

- *If the domain that the RBR system covers is small, non-changing, and well understood, then it's a good idea to use the RBR method. If one tries the RBR approach when these three conditions do not hold, one is asking for trouble.*

Thus, using an RBR system to develop an event correlator that covers the entire domain of the network is not a good idea. The networked domain is large, dynamic, and generally hard to understand.

But this doesn't mean that RBR systems don't have a place in enterprise management. For example, let us think about a single computer system as opposed to an entire enterprise. A single computer system is a much smaller entity than an enterprise. It is reasonable, then, to consider an RBR system to perform event correlation over this small domain.

In fact this is precisely the way that most vendors who build computer monitoring agents do it, for example BMC Patrol, Tivoli TME, Computer Associates Unicenter, and Platinum ProVision. Most of these systems are one-iteration type systems. The reasoning algorithm periodically makes a pass over the memory and the rule base and checks to see if any event (or some set of events) should be escalated to an alarm. Such events include repetitious failures of log-on attempts and thresholds for parameters such as disk space and CPU usage.

3.3.2 Model-Based Reasoning

Recall that model-based reasoning (MBR) in Spectrum corresponds to object collaboration. Let us consider a simple example to explain how MBR works and how it differs from rule-based reasoning. The author often uses this example in lectures and professional talks, and it usually gets the idea across and stimulates further discussion. Refer to Figure 3.6 as we work through the example.

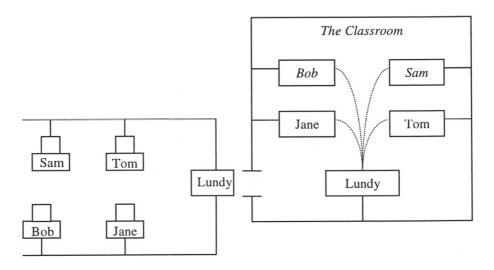

Figure 3.6 A Classroom with Students and a Lecturer

Suppose we have a classroom with several students, and Lundy is the lecturer. Imagine that each student in the class is a model (i.e., a mirror image in software) of some real computer system outside the door. Jane and Tom are models of NT servers, Bob and Sam are models of UNIX workstations, and so forth.

Now imagine that Jane, Tom, Bob, and Sam have a way to communicate with their real-world computer systems. They ping their counterparts every 10 minutes to make sure they are alive, and also collect information about their general health.

The classroom is a model of a subnet. Lundy is a model of the router that hosts the subnet, and Lundy is in communication with the router. Thus there is a real-world system outside the door, and the classroom is a representation of the system.

Lundy and the students are happily pinging their real-world counterparts when all of a sudden Jane pings her NT server and doesn't get a response.

After two more pings with no response, Jane sends a message to Lundy asking if he has heard from his router.

If Lundy answers yes, then Jane infers that there is a fault with her NT server and raises an alarm accordingly. But if Lundy answers no, then Jane reasons that probably her NT server is in good shape, and the real fault is with the router.

The thrust of the example is that event correlation is a collaborative effort among virtual intelligent models, where the models are software representations of real entities in the networked domain.

A general description of a MBR system is as follows:

- An MBR system represents each entity in the network as a model.

- A model is either (i) a representation of a physical entity (e.g., a hub, router, switch, port, computer system) or (ii) a logical entity (e.g., LAN, MAN, WAN, domain, service, business process).

- A model that represents a physical entity is in direct communication with the entity (e.g. via SNMP or other protocols).

- A description of a model includes three categories of information: attributes, relations to other models, and behaviors.

- Examples of attributes for device models are *ip address*, *mac address*, *alarm status*, and myriad others.

- Examples of relations among device models are *connected to*, *depends upon*, *is a kind of*, and *is a part of*.

- An example of a behavior is: *If I am a server model and I get notifications of three "no response" events from my real-world counterpart, then I request status from the model to which I am connected and then make a determination about the value of my alarm status attribute.*

- Event correlation is a result of collaboration among models (i.e. a result of the collective behaviors of all models).

The best example in the industry of the MBR approach is Spectrum. Spectrum contains model types (i.e. classes in object-oriented terminology) for roughly a thousand kinds of physical and logical entities. These model types are used as templates for creating models of the actual entities in network. Each model type contains generic attributes, relations, and behaviors which instances of the type would exhibit.

The first thing one does after installing Spectrum is to run Spectrum's Auto-discovery. Auto-discovery discovers and models the entities in the network, and then fills in the generic characteristics of each model with actual data. Then, as monitoring happens in real time, the models collaborate with respect to their pre-defined behaviors in order to realize the event correlation task.

What happens if there exists an entity for which a Spectrum model type is not available? There are two ways to approach this situation. First, one can exploit the *is a kind of* relation among models. In object-oriented terminology, this relation is called inheritance.

Suppose we have a generic model of a router replete with placeholders for attributes, relations, and behaviors that most all routers share. Then we can define a derivative model of the router and say that it is a kind of generic router. The derivative model inherits the characteristics of its parent, and the job is done.

The second way is to implement a new model type in C++ code and link it with the existing model type hierarchy. Note that this method requires an experienced software engineer.

An alternative way to implement event correlation is to use a Spectrum product called SpectroWatch. SpectroWatch is an RBR system as described in the previous section. It is integrated with Spectrum and it augments Spectrum's core MBR method. One can use SpectroWatch to formulate rules that describe how events are mapped into alarms.

The advantage of this alternate approach is that it is easy to do, since there is a GUI that guides one through the process and C++ programming is not required. The disadvantage is that it may suffer the usual deficiencies of RBR systems: If the domain is large, then the performance of event correlation can be jeopardized.

3.3.3 State Transition Graphs

The key concepts in the STG approach are a token, a state, an arc, a movement of a token from one state to another state via an arc, and an action that is triggered when a token enters a state.

To see how the STG apparatus works, consider the scenario in the preceding section. There was a subnet hosted by a router, and the subnet contained several UNIX workstations and NT servers. One of the NT servers (Jane's server) failed to respond to a ping, but the actual problem was that the router (Lundy's router) had failed.

We want the event correlator to be able to reason that Jane's NT server is only apparently at fault, and Lundy's router is the real fault. Figure 3.7 shows an STG that can reason this through.

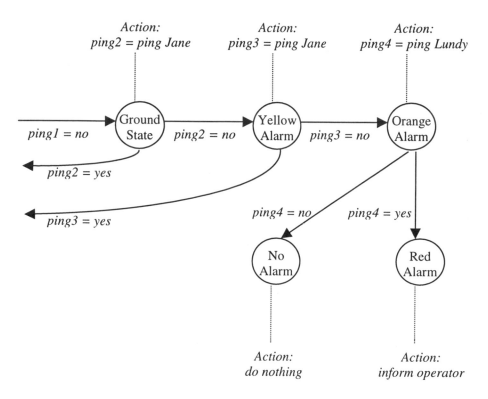

Figure 3.7 A Sample State Transition Graph

The first failure of Jane's NT server causes a token to move into a Ground State. An action of the Ground State is to ping Jane's' NT server after one minute elapses. If the ping doesn't show that Jane's NT server is alive, then the token moves to the Yellow Alarm state, else the token falls off the board. An action of Yellow Alarm is to ping Jane's NT server a second time. If the action returns no, then the token moves to the Orange Alarm state, where the action is to ping Lundy's router. Depending upon the state of Lundy's router, the token moves to either the No Alarm state or the Red Alarm state, and the appropriate action is taken accordingly.

Note that the STG in Figure 3.7 covers a single domain of interest, viz. Jane's NT server. However, a network might contain thousands of diverse kinds of components, and thus it might seem that a large number of STGs may be required to cover the enterprise. Fortunately, since a generic STG can apply to components of the same type, there is no need to build separate STGs for like components.

Further, an action of one state may be to confer with the output of a separate STG. For example the action of the Orange Alarm state in Figure 3.7 was to ping Lundy's router. Instead, it could have been to ping a STG that covers the router. Note that this design comes close to the collaboration of virtual models described earlier in the MBR approach.

The best example of the STG approach is SeaGate's NerveCenter. NerveCenter is typically integrated with HP OpenView, although it can operate in standalone mode by communicating directly with managed devices via SNMP. See Figure 3.8.

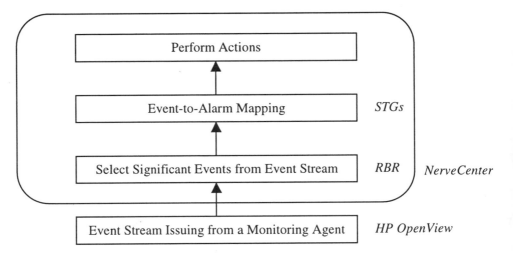

Figure 3.8 The Structure of the OpenView/NerveCenter Integration

The first thing we should notice in Figure 3.8 is that NerveCenter uses the classic RBR method to select significant events from the OpenView event stream, and only these events are passed to a set of STGs to perform the event-to-alarm mapping function. In the commercial literature, one often sees NerveCenter described as a rule-based system, which is somewhat misleading. NerveCenter uses two kinds of representations: rules and STGs.

3.3.4 Codebooks

The major concepts in the codebook approach to event correlation are a correlation matrix, coding, a codebook, and decoding. To see how the codebook apparatus works, let us consider a simple example.

Consider a small domain of interest in which there are four kinds of events e1, e2, e3, and e4 and two kinds of alarms A1 and A2. Now, suppose we know the sets of events which cause each alarm. We organize this information in a correlation matrix as follows:

	A1	A2
e1	1	1
e2	0	0
e3	0	1
e4	0	0

This matrix tells us that an occurrence of events e1 indicates A1, whereas a joint occurrence of e1 and e3 indicate A2.

"Coding" transforms the matrix into a compressed matrix, which is called a codebook. It is not hard to see that the matrix above can be compressed into a much simpler codebook:

	A1	A2
e1	1	1
e3	0	1

The codebook tells us that only e1 and e3 are required to determine whether we have A1, A2, or neither. Now, with this compressed codebook the system is ready to perform event-to-alarm mapping. This is called decoding. The system simply reads events off an event stream and compares them with the codebook in order to infer alarms.

Note that we could also perform the event-to-alarm mapping function with the original correlation matrix as well as the compressed codebook. However, it is not hard to appreciate the gain in speed when we use the latter. The codebook tells us to be on the lookout for two events instead of four events, and there is considerably less codebook lookup as compared with the original matrix.

Second, the codebook approach allows one to compress a very large correlation matrix, which is hard for the human mind to comprehend, into codebooks that are more comprehensible. To see this, consider the correlation matrix and the two derivative codebooks in Figure 3.9.

The first codebook collapses the correlation matrix into three events e1, e2, and e4. The codebook can distinguish among all six alarms; however in some cases it can guarantee distinction only by a single event. For example, A2 and A3 are distinguished by e4. A lost or spurious generation of e4 will result in a potential decoding error (i.e., incorrect event-to-alarm mapping).

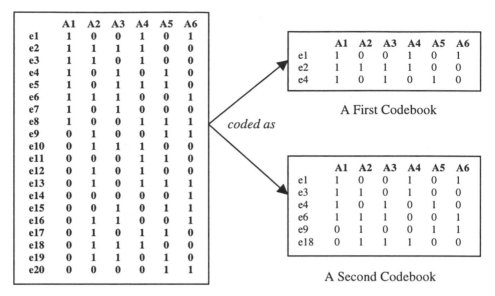

A Correlation Matrix

Figure 3.9 A Correlation Matrix and Two Derivative Codebooks

The second codebook resolves this problem by considering six events e1, e3, e4, e6, e9, and e18. The second codebook is such that a lost or spurious generation of any two events can be detected and any single-event error can be corrected.

There are a few things one has to pay attention to when using the codebook approach to event correlation:

First, how does one come up with the original correlation matrix? If the original matrix is correct, then we have an opportunity to compress the matrix into a codebook that hides noise and irrelevant events. However, if it isn't correct, we run into the familiar problem of garbage-in garbage-out.

Assume that the original matrix is indeed correct. Can we be assured that a high-performance codebook will be generated? Consider the following simple example:

	A1	A2
e1	0	1
e2	1	0

A codebook for this matrix will be equal to the matrix. In general, the compression factor of a correlation matrix depends upon the patterns of data collected in it. Depending upon the patterns, the compression factor may be anywhere from very high to very low.

Finally, how do we choose from multiple codebooks? In general, given any correlation matrix of reasonable size, there will be a very large number of possible codebooks. For example, our discussion of Figure 6 showed that the simplest codebook may not be resilient against errors. On the other hand, a codebook that is resilient to errors may sacrifice simplicity and understandability.

The best example in the industry of the codebook approach is InCharge, developed by System Management Arts (SMARTS). InCharge is typically integrated with either HP OpenView or IBM NetView.

InCharge includes an event modeling language based on classic object-oriented techniques, including class/subclass development, inheritance, and event definition. For example, a class TCPPort and a class UDPPort may inherit the general attributes of a class Port. However, the event PacketLossHigh for a TCPPort has a different definition than PacketLossHigh for a UDPPort.

InCharge contains a generic library of networking classes. Given these classes, one may derive domain-specific classes by adding the appropriate attribute and instrumentation statements to produce an accurate model of the domain. Finally, one adds event definitions to the model. Note that this approach comes close to the MBR approach described earlier.

Thus far we have considered four approaches in the industry for performing event correlation over the enterprise: RBR systems, MBR systems, state transition graphs, and codebooks. Each method represents knowledge and reasoning in different ways. One thing that they have in common is that they rate rather low with respect to learning and adaptability. Our final method, case-based reasoning, compares favorably in this regard.

3.3.5 Case-based Reasoning

The basic idea of CBR is to recall, adapt, and execute episodes of former problem solving in an attempt to deal with a current problem. Former episodes of problem solving are represented as cases in a case library. When confronted with a new problem, a CBR system retrieves a similar case and tries to adapt the case in an attempt to solve the outstanding problem. The experience with the proposed solution is embedded in the library for future reference. The general CBR architecture is shown in Figure 3.10.

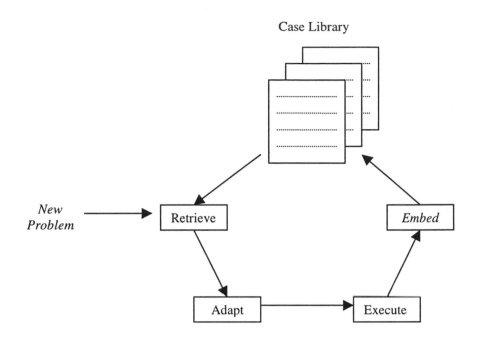

Figure 3.10 The General CBR Architecture

A challenge of the CBR approach is to develop a similarity metric so that useful cases can be retrieved from a case library. We would not want the system to retrieve the case that simply has the largest number of matches with the fields in the outstanding case. Some of the fields in a case are likely to be irrelevant, and thus misguide the system. Thus, relevance criteria are needed to indicate what kinds of information to consider given a particular problem at hand.

An example of a relevance criterion is the following:

> *The solution to the problem "response time is slow" is relevant to bandwidth, network load, packet collision rate, and paging space.*

Note that relevance criteria are not the same as rules in a RBR system. Relevance rules simply tell the system what cases to look at, but not what to do with them.

How does one acquire relevance criteria? Current research involves the application of machine learning algorithms (such as neural networks and induction-based algorithms) to an existing case library. The output of the algorithm is a list of relevance rules. For the present, however, a pragmatic approach is to handcraft relevance rules and test them manually.

An additional challenge for the CBR approach is to develop adaptation techniques by which the system can tweak an old solution to fit a new problem, although the new problem might not be exactly like the old problem. We discuss several kinds of adaptation techniques below.

Consider an outstanding problem "response time is unacceptable" and imagine that only one source case is retrieved from the case library, as shown below. In this example, the resolution is page_space_increase = A, where A is a solution variable that holds the amount by which to increase the page space of a server, determined by the function f.

> Problem: response time = F
> Solution: A = f(F), page_space_increase = A
> Solution status: good

"Parameterized adaptation" is a method for adjusting the solution variable of an outstanding problem relative to the problem variable, based on the relation between the solution and problem variables in a source case. Everything else being equal, an outstanding problem "response time = F*" should propose the solution page_space_increase = A*, where F* and A* stand in the same relation as F and A in the source case. The proposed solution in the outstanding case, therefore, would be like the following:

> Problem: response time = F*
> Solution: A* = f(F*), page_space_increase = A*
> Solution status: ?

How does one acquire functions like f? The safest method is to handcraft and test them, and in general there are several ways to represent f. The simplest is a look-up table, where values of A* not in the table are calculated by interpolation. Also, learning f from a collection of historical performance data can be looked upon as a function approximation task, and thus lends itself to neural network methods which are generally good at function approximation, e.g. counter-propagation and back-propagation.

Note also that f does not have to be a function per se. For other kinds of problems, f might be a sequence of steps or a decision tree. Suppose a retrieved case holds a simple procedure as follows:

> Solution: reboot(device = client1)

where *reboot* is a process and *client* is the value of the variable device. Suppose this case is just like an outstanding case except that in the outstanding case the value of device is server1. Thus, the advised solution is:

Solution: reboot(device = server1).

This adaptation method is called "adaptation by substitution."

Now, since it is impolite to reboot a server without warning, one might wish to prefix the step "issue warning to clients" to the advised solution and enter the case back into the case library. In this example the proposed solution is adapted manually by a user, so this technique is called "critic-based adaptation."

There exist several generic CBR systems in the industry, e.g. CBR Express from the Inference Corporation and SpectroRx from Aprisma Management Technologies. SpectroRx is an add-on application for Spectrum. As described earlier, Spectrum performs the event correlation task using the MBR method. Once a fault is identified, however, there remains the problem of finding a repair for the fault. Clearly, past experiences with similar faults are important, and this is just the kind of knowledge that is provided by SpectroRx.

An interesting story regarding SpectroRx is as follows. Version I of SpectroRx was shipped in 1995 with an empty case base. In the industry, this is sometimes called a knowledge shell. The user was expected to build an initial seed case library manually, after which the system would expand and become increasingly fine-tuned with use.

The problem was that users weren't too keen on the idea of first having to build a seed case library, although they liked the general idea of CBR. Many requests came in to ship SpectroRx with a generic seed case library. But now the engineers who developed SpectroRx had a problem. How could one build a generic case library, when any two networks are likely to be quite different – each having different components, services, and configurations?

After much research to try to understand what a generic case library would look like, and to determine whether there should be just one or several generic case libraries, an engineer proposed a simple, ingenious solution: Suppose we take the event-to-alarm mapping knowledge in Spectrum and transform it into a set of cases?

Part of the beauty of this solution is that although Spectrum contains more than a thousand model types, it is never the case that Auto Discovery will instantiate each model type. Typically, one to two hundred model types are actually instantiated as models. Therefore, the seed case library is based on the event-to-alarm mapping knowledge that is related to only these models.

Version II of SpectroRx was shipped in 1996 with a case library that holds just one case, which says:

Problem: Your case library is empty.

Solution: Depress the Execute Solution button and we will build a seed case library for you in about 10 minutes.
Solution Status: ?

This solution solves the problem elegantly. For any two network management systems, the seed case library will be tailored to reflect the components, services, and configurations that are unique for each network.

3.3.6 Discussion

We have looked at five paradigms by which to build an event correlator for network management systems: rule-based reasoning, model-based reasoning, state transition graphs, codebooks, and case-based reasoning. Table 3.2 summarizes these paradigms along three dimensions: knowledge, reasoning, and learning.

Table 3.2 Comparison of Event Correlation Paradigms

Paradigm	Knowledge	Reasoning	Learning
RBR	Rules	Rule-firing	No
MBR	Models	Message-passing	No
STGs	Graphs	Node-following	No
Codebooks	Tables	Table look-up	No
CBR	Cases	Case retrieval	Yes

In addition, we saw that RBR is not appropriate for an enterprise-wide event correlator, but it is well suited for smaller domains such as computer monitoring and control.

MBR, STG, and Codebooks are used in the products Spectrum, NerveCenter, and InCharge respectively. MBR is built into Spectrum. NerveCenter and InCharge are standalone applications that often are integrated with HP OpenView or IBM NetView.

We saw that the fifth method, CBR, shows promise for learning and adaptation to evolving event correlation scenarios.

The Spectrum Management System employs three of the methods. MBR is the core method, complemented with RBR in a product named SpectroWatch and CBR in a product named SpectroRx.

There are other paradigms that we haven't discussed, e.g. neural networks, fuzzy logic, and genetic algorithms. These methods show promise for increased learning and adaptation with less human intervention; but currently they are in the research realm.

3.4 Integrating Management Applications with Spectrum

In the previous two sections we described Spectrum's object-oriented approach to network management and compared Spectrum's approach to event correlation with other industry approaches.

In this section we examine the ways in which Spectrum can be integrated with other management applications. We provide two detailed examples as illustrations, but leave other examples as exercises at the end of the chapter.

3.4.1 Integration Methods

There are two approaches to integrating SPECTRUM with an external application: the Application Programming Interface (API) approach and the Platform External Interface (PEI) approach.

With the API approach, the exchange of data between two applications requires a programming language API (such as C, C++, Java, or CORBA) for each application. A vendor offers an "open systems" application with libraries, source code, and documentation that a developer uses to build an integrated application. The developer selects modules and functions in each API, and the applications are integrated at the source code level.

With the PEI approach, the exchange of data between applications requires a simple function call. Suppose that management application 1 (MA-1) is required to pass information to MA-2. The name of the function call is provided by MA-2 but the function arguments are provided by MA-1. MA-1 simply executes MA-2's function with a set of MA-1-specific arguments.

There are important trade-offs between the API and PEI approaches to integration, as shown in Table 3.3. A viable method of integration that combines the best of both approaches is to use the PEI approach to develop an integrated system prototype. If the performance or functionality of the system is questionable, then the prototype may be used as a specification for building a more efficient integration using the API approach.

Table 3.3 Pros and Cons of API and PEI Integration Methods

API Approach	
Pros	Cons
1. Good performance	1. Compatible APIs are required
2 PEI independence	2. Support of multiple OSs is difficult
3. Security designed in	3. Comparatively longer development time
4. Flexibility	4. Higher risk in project completion
PEI Approach	
Pros	Cons
1. Little programming required	1. Performance may not be optimal
2. PEIs developed in isolation	2. PEI dependent
3. Integration is achieved quickly	3. Security depends on PEIs
4. Little risk in project completion	4. Little flexibility

In the remainder of this section we describe two integrations using Spectrum PEIs. The integrations could be done using Spectrum C, C++, or CORBA APIs. However, we leave those as exercises.

3.4.2 Alarm-Driven Integration

Recall the discussions of the alarm-driven integration pattern and help desk integration in Chapter 2. Since we discussed the event-to-alarm mapping problem in the preceding section, it is appropriate to show how one may transform Spectrum alarms into trouble tickets for a help desk.

The alarm-driven pattern of integration can be implemented using a Spectrum PEI named AlarmNotifier. Alarms detected by Spectrum are posted in an Alarm Manager View, showing parameters such as date, time, the model on which the alarm occurred, probable cause, recommended repair procedures, and the event messages that underlie the alarm. See Figure 3.11.

This information also can be forwarded to other management applications by enabling the AlarmNotifer (AN). When the AlarmNotifier is enabled, it executes a script when alarms are detected, updated, or cleared. Figure 3.12 shows a portion of the script (SetScript) that is cxccuted when an alarm is detected. The script is quite simple. It displays alarm information on a UNIX terminal. Figure 3.13 shows a sample of output.

Importantly, one can pass these parameters to a function provided by an external application. Suppose the application is a help desk that offers a function EnterTT that can be executed from the command prompt. One can put this function at the bottom of the SetScript in Figure 3.12 with the appropriate arguments, for example:

EnterTT $Date $TIME $MODELNAME $CONDITION $PCAUSE

Note that there are other ways to forward alarm information to external applications. For example, a less elegant way is to drop alarm information into a so-called alarm bucket, whereupon the help desk periodically picks up the alarms in the bucket. In addition, it is possible to wrap alarm information in an SNMP trap structure or an Extended Mark-up Language (XML) structure, and pass that to the external application. The implementation method depends upon the nature of the external application's PEI.

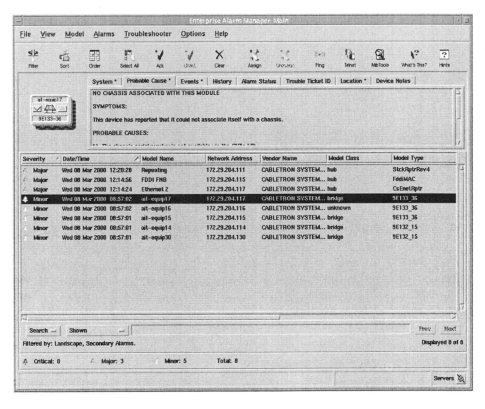

Figure 3.11 A Collection of Alarms in an Alarm Manager View

SetScript

```
echo "Spectrum Alarm Notification "
echo " "
echo "Alarm SET:"
echo ""
echo "Date: " $DATE
echo "Time: " $TIME
echo "Mtype: " $MTYPE
echo "ModelName: " $MNAME
echo "AlarmID: " $AID
echo "Condition: " $COND
echo "CauseCode: " $CAUSE
echo "RepairPerson: " $REPAIRPERSON
echo "AlarmStatus: " $STATUS
echo "SpectroSERVER: " $SERVER
echo "Landscape: " $LANDSCAPE
echo "ModelHandle: " $MHANDLE
echo "ModelTypeHandle: " $MTHANDLE
echo "IPAddress: " $IPADDRESS
echo "SecurityString: " $SECSTR
echo "AlarmState: " $ALARMSTATE
echo "Acknowledged: " $ACKD
echo "UserClearable: " $CLEARABLE
echo "Location: " $LOCATION
echo "AlarmAge: " $AGE
echo "NotificationData:" $NOTIFDATA
echo "ProbableCause: $PCAUSE"
echo "EventMessage: " $EVENTMSG
```

Figure 3.12 Spectrum Alarm Parameters

3.4.3 Database Integration

Recall the discussion of database integration in Chapter 2. Spectrum provides two PEIs for database integration: the Data Export Tool and the Command Line Interface. The former is typically used to transform large chunks of Spectrum data into alternative database formats such as Oracle, SAS, Sybase, IBM DB2, or plain ASCII files.

The Command Line Interface (CLI) can be used to retrieve small portions of data, or to insert new information into the Spectrum database. In this section we consider examples of database integration using the CLI. Table 3.4 shows a subset of CLI commands.

```
Spectrum Alarm Notification

Alarm SET:

Date: 2/14/2000
Time: 12:14:45
Mtype: Pingable
ModelName: graham
AlarmID: 143
Condition: YELLOW
CauseCode: 10519
RepairPerson: French
AlarmStatus: Problem Resolved
SpectroSERVER: coffee
Landscape: 0xd00000
ModelHandle: 0xd002c9
ModelTypeHandle: 0x10290
IPAddress: 132.177.13.37
SecurityString: ADMIN
AlarmState: EXISTING
Acknowledged: FALSE
UserClearable: TRUE
Location: World:U.K.:London:Building1:Lab
AlarmAge: 0
NotificationData: French, DiPietro or Jones:Wong:Desrochers
ProbableCause:  DUPLICATE MAC WITH DIFFERENT IP
                A model exists with the same MAC address but with a
                different IP address than this model. Are there 2
                models with multiple hops on a route?
EventMessage:   Mon 14 February, 2000 - 9:32:30 - Device graham of
                type Pingable was created with a MAC address
                (0:0:C:18:E5:31) already used by another model which
                has a different IP Address than ( 132.177.13.37 ).
                (event [00010911])
```

Figure 3.13 Sample Output of AlarmNotifier

CLI commands fall into two general categories: **create** commands and **show** commands. The **create alarm** command is one way to pass alarms from an external application to Spectrum. A traffic management application, for example, can execute the **create alarm** command with the appropriate arguments. One can use **show** commands to select network topology data from Spectrum and forward it to other applications for further processing. We provide an example below.

Table 3.4 Sample CLI Commands

Command	Result
create event	Creates an event on a model
create alarm	Creates an alarm on a model
create model	Creates a model in a specified domain
create association	Creates an association between two models
show events	Displays a list of events for a model
show alarms	Displays a list of alarms for a model
show models	Displays all models in a domain
show associations	Displays all associations for a model

Recall that Spectrum models participate in a number of relations with each other. For example, the "connects to" relation indicates network connectivity at the port level (LAN802_2 *connects to* graffam_pc), while the "contains" relation indicates containment at a logical, conceptual level (Bldg1 *contains* Room12).

Suppose a design requirement is to list port connectivity in a particular domain. Figure 3.14 show a UNIX script for accomplishing that.

PortConnectivityScript

```
show models >> model_info                                    # (1)
model_list=`cat model_info | cut -f1`                        # (2)
for i in $model_list                                         # (3)
 do                                                          # (4)
   show associations mh=$i | grep "connects to" >> tmp       # (5)
 done                                                        # (6)
sort -u tmp > port_connectivity                              # (7)
```

Figure 3.14 A Script for Extracting Port Connectivity

Line (1) puts all models into a file called model_info. Each line of the model_info file has the following form:

Model ID   Model Name   Model Type ID Model Type

For example, the contents of the model_info contains rows like the following:

0xc40d2d	Gator_MIM2	0x10256	data_relay_prt
0xc40632	Gator_MIM2	0x10256	data_relay_prt
0xc40631	Gator_MIM2	0x10256	data_relay_prt
0xc40531	Gator_MIM2	0x10256	data_relay_prt
0xc40530	Gator_MIM2	0x10256	data_relay_prt

Line (2) cuts the Model ID (i.e. field 1) from each line in the model_info file, and transforms it into a list that is the value of the variable model_list. Note that a model ID is unique whereas the model name isn't necessarily unique, as our example shows.

The "for" loop on lines (3) – (6) walks down the model_info list, picking out all instances of the "connects to" relation with the UNIX grep command, and puts them into a file named tmp.

Finally, line (7) simply eliminates duplicate rows from tmp with the UNIX sort command and puts the results into a file named port_connectivity. The contents of the port_connectivity file contains rows like the following:

| Port ID | Port Name | connects to | Port ID | Port Name |
Port ID	Port Name	connects to	Port ID	Port Name
0xc407a7	Auto FANOUT	connects to	0xc40463	ETH-BRIDGE
0xc4035e	Auto FANOUT	connects to	0xc40463	ETH-BRIDGE
0xc4079c	Auto FANOUT	connects to	0xc4057c	134.141.67.146
0xc4040b	134.141.67.14.1	connects to	0xc4057c	134.141.67.146
0xc402f4	134.141.67.14.1	connects to	0xc40634	134.141.67.224

This information can now be transported to an external application for further processing. Note that our exercise demonstrates how one can carve out select, specialized information from the Spectrum database.

The script PortConnectivityScript is for illustration purposes. One can enhance the script so that it also shows the transmission device on which a port resides (with the "is a part of" relation) and the characteristics of port traffic (with the show attributes command). We leave those as exercises.

3.4.4 Discussion

We have shown two ways in which one can integrate Spectrum with other management applications. Both involve Spectrum PEIs: the AlarmNotifier and the Command Line Interface. The examples are for illustration purposes. With a little ingenuity the reader should be able to find other uses for those PEIs.

We emphasize that the PEI method of integration is just one way to implement a design of an integrated system. The PEI approach to integration is useful for demonstrating proof-of-concept designs. But since the Spectrum PEIs are constructed from the Spectrum APIs, one can always re-implement a PEI-based design in C, C++, Java, or CORBA. In this regard, the reader should keep in mind the pros and cons of the PEI approach and the API approach in Table 3.2.

Chapter Summary

In this chapter we introduced the Spectrum Management System developed by Aprisma Management Technologies in the USA. First we discussed the history of Spectrum. We showed that Spectrum began life as a "network" management system in 1990, for which the requirements were to model and manage popular network devices from Cabletron, Cisco, 3COM, and others.

We argued that Spectrum architects in 1990 made two important design decisions: (i) to use the object-oriented paradigm (OOP) for network modeling and (ii) to use model-based reasoning (MBR) for event correlation.

Those were good decisions. OOP and MBR are considered essential for network management in the 2000s. Further, we showed how those decisions laid the necessary groundwork for allowing Spectrum to evolve during the 1990's decade to cope with the increasing demands and broader scope of network management.

We proceeded to examine OOP and MBR is more detail. We discussed the main concepts in OOP and showed how they map into Spectrum concepts. For example, the brand name in Spectrum for OOP is Inductive Modeling Technology. The relations between OOP terms and Spectrum terms are listed in Table 3.1.

Then we compared the Spectrum MBR approach to event correlation with other approaches in the industry. We examined rule-based reasoning, state transition graphs, codebooks, and case-based reasoning.

Finally, we described implementation methods for integrating Spectrum with other external applications. This discussion complements Chapter 2, where we described integration patterns but didn't discuss the tools of implementation.

Exercises and Discussion Questions

1. Describe how Auto-Discovery works in Spectrum. Run Auto-Discovery on your laboratory network.

2. What is a model type in Spectrum? Produce a list of model types with the Spectrum CLI. Identify some entity (either physical or logical) in the networking domain that is not included in the list.

3. What is the difference between a "relation" and an "association" in Spectrum? Produce a list of relations and a list of associations using the Spectrum CLI.

4. Configure the Spectrum AlarmNotifier so that it sends you an email when a network alarm occurs. Create an alarm with the Spectrum CLI and verify that you receive an email.

5. What is the Spectrum Data Export Tool? How can it be used in an integrated management system? What business requirement would the integration satisfy?

6. What is SpectroWatch? How can it be used in an integrated management system? What business requirement would the integration satisfy?

7. What is Spectrum CsNewView? How can it be used in an integrated management system? What business requirement would the integration satisfy?

8. With either Data Export, SpectroWATCH, or CsNewView, integrate Spectrum with some other management application.

9. Produce a list of Spectrum APIs and describe their purposes.

10. This is a research question. Describe the Common Information Model (CIM). How does the Spectrum modeling language compare with the CIM modeling language?

Further Studies

The web site www.aprisma.com contains material on Spectrum, including white papers, Spectrum manuals, and case studies. The manuals required for answering the exercises and discussion questions are:

- AutoDiscovery User's Guide
- Command Line Interface User's Guide
- AlarmNotifier User's Guide
- Data Export User's Guide
- SpectroWATCH Operator's Reference
- Event Configuration Editor User's Guide
- SPECTRUM Concepts Guide
- SPECTRUM Knowledge Base Guide
- SPECTRUM Guide to Integrating Applications

Other useful web sites that demonstrate Spectrum integrations include www.ics.de, www.metrix.lu, www.opticominc.com, www.itactics.com, and www.geckoware.com. In addition, one can perform a web search on "Cabletron Aprisma Spectrum" and likely turn up many analyst white papers and other useful material.

A list abstracts of Spectrum patents is provided at the end of the book.

The distinction between PEI and API approaches to integrated management is discussed in Ghetie's book *Network and Systems Management Platforms*. The book describes the PEIs and APIs of Spectrum and other commercial management systems.

Two book that focus on Hewlett Packard's OpenView are *HP Openview: A Manager's Guide* by Huntington-Lee et al and *Power Programming in HP OpenView: Developing CMIS Applications* by Kean and Caruso.

A very good textbook on Network Management is Subramanian's *Network Mangement: Principles and Practice*. The book provides (i) an overview of data communications, telecommunications, and management methods of each, (ii) SNMP, Broadband, and TMN Management, and (iii) management tools, systems, and applications, including Spectrum and other commercial management systems.

References

Ghetie, J. *Network and Systems Management Platforms*. Kluwer Academic Publishers. 1997.

Huntington-Lee, J., K Terplan (Contributor), J. Gibson (Contributor). *HP Openview: A Manager's Guide.* McGraw Hill Text. 1997.

Kean, M. and R. Caruso. *Power Programming in HP OpenView: Developing CMIS Applications.* Prentice Hall. 1996.

Subramanian, M. *Network Management: Principles and Practice.* Addison-Wesley. 2000.

Part II
Three Case Studies in
Network Management

In Part II we get our hands dirty. We begin applying the material in Part I to the management of real-world networks.

Each chapter in Part II focuses on a particular type of network that exhibits unique management challenges. The kinds of networks we'll examine are:

- Micro City Networks
- Service Provider Networks
- Internet2 GigaPoP Networks

For each network domain, we discuss the following general themes:

- Definition of the Domain
- Management Challenges
- A Case Study
- Management Architecture, Implementation, and Deployment
- Successes and Challenges for Future Work

Chapter 4 focuses on the management of micro city networks, and the case study is the Camp LeJeune Marine Corps Base. It is challenging because the network is quite large and consists of multi-vendor components.

Chapter 5 focuses on the management of service provider networks, and the case study is the Vitts Network in New England. It is challenging because the network demonstrates the convergence of data and tele-communications networks. In addition, it is one of the first networks of this type to emerge as a result of the Telecommunications Deregulation Act in 1996.

Chapter 6 focuses on the management of Internet2 GigaPoP networks, and the case study is the North Carolina GigaPoP. It is challenging because the purpose of the GigaPoP is to support advanced Internet2 applications such as distance learning, tele-presence, and virtual reality.

Importantly, the management systems in the case studies are not fully completed. Management methods and systems are in place, but there is room for much improvement. Thus, each chapter includes sections on successes and challenges for future work. That should go a long way towards preparing the reader for management challenges in the 21st century.

4 Managing Micro City Networks

As our first case study, we look at the management challenges of networks that support micro cities. We cover the following topics in this chapter:

- What is a Micro City?
- Camp LeJeune's Micro City Network
- Managing Camp LeJeune's Network
- Moving from Network to Enterprise Management
- Towards Integrated End-to-End Management
- Challenges for Integrated Management

First we describe the concept of a micro city. We will see that a micro city is essentially a self-contained city by design, where traditional units such as schools, medical care facilities, the fire department, the utility department, the police department, etc are connected via a shared communications network and managed by a single IT department.

An excellent example of a micro city is the Camp LeJeune Marine Corps Base in the USA. We describe the operations of the Camp Lejuene community and look at the network infrastructure that supports those operations. The main features of the Camp LeJeune network that we are interested in are its size and heterogeneity. The network consists of multi-vendor networking devices, and that imposes special challenges for centralized network management.

Next we describe the methods of network management at Camp LeJeune. The main features of the current system are (i) multi-vendor management and control, (ii) central control from a single workstation, (iii) management down to the port level, and (iv) bandwidth management. We show how this is accomplished with the Spectrum Management System (described in Chapter 3).

Next we discuss Camp LeJeune's plan for moving from network management to enterprise management, including the management of desktop computer systems, applications, and service level management.

The move from network to enterprise management requires extensions to the current system, and that calls for integration with other specialized management products. Thus we describe the integration architecture for the next iteration of the management system, showing how the specialized products are integrated with Spectrum into a single whole.

Finally, we discuss the challenges of deploying and configuring the integrated system so that it satisfies the needs of the Camp LeJeune network overseers.

4.1 What is a Micro City?

In order to avoid confusion, let us distinguish between a "virtual" city and a "micro" city. The phrase "virtual X" usually implies the lack of physical proximity regarding X. For example, virtual reality implies the experience of physical objects although the objects are not real.

Likewise, a virtual city connotes the experience of a city although one is not actually in a city. A florist shop might be in Chicago, a bookstore in New York, a bank in Atlanta, etc, although the "city dweller" conducts transactions with those businesses via the Internet.

In contrast, a micro city is a real, physical city that (i) is to a large extent autonomous and self-governing, (ii) is generally set apart from the public domain, and (iii) provides the necessary facilities and services usually associated with public cities.

A common example of a micro city in the sense that we have defined it is a large university campus. Most people who have enrolled in a large university first find out that the university is practically a city within itself, with its own police department, medical care facilities, day care facilities, and stores and shops. Other good examples of micro cities are large housing developments and businesses that provide private facilities commonly associated with public cities.

The facilities of a micro city are interconnected via a shared communications network. Thus, a micro city also requires a shared information technology (IT) department that is responsible for designing, implementing, and maintaining the network and the business applications used by each facility in the city.

In our case study, we look at the network supporting the Camp LeJeune micro city in the USA. The management of Camp LeJeune's network is particularly challenging because of its sheer size, the heterogeneity of the network infrastructure, and its special requirements for network management. It is an excellent example of a micro city network.

After reading this chapter, the reader should ponder the question of whether cities as we know them today will begin to exhibit features of micro cities in the future. Can we imagine cities such as San Francisco (USA),

Sydney (Australia), or London (UK) having a common network infrastructure and a city-wide IT department to manage the network?

The idea of gradual transformation of public cities into micro cities is not farfetched. Public cities that neighbor Camp LeJeune are already looking at the Camp LeJeune micro city as a model that is worthy of duplicating, e.g. Jacksonville, North Carolina. The officials of those neighboring cities seek advice from Camp LeJeune's network architects regarding networking and network management.

It is an intriguing question whether micro cities will become a trend in 21st century civilization. Perhaps they will become commonplace in our lifetimes.

4.2 Camp LeJeune's Micro City Network

Camp LeJeune is a Marine base on the East Coast of the USA. It is home for 47,000 marines, and it is the largest amphibious training base in the USA. In addition to its training personnel, the base is residence to active duty, dependent, retiree, and civilian employees. Its total population is about 150,000 people.

Camp LeJeune is indeed a self-contained city. In addition to marine training and housing buildings, the city includes hotels, recreational centers, hospitals, schools from kindergarten to the college level, and all other facilities we normally associate with medium to large cities.

All the networks and applications are managed by a single IT department. Figure 4.1 shows the network. The part above the dotted line is a Marine Point of Presence (PoP) that is connected to the Internet. The USA Marine Headquarters manages twenty-seven such PoPs, of which Camp LeJeune is the largest. Camp LeJeune architects know the up/down status of the devices in their PoP, but all other PoP management functions are performed by Marine headquarters.

The main responsibility of the network architects at Camp LeJeune is to manage the part of the network that is below the dotted line. It is a 75-mile, multi-vendor, dual-ring ATM backbone network. There are nine exit points on the ring, where each exit point is a Fore ATM switch and each switch serves one of the nine domains. For example, the switch that serves Domain 7 provides communication services for all the schools and colleges on the base.

In total, the network connects 1000+ buildings and supports 20,000+ users. Domain 2 is the largest of the nine domains, serving about 250 buildings.

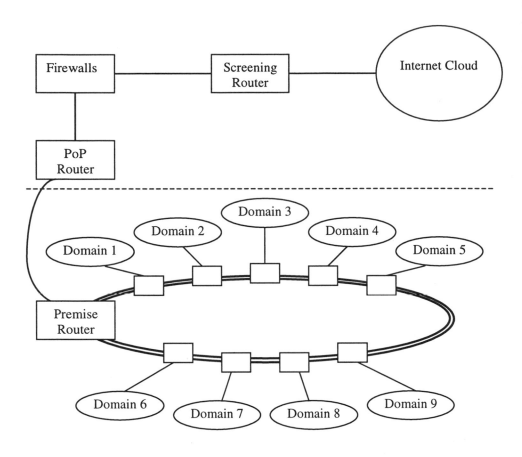

Figure 4.1 Network Topology at Camp LeJeune

The Camp LeJeune micro city network is quite comprehensive and heterogeneous, consisting of network gear from Cisco, Fore, and Enterasys. One approach to managing the network is to do element-by-element management, where each device is managed by the particular element manager provided by Cisco, Fore, or Enterasys. However, it is well known that that approach doesn't scale well for networks of this size. In addition, methods of event correlation are hard to achieve when one is dealing with multiple element management systems.

For these reasons, the architects took the approach of centralized, multi-vendor management. They wished to manage all the network gear from a single network management station. We discuss their specific requirements in the next section.

4.3 Managing Camp LeJeune's Network

In Chapter 2 we looked at a set of sample requirements for network management systems. Those requirements gave the reader a taste of what to expect in the field. We followed that with a discussion of methodology for building network management solutions, and then discussed common patterns of integrated network management.

In this chapter and the following chapters in Part II we start looking at specific requirements of network administrators in the field. Below we list the requirements laid down by the network administrators at Camp LeJeune. We will use those requirements as a starting point for building a management solution.

The first requirements of the Camp LeJeune administrators were these:

- Centralized Management from a Single Workstation – Be able to perform all management functions from a single workstation.

- Multi-Vendor Management – Be able to manage network devices from Cisco, Fore, and Enterasys.

- Port Level Management – Be able to manage Cisco, Fore, and Enterasys devices down to the port level.

- Configuration Management – Be able to configure the operational characteristics of devices from Cisco, Fore, and Enterasys.

- Alarm Management – Be able to view network-wide alarms in a single, consolidated view.

- Web-Based Alarm Management – Be able to view network-wide alarms with a Web browser.

- Bandwidth Monitoring and Allocation -- Be able to monitor bandwidth usage on a weekly schedule and allocate bandwidth accordingly.

- Scaled Management vis-a-vis Network Evolution – Be able to incorporate newly installed devices from Cisco, Fore, Enterasys, and other vendors into the management system.

The network architects at Camp LeJeune evaluated several management proposals and finally settled on Spectrum as their management platform. We described Spectrum in Chapter 3. Spectrum satisfies all the requirements above; however, the main features that sold them on Spectrum were (i) centralized multi-vendor management from a single workstation and (ii) the promise of scalability as the network evolves in the future. Thus, let us say a few words about Spectrum's scalability properties.

The Spectrum Management System is based on a distributed client/server architecture, which was described in Chapter 3. A short review is in order here. See Figure 4.2. The Spectrum servers, called SpectroSERVERS (SSs), monitor and control individual network domains. The Spectrum clients, called SpectroGRAPHS (SGs), may attach to any SS to graphically present the state of that SS's domain, including topological information, event and alarm information, and configuration information.

The SGs are the interfaces to the network administrators, but they do not have direct access to network components. The SSs provide the interfaces and communication links to the network components, but they are not responsible for displaying data. They pass data to remote SGs for display in either synchronous or asynchronous modes of communication.

All domains can be viewed from a single SG. If SG-1 in Figure 4.2 is in communication to SS-1 but one wishes to monitor and control the domain covered by SS-2, one can click on an icon in SG-1 that represents SS-2. Figure 4.2 shows a primary client/server communication between SG-1 and SS-1. Virtual communications between SG-1 and the other SSs are indicated by dotted lines.

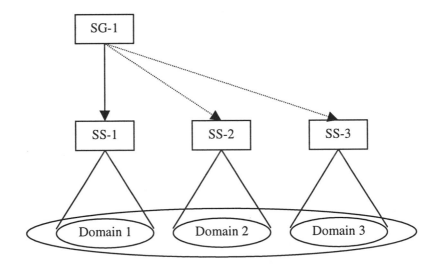

Figure 4.2 Spectrum's Distributed Client/Server Architecture

A sizing tool in Spectrum determines how many SpectroServers are required to manage a network of any given size. It turns out that Camp LeJeune's network required three servers. SS-1 manages domains 1, 5, and 9, SS-2 manages domain 2, and SS-3 manages domains 3, 4, 6, 7, and 8.

The following quotes (with a touch of humor) from network overseers at Camp LeJeune sum up the current system, their challenges, and their desires for the next iteration of the management system:

Our network generally works fine (unless a backhoe interferes), and our network management system helps us keep it up and running. But now the applications are starting to arrive in hordes – some of which are installed illegitimately by young Marines. That calls for careful application monitoring and control, which in turn calls for an extension of the current system into the application domain.

We now wish to start looking at other things, including systems management, application management, and quality of service management. We would like to start thinking of our IT department as a service provider instead of a network manager. Also we would like to be more proactive and less reactive, and we need tools that allow that.

Ninety percent of the problems that cause us headaches have to do with the "loose nut between the keyboard and seat." For example, one caller complained of not getting power to his monitor. Upon investigation, it was found that the monitor wasn't plugged in. When that was pointed out, the user replied "That's just what I said. I'm not getting power to my monitor. I have only two jacks: one for the computer and one for my fan. It's hot in North Carolina!"

Another problem we have is what we call the musical building problem. One third of the base goes overseas every six months, and often they are assigned to another base upon return. Therefore, we can't count on our management staff to be with us very long. And if we are able to keep hold of a well-trained staff member, and she discovers the huge salaries available in the public domain, she's a goner -- understandably.

People play musical buildings around here. They move about, taking different jobs during their tenure on the base. That's the nature of the Marine Corps. We need management tools that (i) are easy to learn and use and (ii) embody as much automation as possible. That would help us be less dependent on human troubleshooters and help us alleviate the musical building problem.

An analysis of these statements shows that the main requirements of the next iteration of the management system are the following:

- Extend the current system so that it also manages systems, applications, and quality of service (for example, see Section 2.1.5 on Service Level Agreements).

- Transfer human management tasks as much as possible to the management system, thereby decreasing the dependency on human troubleshooters.

Unfortunately, not much can be done about the loose nut problem. Perhaps by the year 3000 we'll be able to monitor and control human users remotely with a network management system. We'll leave that as an exercise for the reader's grandchildren.

In the next section we discuss the move from network management to enterprise management, focusing on the two primary requirements listed above.

4.4 Moving From Network to Enterprise Management

Recall that in Chapter 1 we argued that there is more to network management than "network management." We categorized the generic components of a network to help us see that, as shown in Figure 4.3.

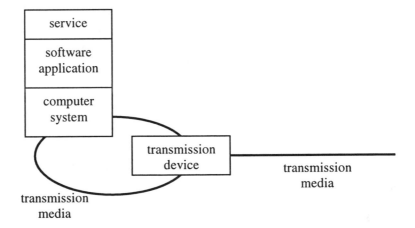

Figure 4.3 The Generic Components of a Network

There are the *transmission devices* that receive traffic from, and forward traffic to, other transmission devices. Examples of such devices are routers, hubs, switches, access devices, cable modems, and satellite stations. There are the *transmission media* over which traffic flows. Examples of such media are copper wire, coaxial cable, fiber-optic cable, telephone lines, and airwaves. There are the *computer systems* that reside on a network, for example desktop computers, workstations, mainframe computers, and laptop computers. There are the *software applications* that run on the computers, for example document writing applications, database applications. Note that distributed applications span multiple computer systems that may be distributed over separate networks.

Finally, there are various *services* that are supported by software applications. The concept of a service is a recent advancement in our understanding of networking technology. A service is an abstraction, or epi-phenomenon, that arises in virtue of the structure and operation of transmission devices, transmission media, computer systems, and applications. Examples of services are electronic commerce, inter-continental email, and accounting and billing.

Let us compare these concepts with our discussion on the evolution of network management in Chapter 1. Recall our table showing the history of network management in data communications, reproduced below in Table 4.1.

Table 4.1 History of Data Communications Network Management

1975	Device management
1990	Network management
1991	Traffic management
1992	Computer system management
1994	Application management
1996	Enterprise management = network + traffic + computer + application management
1998	Enterprise management = network + traffic + computer + application + service management
2000	Enterprise management = network + traffic + computer + application + service + response time management

We showed in Chapter 1 that during the latter 1990's an important shift took place in the direction of network management: (i) the ideas of "enterprise management" and "end-to-end management" became prominent and (ii) vendors began to concentrate on the integration of their products with other products in order to have a complete end-to-end solution.

Now, that is precisely where we are in the Camp LeJeune case study. Network and traffic management are in place and successful, but now the goal is to extend the system to encompass enterprise management, i.e. we wish to extend the current system to include the management of computer systems, applications, and quality of service.

Figure 4.4 shows an architecture for the next iteration of the management system. We wish to combine network, systems, and application management information into a consolidated enterprise management system (EMS). Note: Be careful not to read EMS in this context as *element* management system.

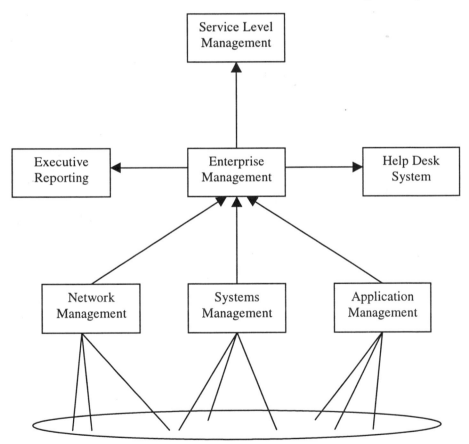

Figure 4.4 Generic Architecture for an Enterprise Management System

The EMS (i) encompasses monitoring and control of networks, computer systems, and software applications, (ii) correlates enterprise-wide events into enterprise alarms, (iii) transforms enterprise alarms into trouble tickets and passes them to the help desk, and (iv) provides enterprise-wide executive reports.

The service level management system will allow one to represent services that the enterprise network offers. Recall that we defined a service as a function of network, system, and application components. Thus, the service level management system sits on top of the enterprise management system. Our task now is to transform this model into a design, and then to a fielded system.

4.5 Towards Integrated End-to-End Management

Before we proceed, let us make a distinction between management *roles* and management *instances*.

The boxes in Figure 4.4 represent management roles. When we begin embodying the system, we have to search for instances of the roles, where instances are construed as real management applications, whether they are commercial systems, public domain systems, or home-grown systems. The distinction between management roles and management instances should remind the reader of the distinction between an analysis model and a design model that was discussed in Chapter 2.

Importantly, the relation between management roles and management instances does not necessarily have to be one-to-one. The relation might very well be many-to-one or one-to-many. That means that it is logically possible for multiple management roles to be played by a single management instance, or vice versa.

With the role/instance distinction in mind, let us describe a candidate embodiment of the generic architecture in Figure 4.4. Figure 4.5 shows a collection of management systems that the Camp LeJeune architects are considering in order to make the move from network management to enterprise management.

Note that Figure 4.5 is just like Figure 4.4, save that we have replaced generic roles with instances of commercial products in the boxes. For example, a candidate management application for the executive reporting function is Opticom's *iView*. A candidate help desk application is the Remedy *Help Desk*, and a candidate service management application is Gecko's *Saman*. Those applications stand in a one-to-one relation with the roles in Figue 4.4.

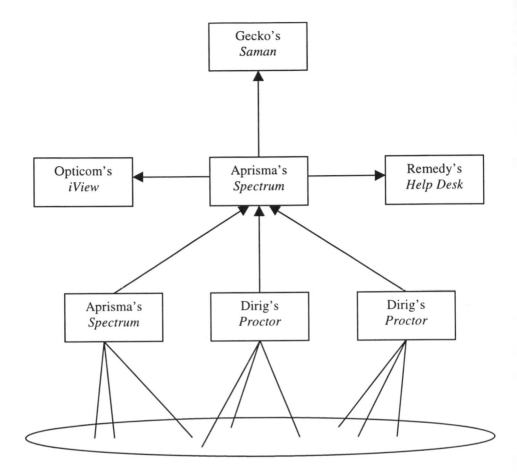

4.5 An Embodiment of the Generic Architecture in Figure 4.4

A candidate application that performs both the system and application management roles is Dirig's *Proctor*. In addition, Aprisma's *Spectrum* plays the roles of both network management and enterprise management. Thus, Proctor and Spectrum both wear two hats, so to speak. Both of them play dual management roles.

Our candidate embodiment makes sense. The idea is to continue using Spectrum as the network management system, but to escalate it to EMS status also. The problem, however, is to make sure that Proctor, iView, Help Desk, and Saman can be integrated with Spectrum in order to achieve centralized end-to-end management with quality of service.

Some good news is that Proctor, iView, Help Desk, and Saman are already integrated with Spectrum. However, they are integrated in different ways. iView and Help Desk are integrated in platform external interface

(PEI) fashion, while Proctor and Saman are integrated in application programming interface (API) fashion. We discussed the PEI and API approaches to integration in Chapter 3, but a short review is in order here.

When two applications are integrated in PEI fashion, they run as standalone systems but they pass information between each other as needed via their external interfaces. The classic example of PEI integration is the transformation of a network alarm into a trouble ticket, and then the passing of the trouble ticket to a system such as Remedy's Help Desk. Note that the two applications are not actually compiled into a single software system. They are compiled separately, but are integrated via their PEIs.

When two applications are integrated in API fashion, they are indeed compiled into a single software system. For example, recall our discussion of the Spectrum model type hierarchy in Chapter 3. The model type hierarchy is like a class hierarchy in object oriented terminology. We argued that a well-designed class hierarchy makes it easy to add new classes in order to extend a network system into other domains.

That is just what Dirig and Gecko software architects have done. Using the Spectrum APIs, they expanded Spectrum's model type hierarchy so that it includes models for systems, application, and service management. Further, they expanded Spectrum's basic event correlation mechanism so that event correlation takes place over system and application events in addition to network events.

It is important that the reader appreciates the difference between PEI and API methods of integration. Given two management applications that need to be integrated in order to satisfy a customer requirement, a major design decision is whether they should be integrated in PEI fashion or API fashion. Many integration projects have failed because the wrong decision was made.

With this distinction is mind, let us proceed to describe Proctor, iView, Help Desk, and Saman in more detail and show how they are integrated with Spectrum.

4.5.1 Dirig's *Proctor*: System and Application Management

Dirig's Proctor utilizes agent technology for system and application management. There are two basic kinds of agents in the Proctor system: master agents and subagents.

Subagents reside on the computers, and thus directly monitor computer and application parameters. Master agents may reside on any NT or UNIX managing station, and are used to deploy and configure a collection of subagents. Data from subagents are forwarded back to master agents for display and further processing. Figure 4.6 shows the master agent (ma) and subagent (sa) relationship.

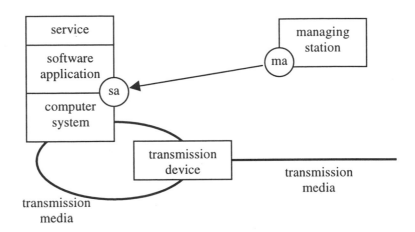

Figure 4.6 The Master Agent and Subagent Relationship

An important concept in Proctor is "management by policy." Consider laptop management. One can set up a domain simply named "laptops" where all laptops connected to the network reside in a policy domain. Each subagent monitors and controls its respective laptop in accordance with some predefined set of policies that hold for the domain of laptop computers.

A policy is of the general form "If X, then Y" where X is some system or application variable and Y is an action. For example: If file F is new and F is in a non-standard directory, then raise a "possible intrusion detection" alarm.

In sum, the master agent is used to perform the following tasks:

- Define a policy domain
- Deploy subagents in the domain
- Define policies than govern subagent behavior
- Forward control messages to subagents
- Collect information from subagents for display
- Forward significant events and alarms to other management applications

There are different kinds of subagents in the Proctor system, each having to do with specific kinds of domains and policies.

A *resource* agent is responsible for monitoring a computer's CPU, memory, file systems, and other system variables. Policies regulate the variables that are to be monitored and the action when a policy is violated.

A *process* agent monitors the processes that are running on the computer. It is useful for reporting machine activity, determining whether a process is consuming too many resources, or determining whether an illegitimate process is running on the machine.

A *logging* agent monitors system, security, and application log files for patterns. A set of policies dictates acceptable and unacceptable patterns.

An *application inventory* agent discovers software applications installed or running on a collection of computers in a domain. It maintains a list of these applications and their vendors, along with any version information.

A *modeling* agent monitors groups of related processes and/or applications. It aggregates statistics on the models, such as combined CPU percentage, memory usage, and total time running. It is useful for getting statistics on distributed client/server applications.

An *action* agent embodies a collection of utilities that can be used to control the workstation (i.e. the *Y* part of the policy "If *X*, then *Y*), including remote pings, URL inspection, and customized scripts. Pings determine network response times. URL inspection tests web access of a client and the availability of web servers. Customized scripts can perform backups, virus checks, or application health tests.

An *Internet service* agent allows one to determine the availability and response time for common Internet services, e.g. email and web transactions. Using a synthetic transaction engine, it emulates protocols such as HTTP, FTP, SMTP, POP3 and TCP/IP ECHO. During emulation, it records the connection time, last transaction time, and average transaction time of each transaction.

For example, using the HTTP protocol, the agent connects to a Web Server and records the connection interval. After the connection, it downloads a specific web page. If successful, the transaction time is stored. A corrective action is taken if the protocol emulation failed, or the initial connection failed. Baseline averages can be determined to define normal response times. When response time is out of the normal range, corrective actions are issued. In addition, historical reports display response time and availability over specified time periods.

Proctor includes a concept called Specific Application Management (SAM) whereby one aggregates subagents into a single software entity in order to manage the application. For example, a SAM such as Apache Web Server management may embody several subagents. Other kinds of SAMs include the management of Oracle Databases and Microsoft Exchange servers.

Thus far we have described the internal components of Proctor. Those same internals are working behind the scenes whether Proctor is run in standalone mode or as a Spectrum integrated application. Consider the

standalone mode. Two primary views in the Proctor system are Policy
Manager and Alert Manager. The policy manager is the means by which one
defines policy domains, organizes policy domains into a domain hierarchy,
lists computers and applications running in a domain, and attaches policies to
them.

Figure 4.7 shows a sample policy view (in standalone mode) in which
policies for server backup, virus checks, Oracle System Log, and Apache
webserver are applied to the computers "boxter" and "augusta" in a "Nashua,
NH" domain, which is part of the East Coast Domain, which in turn is part of
the Dirig Software domain.

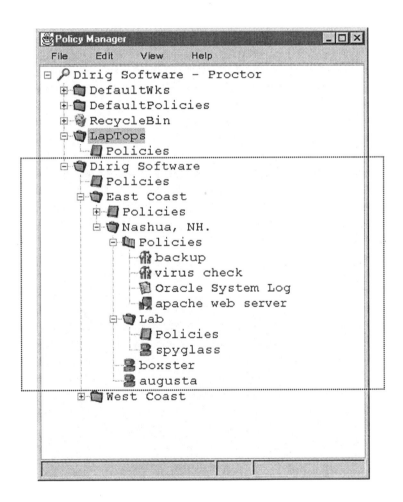

Figure 4.7 A Sample Policy View in Standalone Mode

The Alert Manager displays alerts that are collected by master agents. See Figure 4.8, where alerts are reported on boxster and augusta. The Alert Manager shows information about each alert such as severity, a description, operator annotation, and a probable cause.

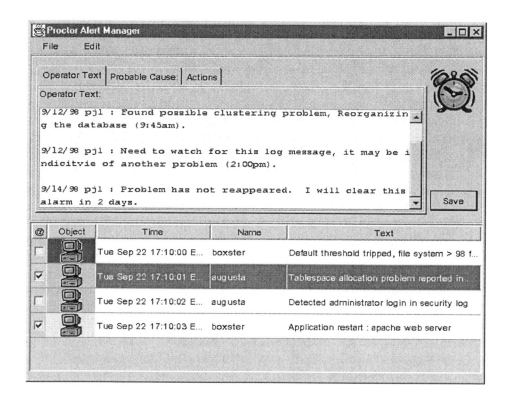

Figure 4.8 A Sample Alert View in Standalone Mode

In addition to these two primary views, there are a large number of reports that show historical information for computer systems and applications in the usual formats of pie charts, bar charts, and timelines.

Proctor is integrated with Spectrum in the following way. New model types and attributes were added to the Spectrum model type hierarchy to allow Proctor data to be stored and manipulated in the Spectrum database (see the description of the Spectrum database in Chapter 3). Intelligence for event correlation was added to provide integration of system and application alerts with network alerts. Finally, new views and icons were added to the SpectroGraph to provide a common "look and feel" and allow one to administer system and application management from a central console.

4.5.2 Opticom's *iView*: Executive Reporting

Opticom's iView is aimed toward business executives rather than technical, specialized network managers. It is integrated with enterprise management systems such as Aprisma Spectrum and HP OpenView.

The following quote from Opticom's marketing literature sums up the goals of iView. The essence and intent of the iView reporting package is clear.

> If you're responsible for the cost-effective performance of the network and technical infrastructure on which your enterprise and your customers depend, the last thing you need is more "raw" information. What you need is an easier, faster way to consolidate, analyze and interpret the vast amount of data that has already been collected. iView is the intelligent infrastructure management and resource planning suite that does just that. Working dynamically with your existing management system, iView automatically consolidates, analyzes and reports on information to provide you with a single, executive-level view of your entire infrastructure.
>
> iView enables senior IT staff and service providers to bring technology and business goals into alignment by giving senior management the necessary information to measure and control financial impacts of the technology on the business through a clear, concise, consolidated view of all aspects of the technical infrastructure which reduces the cost associated with service level measurement and improvement

iView thus collects raw data that has been logged by network, systems, and application management systems and transforms it into information that is useful to business executives. In that way, executives are able to understand the relation between technology expenditures and business goals.

The "business alignment" problem is of paramount importance in industry. Given the recent advancement of networking technology and the dependence of modern business on the technology, there has become a problem in understanding how technology expenditures contribute to the operation and profit of the business. The goal of Opticom's iView is to fill that gap.

Following good software engineering practices, the Opticom software architects first started with a set of requirements expressed by business executives. The requirements are listed as a series of executive-type questions around the general categories of service, capacity, availability, and asset management. We list them below.

Service Management

- What is the perceived availability of the services my IT operations provide?
- Am I meeting my committed Service Level Agreements (SLAs)?
- How many users will be affected by any given network event?
- Do I have enough redundancy built into my network?

Capacity Management

- Are my network resources adequate to support current and projected applications?
- Am I over or under utilizing my network?
- Am I maximizing the bandwidth I have today?
- How efficiently am I utilizing my network?
- When will my current bandwidth no longer support my customers?
- When and where do I need to review my network usage so that I can maximize the existing infrastructure?

Availability Management

- What is the average length of outages by a given vendor/service provider?
- Is this vendor/service provider sensitive to the availability of my critical business applications?
- How responsive is my vendor/service provider?
- Which vendor/service providers are meeting the service levels I am paying for?
- How reliable are my vendor/service providers?
- Which vendor/service providers are effecting my bottom line?

Asset Management:

- Am I meeting the scheduled roll-out?
- When and where do I need to purchase new infrastructure?
- How much growth will my network support before I am forced to purchase more equipment?
- Can I move network resources to maximize capacity?

Given these requirements, the architects began examining ways to transform raw data from enterprise management systems into executive-level reports in order to provide answers to the questions above. There are roughly fifty such reports. We refer the reader to the Further Studies section to examine them.

4.5.3 Gecko's *Saman*: Service Level Management

Saman, as the name suggests, is an application that manages service level agreements (SLAs) for the delivery of IT services, including (i) defining a service and corresponding SLA, (ii) mapping select network, systems, and application elements into services, (iii) tracking the service, (iv) generating alarms if the service is violated, and (v) managing the service within the context of the business organizational structure.

The philosophy of Gecko is this: Any IT equipment, be it a class of network, hardware, software, or a process, may contribute to the provision of a service. Let us call these service elements. Service elements are combined into service level components, and service level components enter into service level agreements.

As an example, consider an email service. This service can be viewed as consisting of the following service level components:

- Telecommunications connectivity to external email post offices
- Email routing and delivery by email application
- Infrastructure connecting e-mail customers to the email server
- Applications used by customers to prepare, post, and receive e-mail

Each service level component, in turn, consists of a collection of service elements. For example, the service level component that provides e-mail routing and delivery is composed of the following kinds of service elements:

- Host computer for the email server application
- Operating systems of the host computers
- Email server application
- Name-server hosts, with operating system and name-server applications

By definition, a service element can be any model in the Spectrum model hierarchy, including models of networks, network devices, transmission media, computer systems, and software applications. Some examples of Spectrum models are these:

- A leased telecommunications link supplied by a telecommunications service provider, e.g. a 64Kbps digital service from British Telecom. In Spectrum, this model is named *WA_LINK*.

- A desktop personal computer used by a customer, e.g. a COMPAQ Presario with Microsoft Windows 98. The Spectrum model is named simply *PC* or *Pingable*.

- An email server application that provides e-mail access and forwarding, e.g. a Lotus ccMail server application. The Spectrum model is *ccMailApp*.

Service elements are monitored by the underlying enterprise management platform (Spectrum). When a service element fails, the impact of the failure is applied to relevant service level components and SLAs.

In Saman, SLAs are defined in terms of the following metrics: availability, reliability, mean time between failure (MTBF), and mean time to repair (MTTR). If an SLA is violated, then an alert is displayed in the Spectrum alarm view. In addition, SLA metrics are stored in the Spectrum database, through which Saman provides historical reports showing whether the SLA has been violated or is likely to be violated.

Figure 4.9 shows a Saman screen shot for illustration purposes. The topmost icon represents an SLA. It is composed of two service components: a collection of small LANs and a collection of small desktop computers. One of the small LANs is a Bay coaxial network, while two desktops are "monet" and "rodin." The LANs and desktop computers are monitored by Spectrum, and the performance metrics are aggregated in the topmost SLA.

In sum, the Saman/Spectrum integration provides an apparatus and methodology for four service management functions:

- Modeling services and SLAs
- Real-time monitoring of service elements
- Alerting on failure to meet SLA criteria
- Historical reporting on SLA metrics

Unfortunately, it not as easy as that. The Gecko architects point out that to use Saman one needs a conceptual model of services, SLAs, and underlying service elements. Good SLA's require interaction with the provider and customer to ensure mutually agreed upon criteria. Determining the elements and components of a SLA may be time-consuming, and it can be a rather complicated process.

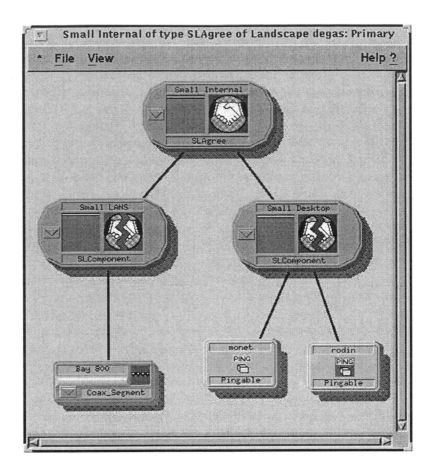

Figure 4.9 A View of an SLA, Service Components, and Service Elements

However, once the structure has been agreed upon, modeling the structure in Saman is relatively straightforward. This means that a lot of thinking should be done before one starts using Saman. Further, after the SLA has been modeled and configured, one should run service reports for a few days to ensure that the conceptual model is correct. It is likely that some configuration changes will be required.

In short, the definitions of services, service level components, service elements, and SLAs are best conceived as a conceptual process, where the implementation of the final structure with Saman is one part of the process.

4.5.4 Remedy's *Help Desk*

The integration of management systems and help desks (sometimes called trouble ticket systems) is fairly well known in the industry. We have discussed some of the design and implementation methods of help desk integration in Chapters 2 and 3 respectively.

There are six primary functions involved in the integration of the Spectrum management system and the Remedy Help Desk:

- Automatic Trouble Ticket Generation (ATTG) – The Spectrum management system collects information about an event or alarm and forwards it to Help Desk.

- Policy-Based ATTG – The administrator sets policies regarding ATTG so that only selective alarms are passed to Help Desk.

- Manual Trouble Ticket Generation – The administrator clicks on a "Make Trouble Ticket" selection in the Spectrum alarm display, thereby entering a trouble ticket into Help Desk.

- Help Desk Drilling – From a trouble ticket in Help Desk, the administrator clicks a button that invokes a detailed view in the Spectrum system having to do with the contents of the trouble ticket, e.g. topology, organization, performance, or port-level views.

- Problem Resolution – From a trouble ticket in Help Desk, the administrator clicks a button that retrieves similar, resolved trouble ticket systems.

- Synchronized Alarm Clearing – If the problem in a Help Desk trouble ticket is resolved, then the alarm is cleared in the Spectrum management system, and vice versa.

An interesting story regarding help desk integration is this: ATTG was introduced in the industry in the early 1990s. However, the mode of integration was event-forwarding. That is, all events were placed in a temporary buffer in the help desk. The help desk administrator would then sift through the events, discarding the majority of them and transforming a few of them into trouble tickets.

People realized rather quickly that that was an awkward and inelegant mode of integration. It results in the so-called event-flooding problem, and places undue burden on the help desk administrator.

A solution to that problem is three-fold: (i) get rid of the temporary buffer in the help desk system, (ii) exploit the event-to-alarm mapping mechanism in the management station, and (iii) set policies on the management station so that only select alarms are forwarded to the help desk.

Recall that the purpose of event-correlation is to transform collections of events scattered in space and time into a single over-arching alarm. (See the discussion of event correlation in Chapter 3). Thus, only those alarms are forwarded to the help desk. On top of that, one can set policies that govern alarm-forwarding.

The variables of alarm policies are numerous, including alarm type, alarm severity, alarm location, and others. An interesting variable is alarm age. A policy regarding alarm age says essentially this: Mr. Alarm, if you live to be 30 minutes old, then you may move to trouble ticket status. Such a policy, for example, is quite useful for SNMP agents that often die (causing an alarm to be born), but then start themselves back up again (causing the alarm to die). In that case, only bona fide SNMP agent deaths are reported to the help desk.

The Spectrum/Help Desk integration includes these functions. It was one of the first integrated systems that was built at Aprisma in the early 90s.

4.6 Challenges for Integrated Management

We have examined instances of the management roles in Figure 4.4. An alternative view of the integrated system is shown in Figure 4.10, where the distinction between API and PEI modes of integration is made clear. Proctor, Saman, and Spectrum are integrated in API-fashion, while iView and Help Desk are integrated in PEI-fashion.

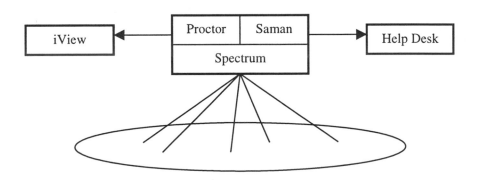

Figure 4.10 An Alternative View of the Integrated System

The architecture of the integrated system is quite simple and reasonable, and it will be easy enough to install the system and get it running.

However, it will not be as simple to configure it so that it is useful in the field. For one thing, there is a lot of functionality available, and there is at least some overlap in functionality across the individual systems. Probably, only about 75% of the total possible functionality of the integrated system will be required to manage the enterprise.

For another thing, as we saw with Gecko's Saman, there should be some conceptual structuring done up front before we proceed to implementation. That problem calls for some careful thinking about the day-to-day goings-on at Camp LeJeune.

And finally, there is the problem of fine-tuning. Examples of fine-tuning are creating the policies that will be used in both Saman and the Help Desk. It is not hard to implement the policies once we know what the policies should be. However, it is a bit hard and requires some work to know what the policies should be in the first place.

Interestingly, these points bring us back around to our discussion of "use cases" in software engineering methodology in Chapter 2. In our discussions in this chapter, we have almost violated our principle of disregarding technical details when we try to understand how a management system should be used. At this juncture, we would start all over again and try to uncover the use cases for Camp LeJeune's management system. In fact, that is happening as this chapter is being written. It is comforting to know that an integrated management system in some form is technically possible, but we shouldn't let that particular system influence us as we construct a use case model.

In Chapter 7 we will revisit the problem of uncovering use cases. We'll look at a methodology called Contextual Inquiry that will help us answer the question "What do network administrators do?" and give us guidance for developing integrated management systems that are user-friendly.

Chapter Summary

In this chapter we discussed our first case study. We described a micro city network at Camp LeJeune in the USA. The current management system at Camp LeJeune is essentially a *network* management system. However, the goal is to transform the network management system into an *enterprise* management system that monitors and controls computer systems, applications, and services in addition to the network. We described a candidate integrated system that includes Aprisma's Spectrum, Dirig's Proctor, Opticom's iView, Gecko's Saman, and Remedy's Help Desk.

Finally, we discussed the challenges of deploying and configuring the integrated systems.

Exercises and Discussion Questions

1. Is the network of a micro city an example of a business network or a service network? Explain.

2. Will micro cities in the sense that we have defined them become commonplace by the year 2010? Is it technologically feasible? Is it sociologically feasible? Will city dwellers allow themselves to be taxed for such purposes?

3. Send an email to network overseers at Camp LeJeune, asking for a brief update on the management of their micro city.

4. Download an evaluation copy of Dirig's Proctor. Use it to manage a set of applications on an NT or Unix workstation. Discuss with your peers.

5. Download an evaluation copy of Gecko's Saman. Use it to manage an email service. Discuss with your peers.

6. What is the "business alignment" problem? How does our integrated architecture alleviate the problem? What other approaches might alleviate the problem?

7. Try to get an interview with a network administrator or executive. Propose the list of executive questions in Section 5.5, and have the administrator rate the importance of each question.

8. Following #7, have the administrator describe special requirements or "management headaches."

9. Following #8, try to sketch a solution to any management headache within our integrated framework. If possible, try to implement a prototype of the solution.

10. Finally, following #9, try to get the administrator to take a look at your solution and evaluate it.

Further Studies

To get a good idea of the operations at Camp LeJeune, the reader should visit their web site at www.lejeune.usmc.mil.

We have been a bit stingy in showing screen shots of the management applications discussed in this chapter. Our main goal was to describe the concepts and methods behind them. For more detail on the management applications, including numerous screen shots, the reader can visit their web sites: www.aprisma.com, www.dirig.com, www.opticominc.com, www.geckoware.com, and www.remedy.com.

Three good books on methods and issues in integrated management are Ghetie's *Network and Systems Management Platforms*, Hegering and Abeck's *Integrated Network and Systems Management*, and Subramanian's *Network Management: Principles and Practice*.

A useful book on the integration of management platforms and help desks is Lewis' book *Managing Computer Networks: A Case Based Reasoning Approach*.

A useful book that discusses many features of the integrated architecture in this chapter is Lewis' *Service Level Management for Enterprise Network*.

Numerous issues and approaches towards integrated management can be found in the proceedings of conferences on network management, including the International Symposium on Integrated Network Management (ISINM, renamed simply Integrated Management (IM) in 1999) and Network Operations and Management Systems (NOMS). Go to the web site of the IEEE Communications Society, www.comsoc.org, to find out about these conferences and others.

References

Ghetie, J. *Network and Systems Management Platforms*. Kluwer Academic Publishers. 1997.

Hegering, H. and S. Abeck. *Integrated Network and Systems Management*. Addison-Wesley. 1994.

Lewis, L. *Managing Computer Networks: A Case Based Reasoning Approach*. Artech House. 1995.

Lewis, L. *Service Level Management for Enterprise Networks*. Artech House. 1999.

Subramanian, M. *Network Management: Principles and Practice*. Addison-Wesley. 2000.

5 Managing Service Provider Networks

In our second case study, we look at the management of a service provider network. We cover the following topics in this chapter:

- What is a Service Provider Network?
- USA's Telecommunications Act of 1996
- Vitts Networks, a Service Provider in the USA
- Network Management Behind the Scenes
- Response Time Management
- Integrated Network Management

First we review the distinction between a business network and a service network that was introduced in Chapter 1.

Second, we describe the political and business landscape in the USA in the wake of the Telecommunications Act of 1996. In Part I of our book we were concerned primarily with the technical aspects of network management. Realistically, however, there is more to the story, especially in the service provider space. It is important that the reader be cognizant of political and business influences on network management practices.

Third, we focus on Vitts Networks in the USA, a prime example of a service provider that emerged after the Telecommunications Act of 1996. Vitts Networks is sometimes called a "data competitive local exchange carrier" (D-CLEC) and sometimes called a "packet-based local exchange carrier" (PLEC). Regardless of branding and nomenclature, Vitts has built a *Protected Service Network* (PSN) that offers data services to homes and businesses in the northeast and mid-Atlantic states in the USA. We discuss the coverage of the PSN, its topology and connections to global and regional networks, and its range of service offerings.

Fourth, we describe Vitts' network management practices, which are two-fold. Vitts has to manage (i) its PSN and services rendered and (ii) numerous networks of other businesses as an outsourcer. We are fortunate to have Vitts architects share their experiences with us, including successes, anomalies, and future directions. Our discussion will take us into issues in multi-domain management, event correlation, and service level management.

137

Fifth, we discuss a recent area called response time management (RTM). In Chapter 1, in which we discussed the evolution of network management, we pointed to RTM as the latest direction in network management practices. Here we give the topic full treatment. We discuss the business case for RTM, six approaches to RTM, and several commercial RTM systems.

Finally, we look at the bigger picture of integrated management in which an RTM system is combined with network and systems management. We describe a design and a phased plan for building an integrated RTM/network management system.

5.1 What is a Service Provider Network?

Let us review the definitions of a business network and a service network in Chapter 1:

- A *business network* is owned by the business enterprise, where the scope of the network is to support the informational and operational requirements of the business such as marketing, sales, accounting, and manufacturing departments, but where the function of the business is to provide some useful commodity for sale to public or private sectors, for example automobiles, pharmaceuticals, and other artifacts.

- A *service network* is owned or leased by a service provider, where the scope of the network is to support communication services for resale to businesses, private end users, and other service providers (e.g. electronic commerce, Internet access, cable modems for the home, banking, tele-medicine, and distance learning), and where the function of a service provider is to provide specialized networking infrastructure, computer systems, business applications, and management methods to support the services.

We argued in Chapter 1 that the distinction between business and service networks is useful for the sake of conceptual clarity, but that in practice the distinction might become somewhat blurred. For example, a business might choose to outsource part of its network operation to a service provider, but choose to keep other parts under its own control.

Further, we saw in the previous chapter that it is not perfectly clear whether the Camp LeJeune network should be considered as a business network or a service network (see question #1 at the end of the Chapter 4). That is OK. The question stretches the reader's imaginative and analytical faculties.

We also argued in Chapter 1 that the face of telecommunications network management changed in the mid-1990s when telephone companies became legally obligated to open up their networks to others as a result of the Telecommunications Act of 1996. An entrepreneur now had the opportunity of leasing the bandwidth and services of independent telephone networks, and adding further value to that in order to provide special services to customers.

At this juncture, we wish to say more about how the 1996 Act influences network management practices, especially in the service provider space. Part of the influence is technical, but another part of the influence is political. Indeed, policies laid down by the US Government affect how service provider networks are built and managed.

5.2 The Telecommunications Act of 1996

In this section we discuss the political aspects of communications in the USA, especially with regard to the Telecommunications Act of 1996. The author apologizes for being USA-centric; however, it is close to home. The political landscape of communications services in other countries is left as an exercise for the interested reader.

5.2.1 ILECs, CLECs, and RBOCs

The telephone arrived in the USA in the early part of the 20th century, providing households with both local telephone services and long distance telephone services. Until the mid-1980s, AT&T was the sole owner of long distance telephone services in the USA, although there existed several regional telephone companies (a.k.a. LECs – Local Exchange Carriers) that provided local telephone services.

However, AT&T came to be seen as a monopoly, and in 1984 a compulsory order was issued to AT&T by the US government to divest AT&T stock.

A side effect of the AT&T divestiture was to open up long distance telephone services to competition. Thus, LECs now had an opportunity to enter the long distance market. That was an attractive proposition to LECs because long distance telephone calls comprise roughly 62% of total telephony revenues, while local calls comprise 18%. The remaining 20% of revenues come from international telephone services, calling cards, toll-free services, and fax services.

There have come to be two main types of LECs that have an interest in the long distance market: *incumbent* local exchange carriers and *competitive* local exchange carriers (ILECS and CLECs).

ILECs are considered typically to have been around for a long time and are mainly telephony-oriented (hence, the adjective "incumbent"). CLECs, on the other hand, are considered to be rather new and are both telephony and data-oriented. CLECs typically offer data services such as Internet access, web hosting, and business applications for the home and business.

For example, a popular notion in the CLEC space is an "Internet dial tone" (a.k.a. "web tone"), a familiar concept borrowed from the telephony world. In the same way that we get a dial tone when we pick up our telephones, CLECs would like to provide an Internet "dial tone" when we turn on our computers.

Generally, we may consider ILECs as having control over telephony networks and CLECs as offering data services via their private networks (which, in turn, are connected to telephony networks). We should point out, however, that some ILECs are beginning to offer data services also. A Regional Bell Operating Company (RBOC) such as Bell Atlantic is an ILEC, whereas Vitts Networks in the northeast region of the USA is a CLEC.

5.2.2 The Federal Communications Commission

Now the story continues: The Federal Communications Commission (FCC) in the USA is responsible for setting up policies and guidelines for ILECs, RBOCs, and CLECs that wish to offer communications services. The goal of the FCC is to promote fair competition in the wake of the AT&T divestiture in 1984, which culminated in the 1996 Telecommunications Act.

Section 271 of the 1996 Act has become rather famous (and controversial). It lays down a checklist for ILECs who wish to enter the long distance market. For example, a new ILEC entrant has to demonstrate the provision of nondiscriminatory access to unbundled network elements (UNEs), poles, ducts, conduits, and rights of way. In addition, the 1996 Act lays down qualifications required for a company to have CLEC status.

The concept of a UNE access is of special significance to CLECs. We may consider UNEs as the telephony devices and circuits that make up the local telephone loop, thus rendering our familiar telephone services possible (review the Telephone Network Architecture in Figure 1.2 of Chapter 1). Thus, CLECs have to depend upon ILECs to abide by specific FCC policies in order to combine their data networks with existing telephony networks.

As of this writing, the FCC has denied five ILEC applications since the 1996 Act because they didn't adhere to the checklist. Only one RBOC, Bell

Atlantic in New York (BA-NY), has been approved to enter the long distance market. BA-NY is now focused on a performance assurance plan (PAP).

Now the political landscape gets a little more complex: The Competitive Telecommunications Association (CompTel) in the USA exists to promote fair competition in the long distance market, arguing that any divergence from the checklist or any relaxation of an ILEC's PAP will compromise fairness as CLECs enter the market.

For example, CompTel argues that the BA-NY PAP does not ensure that BA-NY will provide CLECs with UNE access, interconnection, collocation of equipment, and services for re-sale that are at least equal to the access that BA-NY provides to itself and its affiliates.

CompTel has proposed further guidelines to the FCC regarding access to UNEs, where UNEs include (i) loops used to provide high-capacity and advanced telecom services, (ii) network interface devices, (iii) local circuit switching, (iv) dedicated and shared transport, (v) signaling and call-related databases, and (vi) operations support systems.

In general, CompTel argues that the 1996 Act requires ILECs to provide any requesting carrier access to network elements on an unbundled basis at any technically feasible point on rates, terms, and conditions that are just, reasonable, and nondiscriminatory.

5.2.3 Discussion

It is fair to say that the political landscape of communications in the USA is a bit complex. That is not uncommon when several parties have business interests at stake. The main interest of an ILEC is to take advantage of the lucrative long distance telephony market. However, ILECs are scrutinized by the FCC and special interest groups such as CompTel so that they don't block competition and create a monopoly.

At the same time, the main interest of CLECs is to provide data services, but they are dependent upon an ILEC's telephony network in order to provide them. The consumer, who is generally not interested in any of this, simply wants reliable, simple, and economical deliverance of both data and telephony services. Indeed, another party in our political landscape is the Consumer Federation of America, although we won't go into details of its activities here.

Let us reiterate and close our discussion with the following definition of a CLEC from the "Webopedia," an on-line encyclopedia dedicated to computer technology:

CLEC (pronounced see-lek): A Competitive Local Exchange Carrier is a telephone company that competes with an Incumbent Local Exchange Carrier (ILEC) such as a Regional Bell Operating Company (RBOC), GTE, ALLNET, etc. (Note: GTE and Bell Atlantic have now joined together to form VERIZON.)

With the passage of the Telecommunications Act of 1996, there has been a explosion in the number of CLECs. The Act allows companies with CLEC status to use ILEC infrastructure in two ways:

1. *Access to UNEs.* Important to CLEC telecommunications networking is the availability of unbundled network elements or UNEs (through a collocation arrangement). UNEs are defined by the Act as any "facility or equipment used in the provision of a telecommunications service," as well as "features, functions, and capabilities that are provided by means of such facility or equipment." For CLECs the most important UNE available to them is the local loop, which connects the ILEC switches to the ILEC's present customers. With the local loop, CLECs will be able to connect their switches with the ILEC's switches, thus giving them access to ILEC customers.

2. *Resale.* Another option open to CLECs is the resale strategy. The Act states that any telecommunications services ILECs offer at retail, must be offered to CLECs at a wholesale discount. This saves the CLEC from having to invest in switches, fiber optic transmission facilities, or collocation arrangements.

In any case, a CLEC may decide on one or the other or even both. So, you can see why obtaining CLEC status is very beneficial, especially for ISPs, who may easily get access to the copper loops and other switching elements necessary to provide Internet services. Recently courts, in response to the growth of cable Internet access, have also required cable companies to follow the same guidelines as ILECs.

Applying for CLEC status is a very tedious and complex process that involves a Regulatory Attorney or Consultant, the State Public Utilities Commission, and about 50 other steps. But remember, it will be worth it, and now is a good time, because the courts continually are trying to force ILEC costs down and are making access to UNEs easier in the name of fair competition. So, get in before regulators begin to re-regulate the other way.

5.2.4 The Political Landscape Affects Network Management Practices

The reader should begin to see how the political landscape influences network management practices. The situation is this: In general, a service provider network is not a self-contained standalone network like the Micro City Network at Camp LeJeune. The services of a service provider might well depend upon supporting networks that are managed independently by other vendors.

So far, that is fine and good. But recall from Chapter 2 that customers are beginning to call for service level agreements (SLAs). They wish to have a quantitative guarantee that specified service levels will be met.

But now, how can a service provider guarantee a service level when part of the network upon which the service depends is under someone else's control? That is one of the main questions that service providers have to face. It is first a political question, and secondly it is a technical question.

In its simplest form, the problem is illustrated in Figure 5.1. Suppose a data network is managed by CLEC *B*, but a service offered by *B* (represented by the bold horizontal line) depends upon a telecommunications network that is managed by ILEC *A*.

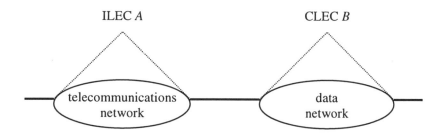

Figure 5.1 The Problem of Multi-Network Management

Logically, there are at least four approaches to the problem:

1. The CLEC limits its service offerings to those that depend upon the networks under its control.

2. The CLEC doesn't offer service guarantees in cases where the service depends upon networks not under its control.

3. The CLEC and ILEC enter an arrangement whereby network operators collaborate to handle service degradations and faults.

4. The ILEC opens it's UNEs to the CLEC's management system, or vice versa.

Note that the four approaches are not mutually exclusive. Further, note that the fourth approach takes us directly into the technical challenges of integrated network management. We have discussed such challenges in a fair amount of detail in the preparatory chapters in Part I of the book; thus, the reader is advised to skim through those chapters before entering the case study.

5.3 Vitts Networks, a Service Provider in the USA

Vitts Networks in the USA is a prime example of a service provider that emerged in the wake of the Telecommunications Act of 1996. The company was incorporated in 1996 and began offering data services in 1998. Vitts engineers built a data network that covers most of the northeast of the USA.

Vitts is not a pure CLEC according to the definition in the preceding section – i.e. it is not a telephone company. It is often referred to as a "data competitive local exchange carrier" (D-CLEC) or a "packet-based local exchange carrier" (PLEC).

The brand name of Vitts' data network is the *Protected Services Network* (PSN), and the brand name of the collection of IP connectivity services offered to customers is *FastReach*.   We can think of Vitts' PSN as superimposed on regional ILEC networks and the Internet, where the PSN is connected to the Internet and ILEC UNEs.

The backbone of the PSN is a high-speed, packet-based, fiber-optic, redundant ring network. The network is made up of 75-gigabit per second IP switching systems that guarantee no more than 0.00001 seconds of switching time between interfaces. In comparison, the average Internet Service Provider's routing time to the Internet is as much as .01 seconds.

The PSN interconnects two types of Vitts facilities: Central Data Offices (CDOs) and Internet Data Centers (IDCs). CDOs are housed at ILEC facilities, where Vitts has collocated networking gear. IDCs are pure Vitts facilities that serve two main functions: (i) customers may collocate their networking equipment there and (ii) they are the places from which the entire PSN is monitored and managed.

At the writing of this book there are some 300 CDOs, with plans to expand that number to more than 1,500 by the end of 2001. There are plans for roughly 12 IDCs to be located throughout the thirteen states of the northeast and mid-Atlantic USA.

The services offered by Vitts are categorized into (i) high-speed Internet access services, (ii) hosting and Internet services, (iii) network security and enhancement services, and (iv) outsourced network management services. For illustration purposes, Figure 5.2 shows an arbitrary number of CDOs on the PSN, where some are connected to customer devices and others are connected to the Internet. Vitts employs four Internet service providers (ISPs) for multiple gateways to the Internet, as shown in the figure.

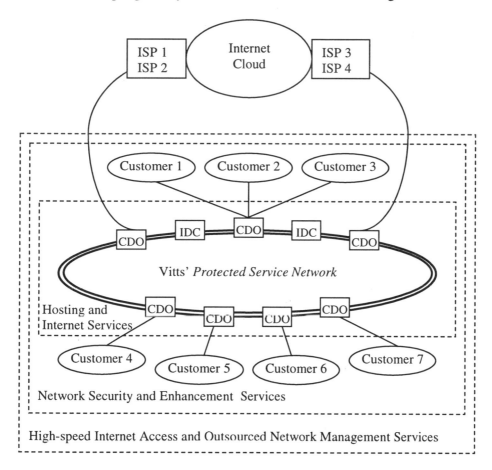

Figure 5.2 Vitts' *FastReach* Line of Services

The innermost rectangle in Figure 5.2 represents those services that are dependent on hardware and software that reside in Vitts' CDOs. The next rectangle out represents those services that are dependent on hardware and software that reside on customer premises. Finally, the outermost rectangle represents broadband access services and network management services.

One thing that Vitts' architects have to worry about is the management of their PSN. In addition, new service packages impose further complexity in Vitts' management practices since each package requires more hardware and software located at CDOs, IDCs, and at customer sites.

In addition, new customers select new sets of services, and old customers modify their existing service packages over time. That also causes fluctuations in bandwidth, device, and application requirements. And since the PSN is expanding to other regions of the USA and opening up to new customers, there are further fluctuations in management requirements.

In sum, Vitts architects and engineers have a lot to deal with in order to configure, provision, and maintain their network and keep their customers satisfied. They have to have a flexible management system. The reader should begin to appreciate the complexity of managing a service provider network.

5.3.1 Services Provided by Vitts Networks

Below we briefly describe the particular services that fall under each service category in Figure 5.2. The reader should try to imagine how these services increase the complexity of managing the networks. A clue is to make a mental note of any additional workstations, servers, applications, or transmission devices that are mentioned in the descriptions of the services.

Hosting and Internet Services

- Media Streaming – Allows encoded audio and video to be broadcast across the Internet, either live or pre-recorded and archived to be played on demand. Provided via a partnership with Real Networks, where Vitts provides required storage space and bandwidth.

- Server Collocation – Allows customers to place their servers in Vitts' facilities, where Vitts provides connectivity to the Internet, security, and facility management.

- E-mail Hosting – Allows customers to place their e-mail services within Vitts' facilities, where email servers are redundant and fault-tolerant.

- Domain Name Service (DNS) Hosting – Allows customers to place DNS services within servers that reside in Vitts' facilities.

- Web Hosting – Allows customers to place web servers in Vitts' facilities.

Network Security and Enhancement Services

- Enhanced Routing Services – Allows customers to connect a workgroup LAN to the PSN via on-site routers. Vitts installs, configures, and manages the on-site routers.

- Access Security Firewall Services – Coupled with Internet Access service. Provides stateful packet inspection to protect customer's private LAN from hackers and intrusions.

- Secure IP Addresses – Provides a network address translation (NAT) server. Users' local LANs and computers behind the NAT server are unrecognizable from the Internet.

- Secure Internet Transit Service – Provides protection of corporate data by encrypting it as it crosses the Internet. Achieved with specially designed hardware platform from Vitts.

High-speed Internet Access Services

- Internet Access – Customers are connected continuously to Vitts' PSN, which in turn is connected continuously to the Internet. Thus there is no waiting for dial-up time, setup time, or modem training before accessing the Internet. The service includes the necessary equipment and configurations billed at a fixed monthly price.

- VIP Private LANs – Allows geographically separated businesses to share information and resources as though they were on the same local area network. Customers sites can be located in Vitts' PSN service area. Thus there are no long distance charges.

Outsourced Network Management Services

- Network Management – Provides customers with a suite of remote network management services designed to maximize network up time and alleviate the network management burden.

Let us focus on Vitts' network management service -- the subject of this book. The challenge of Vitts' network management practice is two-fold. First, it has to manage its PSN and the services it supports. Second, it offers a network management solution for customers' external networks as well, i.e. it manages into a customer's network remotely from IDCs. That should be reassuring to customers with pure business networks, or customers with hybrid business/service networks, given that Vitts has to develop in house expertise in order to manage the complexities of its PSN.

Below we show what Vitts is offering to customers in their network management glossy. Following that, we dig deeper into the internals of their network management practices. The latter is something that customers rarely see. However, it is good to see the kind of language that customers read, and then to understand how it is backed up from an engineering perspective, including successes, glitches, challenges, and future directions.

5.3.2 The Network Management "Glossy"

Vitt's Network Outsourcing Professional Services are designed to provide solutions to many of today's e-business challenges. Using industry-leading hardware and software solutions, Vitts makes the power and scalability of "big company" Internet-oriented applications available to everyone, without the need for substantial investment or in-depth expertise.

Outsource Network Management

In today's global environment, the network is how one does business. The availability of network infrastructure is a critical part of business success. Identifying problems and minimizing downtime through proactive network monitoring is essential.

Vitts offers a suite of services designed to maximize network up-time and alleviate the network management burden, which until recently only Fortune 500 companies could afford. Vitts provides a customized solution of value-added managed services along with leading-edge connectivity packages designed for specific business needs. This integrated approach allows Vitts to become the complete solution provider.

By leveraging the existing connectivity provided to customers and the investment into network management tools and staff, this service provides value to customers for considerably less money than they would spend developing similar services on their own. Utilizing the 24x7 Network Operations Center (NOC), and employing best of breed management techniques, Vitts can customize a management solution that best fits business needs.

Network Device and Server Management

All SNMP-compliant devices can be managed around-the-clock from Vitts' NOC. The NOC can isolate a problem, notify the customer, and execute well-defined troubleshooting procedures. If a third party Service Level Agreement (SLA) covers the device, the NOC can notify the vendor or dispatch the required personnel based on pre-defined customer instructions.

Reports detailing utilization, trending and connectivity are displayed on daily, weekly, monthly and yearly graphs via the Web. Server management provides CPU, memory and disk utilization monitoring for UNIX or NT based servers. Thresholds can be set against any process running on the system being monitored.

Application and Desktop Monitoring

Applications that reside on the servers can also be managed. Thresholds can be set to match customer-defined SLAs to insure the desired Quality of Services (QoS).

Desktop monitoring provides CPU, memory, and disk utilization monitoring for desktop devices. Thresholds can be set against processes running on the system. Vitts offers a comprehensive suite of services designed to alleviate the burden and cost of managing complex networks and business applications. Services can be selected "a la carte" to tailor a managed service program that meets the customers needs. All services offer fault isolation and notifications based on customer defined SLAs and Web-accessible reports.

5.4 Network Management Behind the Scenes

Spectrum is used as the core management system of Vitts' network infrastructure, including (i) the management of devices and circuits that comprise the PSN and (ii) the management of devices and circuits that are added to support IDC and on-site services.

Vitts selected Spectrum because its distributed architecture promised scalability and adaptability in the midst of expansion and fluctuation of managed devices and services. Clearly, that is just what a fast-growing service provider needs.

We discussed Spectrum's scalability properties in Chapter 3. We won't repeat all the details here, but a quick review is in order: Spectrum is based on a distributed client/server architecture. A large network is partitioned into multiple domains, where SpectroServers SS_1, SS_2, ... , SS_N are assigned domains D_1, D_2, ... , D_N. A single SS_N monitors and controls the devices in D_N, performing event-to-alarm mapping with respect to D_N. The alarms are passed to a higher-level SS that performs multi-domain alarm correlation.

Mechanically, that is fine and good. However, a prior conceptual problem is to decide how to partition a large network into domains in the first place. Recall that that was the essence of our discussion of multi-domain management in Chapter 2. We saw that a large network can be partitioned along various dimensions, e.g. with respect to geographical location, business organizational structure, business operations, or other dimensions.

We now look at how Vitts chose to partition the PSN network and services. The interested reader may wish to glance back at Section 2.1.1 and Section 3.1.4 before proceeding.

5.4.1 Multi-Domain Management at Vitts

The first partitioning principle of Vitts' management architecture is based on geographical location and customer density. Figure 5.3 shows the coverage of the PSN as this book is written. It covers the northeast and mid-Atlantic states in the USA.

Region 1 (the white region) includes Maine (ME), New Hampshire (NH), Vermont (VT), Massachusetts (MA), Connecticut (CT), and Rhode Island (RI). Region 2 (the light gray region) includes New York (NY) and New Jersey (NJ). Region 3 (the darker region) includes Pennsylvania (PA), Maryland (MD), Delaware (DE), West Virginia (WV), Virginia (VA), and Washington, D. C.

Figure 5.3 also shows four categories of IDCs. Recall that IDCs serve two purposes: they house customer collocated equipment and they house Vitts' network management equipment. There are four categories of IDCs:

The *Corporate Network Operations Center* (CNOC) is the center of the Vitts management infrastructure. It is located at Vitts' headquarters in New Hampshire.

The *Regional NOC* (RNOC) acts as the focal point within a region. Note that the CNOC in New Hampshire also serves as the RNOC for Region 1. The RNOC for Region 2 is in New Jersey, and the RNOC for Region 3 is in Washington D.C.

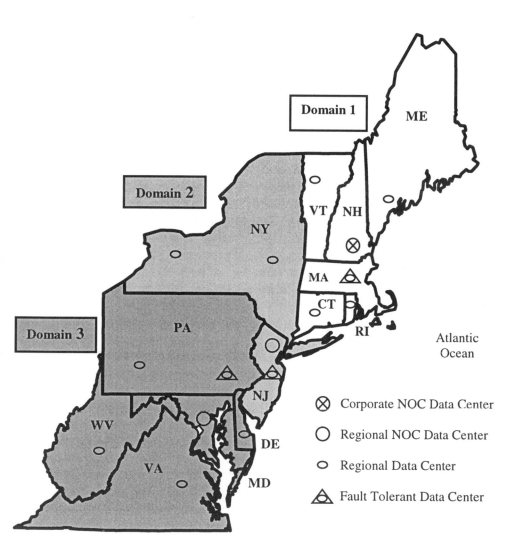

Figure 5.3 Distribution of Vitts' Current and Planned Internet Data Centers

Regional Data Centers (RDCs) are deployed at choice locations within a domain based on customer density and the requirement of a two-hour or less driving distance from an RDC to a customer site.

Finally, a *Fault Tolerant Data Center* (FTDC) is deployed in each region to provide redundancy and disaster control, thereby protecting the management of services against major power outages or catastrophic events. A region's FTDC is collocated at a RDC near the region's RNOC.

Vitts' second partitioning principle is based on classes of managed objects. The managed objects are categorized as follows: (i) equipment collocated at ILEC facilities that comprise the PSN, (ii) equipment that supports the delivery of data services to customer locations, and (iii) equipment at customer locations for which Vitts provides outsourced network management. Thus, Vitts has designated different types of SpectroServers for each class of managed object.

An RNOC SpectroServer (RNOC-SS) monitors PSN equipment that comprises the Vitts backbone network in each region, including equipment collocated at ILEC facilities and pure Vitts facilities. Thus there are three RNOC-SSs at the three regional NOC data centers, as shown in Figure 5.3.

A Delivery Equipment SpectroServer (DE-SS) manages all circuits and devices associated with delivery of data services to a customer site, where the number of circuits and devices determines the number of DE-SSs needed in each IDC.

An Outsource Management SpectroServer (OM-SS) manages customer networks, where Vitts manages into the network remotely from an IDC. The number and size of customer networks determine the number of OM-SSs needed in an IDC.

A "Manager of Managers" SpectroServer (MOM-SS) contains logical models of all DE-SSs and OM-SSs within a region. The CNOC MOM-SS additionally contains models of the RNOC-SSs for regions 2 and 3. Thus, network operators can drill down into details of the PSN, down to the port level if required, from a single console as described in Chapter 3.

Finally, fault tolerant SpectroServers (FT-SSs) provide redundancy and disaster control. Each primary SpectroServer is backed up by an exact copy in an FT-SS.

In general, any particular IDC can wear multiple hats and therefore host several types of SpectroServers. For example, Table 5.1 characterizes the Fault Tolerant IDC in Massachusetts.

Table 5.1 A Characterization of the Data Center in Massachusetts

	CNOC	RNOC	RDC	FTDC
RNOC-SS				
DE-SS			2	
OM-SS			2	
MOM-SS				
FT-SS				11

Wearing its RDC hat, it houses two DE-SSs and two OM-SSs. Wearing its FTDC hat, it houses eleven FT-SSs. Thus, there are fifteen SSs in the Massachusetts IDC.

5.4.2 Event Correlation: An Unexpected Side-Effect

In Chapter 3 we described the benefits of event correlation and how various products approach it. While generally event correlation is a useful feature of a management system, Vitts' architects discovered an unexpected side-effect of event correlation that customers didn't appreciate, viz. that in some cases the customers would not be forewarned of an outage. Fortunately, the problem was overcome rather easily. Let us explain as follows.

Figure 5.4 shows the essential relationships among the different types of SpectroServers in Vitts' overall management architecture (excluding FT-SSs). RNOC-SSs manage PSN backbone equipment, DE-SSs manage equipment associated with the delivery of services to customer sites, and OM-SSs manage equipment located at customer sites.

Each SS performs event correlation and event-to-alarm mapping with respect to its particular domain, as described in Chapter 3. Importantly, note that the each SS passes its alarms to the MOM-SS at the CNOC in New Hampshire, whereby CNOC operators have a birds-eye view of the overall health of the PSN.

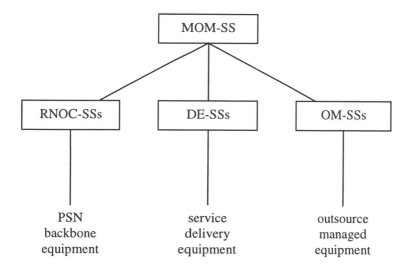

Figure 5.4 The Relationships of Different SpectroServer Types

Figure 5.5 shows a classic scenario involving event correlation. If a crucial transmission device in the topmost CDO fails, then without event correlation there would be a flood of alarms on devices at the sites of customers 1, 2, and 3 (shown by the Xs). With Spectrum's event correlation mechanism, however, the alarms on devices at the sites of the customers are suppressed, and only the culprit alarm on the failed device at the CDO is displayed.

In the Spectrum display, suppressed alarms are indicated by a model turning from green (i.e. healthy) to gray, whereas an authentic culprit alarm is indicated by a model flashing red. Further, the alarm text that accompanies a gray alarm explains that the real fault lies elsewhere. Of course, that is quite useful information when troubleshooters begin trying to pinpoint and resolve the fault.

Now, a common business practice at Vitts is to notify a customer if network faults occur that will affect the customer's Internet services. Thus, before the PSN went on-line in 1998, Vitts' operations staff was trained to notify a customer immediately if a device at the customer site were flashing red. The customer was to be forewarned of a temporary outage and the expected time to normalcy.

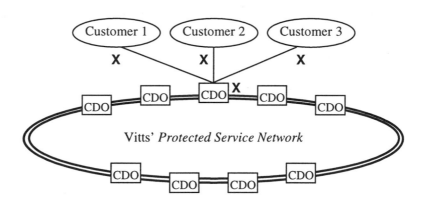

Figure 5.5 A Classic Event Correlation Scenario

It turns out that the scenario in Figure 5.5 actually occurred in the early stage of the PSN deployment. A CDO device was flashing red, but devices at several customer sites were colored gray, thanks to event correlation. The staff followed their instructions properly and concentrated their efforts on resolving the problem with the device in the CDO. They didn't bother to notify customers of pending outages, according to instruction. But afterwards, Vitts' help desk received complaints from several customers because they experienced an outage of which they weren't forewarned.

Fortunately, the problem was easily overcome. The operations staff had to be re-educated about the semantics of alarms and how to respond to them. In particular: If an alarm on a device at a customer site is gray, then notify the customer of a pending outage; but don't spend time trying to diagnose the gray alarm. Instead, expend time to diagnose the red alarm that is the root cause of the gray alarm.

5.4.3 Service Level Agreements

Vitts makes the following guarantees to customers that subscribe to its FastReach Internet services:

1. Availability: There will be at least 99% service availability. That is, the Internet dial tone will be on 99% of the time, regardless of whether somebody is there to hear it.

2. Reliability: There will be a packet loss rate of 5% or less of all packets sent out from a customer site. Note that this does *not* mean that only 95% of emails, remote transactions, etc. will actually make it to their destinations, since dropped packets are re-sent. Rather, it is a measure of network congestion, which in turn is a measure of reliability.

3. Usability: There will be a round trip delay of packets sent from the customer site to the edge of the Internet of 50 milliseconds or less. This is a measure of service usability. It is well known that lags in web transactions are often unbearable and actually interfere with business.

4. Security: Security is built into the PSN (recall the "protected" in PSN). Further, customers may subscribe to various levels of security by selecting certain service packages (e.g. firewalls, IP addressing, and encryption). Importantly, note that security is not quantitatively measured by the management system. That topic has received little attention in the industry, but it is important. We leave it as an exercise.

The first two items are accomplished with Spectrum monitoring and reporting. It is fairly straightforward to aggregate the availability of the devices upon which a service depends into an overall measure of customer service availability. The measurement and reporting of packet loss is straightforward also, and is well known in the industry.

However, the third item is tricky. In Chapter 1, in which we discussed the evolution of network management, we pointed to response time management as a recent direction in network management practices. It is appropriate at this juncture to discuss the topic in more detail.

5.5 Response Time Management

Response time management (RTM) is a method for measuring the performance of application transactions across a network. For a distributed client/server business application, RTM should measure packet delay as the packet moves from the client, to the network, to neighboring networks, to the server, and back to the client.

RTM should identify points of increasing transit delay in the overall system before normal business operations are compromised. That is a good example of proactive performance management, in which problems are identified and repaired before they cause noticeable trouble.

5.5.1 The Business Case for Response Time Management

Businesses are beginning to understand the price they pay when their computer-based tools begin to suffer from poor performance.

According to a 1999 study by Infonetics Research in the USA, the service degradations suffered by US businesses cost them a yearly average of $900,000. Interestingly, this amount is calculated by tallying (i) portions of the salaries of employees who report some percentage of non-productivity and (ii) the loss in company revenue which resulted from employees whose work contributes directly to revenue.

Note that the amount does not include losses resulting from a dysfunctional web site. Those losses are not easy to calculate, although we can appreciate how the company would lose money. For example, if a customer is trying to purchase an item from an e-commerce site and the site is unbearably slow, he might go to a different site to purchase the same item (everything else being equal). Further, the customer may get in the habit of always visiting the second site, and thus the loss is compounded.

Another classic example is this: An investor instructs a stockbroker to execute a large trade. But the transaction has to be completed by the close of business, which is just ten minutes away. Now, if poor system performance causes the transaction to be a minute late... The rest of the story is obvious. One gets the idea. The example is a bit dramatic, but it has happened.

Businesses are beginning to ask for SLAs that hold service providers accountable for application performance. In the past, performance degradations were largely indicated by users calling a helpdesk to report that an application is prohibitively sluggish. Of course, subjective indicators are important, but they are not cold, quantifiable measurements that could be included in an SLA. It would be a step in the right direction to have some hard measurements, and that is what RTM practices offer.

5.5.2 Three Approaches to Response Time Management

Below we discuss three common approaches to RTM: (i) using software agents, (ii) using standard probes such as RMON, and (iii) using humans. We should keep in mind that "true" response time depends upon the user, the software application, the computer, the local network, and the core network.

Using Agents

Agents are software entities that reside on network components such as end stations, servers, dedicated computers, or transmission devices. They typically have a small footprint with respect to memory and CPU consumption, allowing them to be deployed without adversely affecting the performance of the machines on which they are running.

One approach to RTM is to build an agent that resides on user stations and measures the response time of the actual transactions initiated from the station. Thus, the approach is a good indicator of the end user experience. The agent can send alarms to troubleshooters when predefined thresholds or policies are violated. In some cases, a troubleshooter can see that a user is having a performance problem before the user realizes it.

These agents can correlate response time data with performance data such as CPU utilization, disk I/O, etc. Some of them allow the helpdesk to connect to a user's machine and perform diagnostics through the agent.

Because these agents track what the user is doing, the helpdesk can sometimes detect user-error problems. For example, a user might build a database query that is not optimal, and thus experience slow response time. A motivated troubleshooter might send the user an email explaining how response time could be improved.

A second approach to RTM is to build an agent that sends artificial transactions to the application server and measures response time of the transaction. This approach allows transactions to be scheduled and provides good control over how the application performance is managed.

There are several advantages of the artificial transaction approach that are not enjoyed by the end station monitoring approach. Consider thresholding, where a response time greater than some pre-defined value raises an alarm. The artificial transaction approach uses a sequence of transactions to measure response time. The sequence is constant, repeatable, and quantifiable.

On the other hand, with the end station monitoring approach, a user clearly can execute two database queries where one requires more parsing on the server, thereby causing a longer response time as expected. This simple observation makes it difficult to apply response time thresholding consistently.

Another clear advantage of artificial transactions is in web server management. Of course, the owner of a web server farm cannot put agents on all customers' computers. However, the owner can indeed deploy desktops and agents in geographical regions where customer activity is expected. Many businesses that depend upon e-commerce will accept that as part of an SLA.

Finally, the artificial transaction is flexible. The transactions can be set up to take place during custom time frames such as business hours, during nightly backups, etc. With the end station monitoring approach, response time is measured only when the user is making a transaction.

A third approach to RTM is to build an agent that sends transactions to another agent. Simply put, the first agent sends a simulated transaction through the network infrastructure to a second agent, whereupon the second agent replies to the first. The first agent measures the response time of the transaction.

The agent simulates transactions based on the application protocol, packet size, etc. This approach also provides a measurement that is repeatable and schedulable. It gives a very good representation of how the network handles the application traffic.

Although the approach is good at gauging network performance, it does not include all the variables that might affect application performance, for example CPU utilization and disk I/O on client and server machines.

Using Probes

Probes (a.k.a. sniffers or traffic monitoring systems) have been used in network management for over ten years. Probes are passive readers of packets that flow through a device. By archiving data such as source, destination, time stamp, protocol, and size, software can be developed that infers useful information about application performance.

There are several types of probes in the industry, including proprietary probes and standards-based probes such as RMON and RMON II. In fact, the RMON II working group is currently working on RTM standards.

One approach to probe-based RTM is to configure a probe so that it pings a TCP or UDP port on another device and checks the response time through the network. Note that this basic measurement does not include CPU congestion on the server or I/O problems, and therefore does not give a very good representation of the application response time from the user's point of view.

However, the approach can be used by an IT manager to interrogate a device on the network to see what ports respond, and thus infer the applications that are available on that device.

A second approach to probe-based RTM is to enhance a probe so that it watches the start and stop packets for various application transactions on the network and infers a response time.

The use of a probe to infer application response time complements other well known uses of probes, e.g. calculating the total bandwidth used by a particular application over some period of time. In fact, a few agent-based products exploit RMON statistics in order to make an overall evaluation of application performance.

Using Humans

For the sake of completeness, we should point out some companies are hiring humans to monitor and measure availability and response time of business applications. Companies have emerged in the USA who provide such services to large businesses.

For all practical purposes, the approach corresponds to the artificial transaction approach in the agent category, except that the agent is a human entity instead of a software entity. One can imagine a human with a stopwatch who executes a transaction every ten minutes and counts the seconds until it comes back.

This phenomenon is interesting because it is almost the reverse of the common complaint that computers are putting humans out of work. In this case humans are challenging RTM systems and might possibly put *them* out of work.

Summary and Discussion

A summary of the various approaches to RTM is as follows:

1. Using Agents
    1.1 Agents that monitor actual transactions at user stations
    1.2 Agents that send and monitor artificial transactions to a server
    1.3 Agents that send and monitor transactions between themselves

2. Using Probes
    2.1 Probes that interrogate device ports
    2.2 Probes that infer response time by reading packets

3. Using Humans
    3.1 Humans who execute and monitor actual transactions

These are the generic approaches to RTM. Several products on the market combine several approaches in a single RTM system. Table 5.2 shows the methods used by several commercial RTM systems.

Table 5.2 Methods Included in Commercial RTM Systems

	1.1	1.2	1.3	2.1	2.2	3.1
Candle *ETEWatch*	X					
Dirig *Proctor*		X				
FirstSense *Enterprise*	X					
Ganymede *Pegasus*	X		X			
Lucent *VitalSuite*	X	X			X	
NetScout *AppScout*					X	
NextPoint *S3*		X		X	X	
Progress *IPQoS*				X		
SiteRock						X

Now, with this knowledge under our belts, let us revisit Vitts' guarantee to customers:

There will be a round trip delay of packets sent from the customer site to the edge of the Internet of 50 milliseconds or less.

Which approach is best suited for Vitts? Should Vitts purchase a commercial RTM system or build one from scratch? If the former is the case, which commercial RTM system will do job?

Those are the questions that Vitts' architects are unraveling as this book is written. It is not an easy question.

Commonsense tells us that since the requirement focuses on packet delay, Vitts should favor a product that takes the probe-based approach. In fact, Vitts is favoring NextPoint's *S3*. But the question is under study and the final decision remains to be seen. We'll leave it as an exercise for the reader to find out how the work is progressing. The results should be available by the time this book is published and circulated.

5.6 Integrated Network Management

Our discussion so far should remind us that there is more to network management than "network management." Managing the network and the servers does not guarantee that a business application will perform at required levels. RTM complements network management by measuring application response time from the user's point of view. That is more-or-less an authentic measure of how well all systems are working together to support the applications.

How might RTM systems and network management systems work together? Prior to that, is there a good business case for going to the trouble to integrate them?

RTM systems are indicators of application performance, but they aren't designed to manage a network. One can imagine a case in which a network management system detects a network problem that will eventually show up in the RTM system as a performance problem. In the reverse, one can imagine an RTM system detecting a trend towards performance degradation that will eventually show up in the network management system as a fault.

The two classes of information are useful for troubleshooters who are diagnosing a misbehaving network. There is money saved by decreasing downtime and increasing customer satisfaction. That is the business case for integrating RTM systems and network management systems.

Consider a design and a plan for integrated RTM and network management. Spectrum will play the role of the network management and NextPoint's S3 will play the role of the RTM. Note that we could pick other players for each role, e.g. Spectrum and Lucent's VitalSuite. The general architecture is applicable in each case.

Figure 5.6 is a proposal for a five-phased integration plan, where each phase in order of increasing difficulty with respect to implementation.

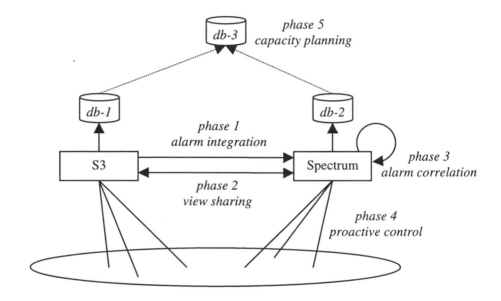

Figure 5.6 A Phased Plan for Integrated RTM and Network Management

- Phase 1: Alarm Integration. S3 passes select alarms to Spectrum, whereupon RTM alarms and NM alarms are grouped according to logical principles.

- Phase 2: View Sharing. S3 will have a mechanism by which to invoke an in-context view provided by Spectrum, and vice-versa.

- Phase 3: Alarm Correlation. Spectrum will correlate its alarms with S3's RTM alarms, suppressing all dependent alarms, highlighting authentic culprit alarms, and providing explanations and recommendations.

- Phase 4: Proactive Control.   Where possible, Spectrum will make changes to the network to repair a fault, in either supervised or unsupervised mode.

- Phase 5: Capacity Planning. Classes of performance data collected by S3 and Spectrum are forwarded to a historical database, whereupon special-purpose algorithms infer trends, potential bottlenecks, and recommendations for network modifications and/or expansion.

Several observations are in order. First, note that the design is rather one-dimensional. That is, Figure 5.6 looks as if we're only considering the integration of a single Spectrum system and a single S3 system.

The second dimension, of course, is that there are about twenty-five SpectroServers covering Vitts' marketing region. Further, there will be at least twice as many S3 agents. The deployment of SpectroServers has been worked out, as we saw in the preceding section. However, the deployment of S3 agents and S3 servers remains to be worked out. That is a crucial task that our plan doesn't address, although Vitts' architects are working on it as this book is written.

Second, note that in Phase 1 the burden of alarm correlation is placed on the human observer of alarms. The burden is not so bad, however, because all alarms are visible in a single console. Further, it is straightforward to group alarms according to pre-defined rules, e.g. by region or customer site. That makes the alarm correlation task less difficult for regional operators.

When operators gain experience in alarm correlation, then that knowledge can be translated to the automated alarm correlation task in Phase 3. This strategy is in line with our approach to start simple and add increasingly challenging functions incrementally.

Third, we should point out that the Phase 2 View Sharing task is quite simple to implement, but offers a useful feature. If an operator observes a Spectrum alarm on workstation *A*, then it would be useful to invoke S3's view of *A* to get further insight into the problem. The same feature is useful in the reverse direction. This is sometimes called "launching in state," and it is different from simply launching one application from another.

Fourth, the Phase 4 Proactive Control feature is likewise simple to implement, but it is dangerous. Generally, one should beware of phases such as "lights-out management," "interventionless management," "automated management," and the like in the marketing literature. The best way to think of automated management is that in principle it can be done, but one should think hard before doing it.

A candidate case for automated management is a "Failed SNMP Agent" scenario. It is quite easy to write a script that is run whenever such an alarm occurs, where the script sends a re-start command to the SNMP agent and reports the results (see Chapter 3 for details). Not much can go wrong there. But if a transmission device is reconfigured automatically, there is the possibility of unforeseen consequences. A middle ground is *supervised* automated control, in which a management system proposes an action to an operator, and the operator chooses whether to execute it.

Finally, the Phase 5 Capacity Planning task is rather ill-defined as we have described it. The problems are (i) understanding the goals of capacity planning, (ii) selecting the proper data that is required for capacity planning algorithms, (iii) organizing and synchronizing data from multiple sources (e.g. as a time series), and (iv) selecting or building appropriate algorithms and methods.

In sum, this is where Vitts' architects are with respect to network management. A good, working management system is in place but there is plenty of work to be done.

Chapter Summary

In this chapter we focused on the management practices of service providers. First we distinguished between a business network and a service network. Next we discussed the political and business landscape in the USA after AT&T deregulation in 1984 and the Telecommunications Act of 1996. Those events affect the management practices of service providers. We saw that most service providers face a special challenge, viz. that the services they offer might depend upon networks over which they have no control. As a case study, we focussed on Vitts Networks in the USA. We described Vitts' *Protected Service Network* and delineated the services Vitts provides to customers. We discussed Vitts' management architecture using Spectrum, paying special attention to multi-domain management, alarm correlation, and service level management. Finally, response time management was explained in a fair amount of detail, after which we proposed a design and plan for integrating RTM systems with network management systems.

Exercises and Discussion Questions

1. Pick a country other than the USA and describe the political and business landscape of telecommunications and data communications.

2. The word "content" has become popular in the industry, e.g. company X provide network infrastructure and company Y provides content. What is content? What is content management? How does it differ from the types of management discussed so far in this book (i.e. network, traffic, systems, application, service level, and response time management)?

3. What is the difference between an Internet Service Provider and a service provider such as Vitts Neworks? What other kinds of LECs exist besides the ones discussed in this chapter?

4. Find a CLEC other than Vitts Networks. Describe the services it offers to customers. Does the CLEC own its network, or does it lease bandwidth from other companies? Try to find out its management practices and any special challenges it faces.

5. The discussion in the section "Event Correlation: An Unexpected Side Effect" is sometimes referred to as Impact Analysis. What is Impact Analysis? Describe and discuss alternative ways of performing Impact Analysis.

6. What is security management? Is network security measurable?

7. Categorize the different types of security violations. Determine which ones can be detected by a management platform.

8. Send an email to Vitts Networks to see how the RTM work is progressing.

9. We argued that a "Failed SNMP agent" scenario is a relatively safe scenario for implementing automated control. Describe two other safe scenarios. Describe two risky scenarios.

10. Get an evaluation copy of one of the RTM systems in Table 5.2. Try to do the Phase 1 integration of the RTM system and Spectrum. Extra credit: Do the Phase 2, 3, and 4 integrations.

Further Studies

For news on the Federal Communications Commission, CLECs, ILECS, and RBOCS in the USA, visit www.fcc.gov. In addition, there are many industry analysts that study the business and technical aspects in the service provider space. A good one is The Yankee Group at www.yankeegroup.com.

The Telecommunication Magazine covers service provider technologies and applications worldwide. It features articles on service provider challenges and solutions, both technical and business-wise. The motivated reader should go to a technical library and skim through past installments of it. The on-line version is at www.telecommagazine.com.

For information on the activities of the Competitive Telecommunications Association (CompTel) in the USA, visit www.comptel.org.

The Webopedia is at www.webopedia.com It is rather fun and worthwhile to spend a little time looking up definitions of one's favorite network-related terms.

For more information on Vitts Networks, visit www.vitts.com.

The discussion of RTM was based on the white paper "An Introduction to Response Time Management" at www.aprisma.com.

The web sites of the commercial RTM systems listed in Table 5.2 are as follows:

Candle *ETEWatch*	www.candle.com
Dirig *Proctor*	www.dirig.com
FirstSense *Enterprise*	www.firstsense.com
Ganymede *Pegasus*	www.ganymede.com
Lucent *VitalSuite*	www.lucent.com
NetScout *AppScout*	www.netscout.com
NextPoint *S3*	www.nextpoint.com
Progress *IPQoS*	www.progress.com
SiteRock	www.siterock.com

The papers and books in the References section are samples of recent work in service level management, application management, and response time management.

References

Bhoj, P., S. Signhal, and S. Chutani. "SLA Management in Federated Environments." In M. Sloman and S. Mazumdar (eds), *Integrated network Management VII*. New York: IEEE Publications, 1999.

Dreo-Rodosek, G., and T. Kaiser. "Determining the Availability of Distributed Applications." In A. Lazar, R. Saracco, and R. Stodler (eds), *Integrated network Management V*. London: Chapman and Hall, 1997.

Dreo-Rodosek, G., T. Kaiser, and R. Rodosek. "A CSP Approach to IT Service Management." In M. Sloman and S. Mazumdar (eds), *Integrated Network Management VII*. New York: IEEE Publications, 1999.

Frolund, S., M. Jain, and J. Pruyne. "SoLOMon: Monitoring End-User Service Levels." In M. Sloman and S. Mazumdar (eds), *Integrated Network Management VII*. New York: IEEE Publications, 1999.

Hegering, H.-G., S. Abeck, and R. Weis. "A Corporate Operation Framework for Network Service Management." *IEEE Communications Magazine,* Jan. 1996.

Hellerstein, J.-L., F. Zhang, and P. Shahabudin. "An Approach to Predictive Detection for Service Management." In M. Sloman and S. Mazumdar (eds), *Integrated Network Management VII.* New York: IEEE Publications, 1999.

Kuepper, A., C. Popien, and B. Meyer. "Service Management Using Up-to-Date quality properties." *Proc. IFIP/IEEE International Conf. On Distributed Platforms: Client/Server and Beyond: DCE, CORBA, ODP and Advanced Distributed Applications.* London: Chapman and Hall, 1996.

Lewis, L. *Service Level Management for Enterprise Networks.* Norwood, MA: Artech House, 1999.

Ramanathan, S., and C. Darst. "Measurement and Management of Internet Services Using HP Firehunter." In M. Sloman and S. Mazumdar (eds), *Integrated Network Management VII.* New York: IEEE Publications, 1999.

Subramanian, M. *Network Management: Principles and Practice.* Addison-Wesley. 2000.

6 Managing Internet2 GigaPoP Networks

As our final case study, we look at the challenges of managing an Internet2 GigaPOP. Our topics are:

- The Internet and the Internet2 Project
- What is an Internet2 GigaPoP?
- The Internet2 GigaPoP in North Carolina (USA)
- GigaPoP Management
- University Research in GigaPoP Management

First we discuss the relation between the Internet and the Internet2 Project. The "Internet2 Project" refers to joint work among universities, industry, and federal agencies towards advancing Internet applications into spaces such as tele-medicine, remote laboratory work, and distance education.

Second, we look at an important goal of the Internet2 Project – the development of Internet2 Gigabit Points of Presence (GigaPoPs). Given advances in fiber optic technology, the Internet backbone has become more or less a limitless, reliable medium for moving large volumes of traffic from one geographical area to another. We may consider GigaPoPs as the on/off ramps between the Internet backbone and commercial businesses, university campuses, and government agencies. Thus, the GigaPoP is an intermediary network that regulates traffic between the Internet backbone and those other networks.

Third, in our case study, we examine the Internet2 GigaPoP in North Carolina (NC) in the USA. There are many GigaPoPs being constructed throughout the world. However, the NC GigaPoP is considered one of several frontrunners in terms of research and development. Advanced applications such as distance education and remote laboratory work impose special requirements for managing the NC GigaPoP.

Fourth, we describe a project underway by scientists in North Carolina and scientists at Aprisma. The project focuses specifically on GigaPoP management. The goals of the project are (i) to understand the special requirements of GigaPoP management and (ii) to implement a working GigaPoP management system. We describe the state of the project at the writing of this book, including successes, challenges, and future directions.

Finally, we look at how industry-sponsored research contributes to Internet2 GigaPoP management. Specifically, we discuss (i) the Aprisma Scholarship Program, (ii) Aprisma-sponsored research at Duke University, the University of North Carolina, and North Carolina State University, and (iii) their contribution to GigaPoP management.

6.1 The Internet and the Internet2 Project

An exercise in Chapter 1 asked the reader to write an essay on the history of the Internet, including discussions of Internet2, the anticipated advantages of Internet2, and the current state of Internet2. A short, concise answer to that question is as follows.

Internet2 is a research and development project whose goal is to advance Internet technology and applications vital to the missions of universities, federal agencies, and commercial businesses. Universities lead the Internet2 Project. The ultimate goal of the project is to enable applications such as tele-medicine, digital libraries, and virtual laboratories that are not possible with the technology underlying today's Internet. The results are intended to benefit all sectors of society.

Consider that the Internet arose from pure research in academia and federal agencies in the early 1980's. The Internet2 Project is the 2000s's version of the 1980's research. Internet2 members join their efforts to develop and test new technologies such as IPv6, multicasting, network management, and quality of service.

The commercial sector is an equal partner in the Internet2 Project and is expected to benefit from applications and technology developed by Internet2 research. Just as email and e-commerce are legacies of 1980's investments in academic and federal research, commercial applications such as tele-medicine and distance education are expected to be legacies of Internet2 research.

It is important to understand that Internet2 is not a physical network that will replace the current Internet. Rather, Internet2 brings together resources from academia, industry, and government in order to develop new technologies and capabilities that build upon the current Internet.

In sum, the mission of the Internet2 project is to expedite the development and deployment of next generation Internet applications, starting with applications that are important to the education and research community, and then migrating proven technologies to the commercial sector. In particular:

- Create a university research environment whose purpose is to deploy and evaluate new networking infrastructure technologies.

- In the beginning, focus on applications and services that promote university education and specialized scientific research.

- Specifically, develop and demonstrate the delivery of remote learning and distance education.

- Further, develop and demonstrate applications that allow remote experimentation and collaboration among researchers in scientific domains such as biology, chemistry, medicine, astronomy, et al.

- Support the migration of proven technologies by providing direction and development tools to federal agencies and commercial businesses.

- Assist in the definition of networking standards and common practices among universities, federal agencies, commercial businesses, and the Internet community in general.

It is easy to see that Internet2 research is inter-disciplinary. On the one hand, the research involves experimentation and evaluation of networking technology. However, the evaluation of the technology depends upon the requirements of innovative applications in other scientific disciplines. Therefore, researchers in networking technology and researchers in the sciences collaborate to prepare the way for next generation Internet applications. We will see some specific examples later in the chapter.

6.2 What is an Internet2 GigaPoP?

The first Internet2 meeting was held in June 1996. At that time, researchers began to define the issues surrounding the development of a new Internet to serve the research and education community. In July 1996, the initial architecture for the emerging Internet2 project was created. At the core of the Internet2 design was a new technology referred to as a GigaPoP. A GigaPoP is the point of interconnection and service delivery between institutional members of the Internet2 project and one or more Internet service providers.

The rationale for GigaPoP development is as follows: Important as a very high-performance backbone is to the next generation of Internet applications, it is no less important that the points at which people connect to the backbone, the so-called points of presence (PoPs), provide an equivalent level of performance. Recall the old adage that a chain is only as strong as its weakest link. Likewise, the provision of an Internet application, from the desktop, across the Internet, and back again, is only as strong as its weakest link.

The requirement, then, is to build a network that can serve as a PoP handling the multi-gigabit traffic to be delivered by the next-generation Internet. Thence comes its name: a GigaPoP. The GigaPoP is a central distribution point where large amounts of digital traffic are moved between various end points and the main line. Since there will be diverse kinds of applications that are downstream from the GigaPoP, each with special bandwidth and priority requirements, it is important that the GigaPoP be able to regulate and prioritize traffic accordingly.

The Internet2 design calls for GigaPoPs that support several crucial features. Each GigaPoP must have high capacity (at least 622 Mb/s) and high reliability and availability. It must use the Internet Protocol (IP) as a bearer service, and must be able to support emerging protocols and applications. It must be capable of serving simultaneously as a workaday environment and as a research test bed. It must allow for traffic measurement and data gathering. Lastly, it must permit migration to differentiated services and application-aware networking.

Figure 6.1 shows the GigaPoPs under development in the USA. We have put a pointer to the North Carolina GigaPoP since that will be our case study in the next section. Note that the figure doesn't include Internet2 backbone structures such as NGI, vBNS, and the commodity Internet.

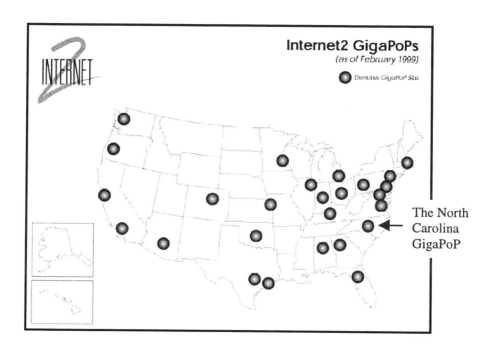

Figure 6.1 Internet2 GigaPoPs in the USA (February 1999)

6.3 The North Carolina GigaPoP

The academic, research, and business community in the North Carolina region known as Research Triangle Park (the area lying amid the cities of Raleigh, Durham, and Chapel Hill) has been working to create a high-performance GigaPoP network as part of the North Carolina Network Initiative (NCNI).

NCNI built an intermediate GigaPoP network between the Internet2 backbone and the research community, with the goal of resolving bottlenecks in the commodity Internet typically caused by high traffic demands of distributed applications. The purposes of the GigaPOP are (i) to keep local traffic local (ii) to provide optimized access to research and education applications that depend upon the Internet, and importantly (iii) to insure an acceptable quality of service for all local and Internet-driven applications.

A GigaPoP is much like any other network. It consists of a collection of nodes and links. Figure 6.2 illustrates the topology of the NC GigaPoP.

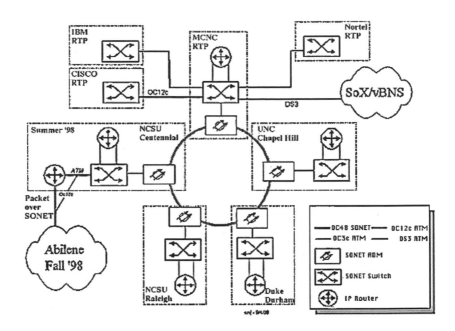

Figure 6.2 The North Carolina GigaPoP

A node is a geographic location where GigaPoP devices reside. There are five primary nodes at North Carolina State University (NCSU) Centennial campus, NCSU Raleigh campus, Duke University, University of North Carolina at Chapel Hill, and MCNC. These primary nodes perform core routing and operational functions for the GigaPOP. They also serve as connection points (on-ramps) to national networks, including the vBNS and the Abilene network. Equipment at primary node sites includes optical-fiber terminating equipment, virtual-circuit switches, data routers, and network monitoring devices.

Secondary nodes reside at NCNI industry sites located in the RTP area, including Cisco Systems, IBM, and Nortel Networks. These secondary nodes are connected to the primary nodes via tributary optical-fiber links.

Importantly, note that the NC GigaPoP is an intermediary network. The campus networks at NC State, Duke, and UNC at Chapel Hill are outside the scope of the GigaPoP, but connected to it. The specific management requirements of a campus network deserve separate treatment; but in this section we wish to focus on the special management requirements of the GigaPoP.

GigaPoP management experiments have been conducted jointly by Aprisma Management Technologies and NCNI. The general goal of the project is to understand requirements and to work out bugs in GigaPoP management in the early stages of Internet2 research and development. We describe the state of the project at the time of this writing, including successes, challenges, and plans for the remainder of the project.

6.4 GigaPoP Management

We will describe GigaPoP management a bit differently than the way we described the management of the Camp LeJeune network and the Vitts' network in the preceding case studies.

The management of the NC GigaPoP is considered as a research exercise. Architects and scientists at Aprisma, NCNI, and North Carolina universities have initiated a joint research project whose goal is to understand the special requirements and challenges of GigaPoP management and to work out bugs in an R&D setting in preparation for commercial and industrial deployment.

In good scientific fashion, the experiments are incremental, where the results of one set of experiments provide input for the definition of the next set of experiments. As of this writing, the researchers are in the midst of the third set of experiments. Below, we describe the results achieved thus far.

6.4.1 Phase 1. Goals for the First Set of Experiments

1. Understand the topology of the NC GigaPOP, including the types of devices and networking technology that have to be managed.

2. Understand (i) the parts of the topology we wish to manage and (ii) the Spectrum management modules required.

3. Based on #2, install, configure, and commence monitoring and control of the GigaPoP with Spectrum.

4. Perform the following experiments: simple up/down monitoring, port threshold monitoring, fault scenarios (either real or simulated), event correlation scenarios, alarm notification via email, trouble ticket

generation from the management system, reports on downtime, and collection of management data for off-line processing.

5. Write a synopsis of Phase 1 results, including an evaluation of the results and recommendations for the next set of experiments.

Synopsis of Phase 1 Results

Figure 6.2 showed the overall topology of the NC GigaPoP. The North Carolina Research and Education Network (NCREN) distance learning application was selected for the experiments. Thus, the experiments focus on the GigaPoP devices that support distance learning in North Carolina.

Spectrum was installed and the discovery of the GigaPoP proceeded without mishap. Figure 6.3 shows the initial Spectrum screenshot of the topology after running Spectrum's auto-discovery application.

Spectrum did not automatically discover CAMVision video applications running on instructors' and students' NT workstations (CAMVision is an MPEG-2 video encoder/decoder). CAMVision management is required in order to achieve (i) end-to-end management of the distance learning service and (ii) stronger event correlation and fault isolation over the complete set of elements that supports the distance learning service. CAMVision management, then, is recommended as a task in Phase 2 experiments.

The experiments involving (i) alarm notification via email and (ii) automatic trouble ticket generation were declared as relatively straightforward. Thus, in the interest of time, they were not carried out. Otherwise, the remaining experiments were performed satisfactorily.

Three useful ideas arose as a result of the initial experiments and brainstorming:

(1) Perform a correlation between unexplained anomalies in the distance learning service and the state of the GigaPoP as a whole, and investigate whether such knowledge could be used to achieve (2) and (3) below.

(2) Be able to answer the question: Can the network accommodate such-and-such new video session.

(3) The ultimate goal is proactive management: Enhance Spectrum so that it can predict when an anomaly is about to happen and possibly prevent it.

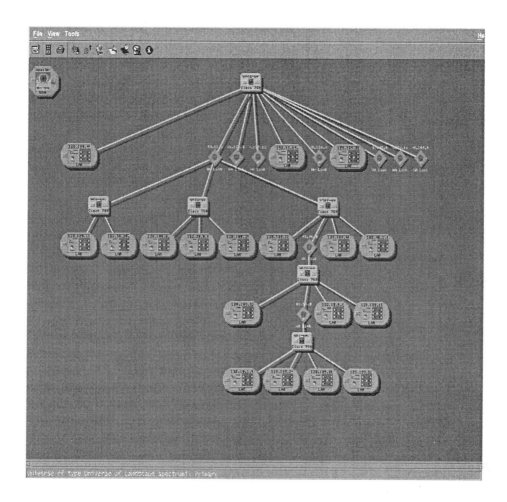

Figure 6.3 Spectrum Screenshot of NCREN Infrastructure (Tree View)

Note: Aprisma awarded a fellowship to North Carolina State University, the subject of which addresses #1. (We describe that work in the next section.) It is possible that the achievement of #1 can be used to achieve #2 and #3. However, those are hard challenges. Although it is premature to tackle them in Phase 2, we wish to keep them in mind as we proceed, saving them for later experiments.

The recommendations for Phase 2 are to evaluate the usability and intuitiveness of the initial management system, perform further routine management tasks, and investigate CAMVision management.

6.4.2 Phase 2. Goals for the Second Set of Experiments

1. Evaluate and criticize the initial screenshot in Figure 6.3, focusing on intuitiveness, monitoring and control facilities, and modifiability. For example, from the perspective of a user or network operator, determine in what ways the picture in Figure 6.3 could be re-organized to represent the NCREN video infrastructure more intuitively. What kinds of actions or views would a user likely want to navigate to from this view?

2. Design/develop monthly reports showing uptime/downtime of elements in the NCREN.

3. Design/develop monthly reports showing packet rate, load, and packets dropped with respect to elements in the NCREN.

4. Set thresholds on router ports (packet rate, load, and packets dropped), raise alarms when thresholds are crossed. Develop formula to handle the problems of thrashing and oscillation.

5. Understand the requirements for CAMVision application management and devise a plan by which to incorporate CAMVision management in the existing Spectrum management framework.

6. Write a synopsis of Phase 2 results, including an evaluation of the results and recommendations for the next set of experiments.

Synopsis of Phase 2 Results

Discovery. Discovering network elements was simple and largely intuitive. For this study, mapping of the network was limited to those Universities that are participating in the distance learning trials.

The core router elements were added to Spectrum using the "model by IP" method. Spectrum retrieved MIB information from the routers, collected interface identifications and IP addresses, and discovered the logical and physical connections between the routers. However, Spectrum did not recognize and categorize the ATM links. Additional manual methods were performed to complete the map.

Intuitiveness. While Spectrum will lay out all the elements in either a spiral or tree-like fashion, it doesn't have the data necessary to make the layout intuitive. However, Spectrum's graphical layout editor is straightforward and allows some fine grain controls for placing elements.

In comparing the spiral vs. tree views, the spiral version seems more intuitive. The initial view was manipulated to align with the star nature of the network, moving the core routers nearer together on the map. See Figure 6.4.

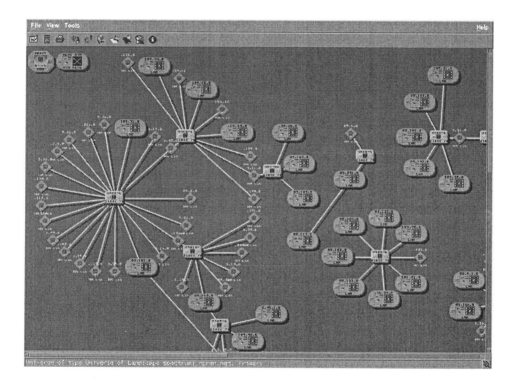

Figure 6.4 Spectrum Screenshot of NCREN Infrastructure (Spiral View)

Now, since the naming of network elements is commonly related to a combination of function and geographic location, it would make sense to provide a view that is geographically accurate. For future versions, Aprisma should consider including an online mapping service, giving users the ability to arrange the network view by associating map coordinates with information in the location field, which is part of the standard enterprise MIB.

Re-sizing the view to accommodate all the GigaPoP elements results in lost detail. Spectrum helps manage this by providing a popup information box when the cursor is pointed to a specific network element.

Another useful feature to consider in future versions of Spectrum is to allow the view to have different line styles for different link types and link speeds. There might also be a different color for those links that are designated as backups, changing state when the backup link is in use.

General Interface. Getting current information about specific routers is intuitive, with the specific "click-zones" on the network elements providing popup clues about what information is available. The performance, device interface, and topology views are well laid out. The performance view is useful for day-to-day management purposes, while the other views are helpful when configuring or troubleshooting.

Alarms/Events. The Spectrum Alarm Manager provides useful functions, including automated popup when an alarm occurs and the ability to capture notes, probable causes, and other related data when acknowledging an alarm.

Reports. Spectrum reports are intuitive, easy to obtain, and useful. Figure 6.5 shows a sample of a Device Up/Down Executive Summary Report.

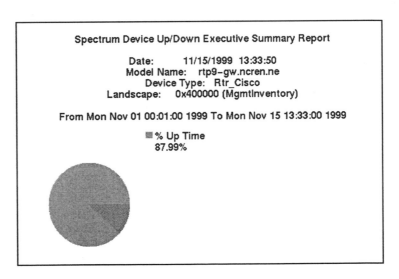

Figure 6.5 Device Up/Down Executive Summary Report

Setting Thresholds. Setting thresholds and threshold formula are largely straightforward. The hardest part of this process is deciding what level to set the thresholds and devising advance threshold formula in the first place.

CAMVision Management. We wish to include CAMVision-2 Codec (CV2) management in the overall NCREN management system. CV2s are manufactured by the Litton Corporation. Thus, Litton architects will begin to participate in this aspect of the experiments.

The approach is to develop a model in Spectrum that represents CV2s and communicates with them via SNMP, in the same way that we have management modules for other physical and logical NCREN objects. Litton has provided the CV2 SNMP MIB, which piggybacks on the standard NT MIB. CV2, then, is considered an application that runs on an NT box.

In Spectrum there is a standard NT management module that provides the means to import additional NT application MIBs. One can do that with the Spectrum Level-1 Toolkit, which means essentially that it can be done on site with no additional programming. When we have the CV2/NT module in place, we can proceed to model each CV2 for purposes of monitoring and control.

Importantly, we wish to understand the extent to which the information we get from CV2/NT is useful for management purposes. For example, are there CV2 MIB variables whose values indicate poor video quality? If so, then that would provide the means for a NOC engineer to receive an alarm or page whenever poor video quality occurs or is about to occur. Further, historical data could be analyzed to infer conditions that typically lead to poor video performance, along with recommendations for correction or possibly automated correction.

It turns out, however, that the only feedback regarding video quality that is available at the application layer is the CV2 restart mechanism. That is, when the data buffers in a CV2 application are well beyond the full mark, the method of recovery is to flush the buffer and restart the sending stream. However, there is not such a trap in the current CV2 MIB. The insertion of a restart trap into the CV2 MIB would be useful for management purposes.

Our hypothesis is that the restart variable is the index into poor video quality; it correlates with poor quality of service from the user's point of view. If further experiments corroborate the hypothesis, then we will have made a large step towards end-to-end management of the distance learning service, and we will have an approach to the ultimate goal of proactive management discussed at the beginning of the project. Therefore, a recommendation for the next set of experiments is to confer with Litton architects about this solution.

Web-based Management. While the current facilities for managing the GigaPoP with Spectrum are useful, there is a need to be able to manage the GigaPoP via a web browser. A requirement is to set up specialized management views per customer, where in this case the customers are the NOC operators at Duke, North Carolina State University, and the University of North Carolina.

6.4.3 Phase 3. Goals for the Third Set of Experiments

1. Create a model of the CAMVision application as instructed in the Phase 2 synopsis. Use the Level-1 toolkit to model NT workstations, and then import the CV2 MIB into the NT model. Report any snags or anomalies.

2. Develop standard reports and alarming facilities for NT/CV2 management.

3. Confer with Litton architects to explore the question of inserting a restart trap into the CV2 MIB.

4. Procure and install the Spectrum Web Console developed by Metrix Systems in France. Partition the GigaPOP with respect to some logical criteria.   Report any snags or anomalies. Evaluate and criticize the effectiveness and intuitiveness of the Web Console.

5. Explore alternative methods for doing capacity planning with respect to the distance learning application. Specifically, in what ways can we answer the question "Can the network accommodate X_1, X_2, ... X_n new video sessions during time intervals T_1, T_2, ... T_n respectively?" Characterize the problem, evaluate alternatives, and formulate an implementation plan to be carried out in Phase 4.

6. Write a synopsis of Phase 3 results, including an evaluation of the results and recommendations for the next set of experiments.

6.4.4 Summary of the GigaPoP Management Project

Phase 3 is currently in progress. The Web Console is operational, but its effectiveness and intuitiveness remain to be reported. Further, the idea of inserting a restart trap into the CV2 MIB remains under exploration.

We can summarize the results of the project so far as follows:

- The standard FCAPS style of managing a GigaPoP with Spectrum is relatively straightforward (see Section 1.5.1 for a discussion of FCAPS). That shouldn't be surprising, however, since the GigaPoP is basically a network like any other.

- Some improvements were suggested regarding the layout of topology in the Spectrum views. Specifically, we wish to provide a web interface into Spectrum via the Spectrum Web Console. A useful feature of the Web Console is that campus administrators will be able to view just the portion of the GigaPoP that affects their applications.

- The end-to-end management of NC's distance learning application requires some additional customization. Since Litton's CAMVision product runs on an NT workstation as an NT application, it is required that we use the Spectrum NT Management Module to import the additional application MIB. With that in place, we will have modeled all the elements upon which the distance education application depends.

- An important insight into quality of service from the user's point of view is to depend upon a simple application MIB variable -- the buffer restart variable. However, this should be considered a hypothesis at this stage of research. Aprisma, NCNI, and Litton architects agree that the hypothesis is promising, and thus Litton engineers are investigating the feasibility of inserting the restart trap into the CAMVision MIB.

- If the restart variable proves to be a good index into quality of service from the user's point of view, then Spectrum will raise an alarm if say, the variable is reset twice in less than a minute. But note that this is classic reactive management, i.e. dealing with the problem after it occurs. While that is useful, clearly a higher goal is to be able to predict poor video performance and correct it before it occurs.

Interestingly, the progression of work on the project takes us back to the ideas in the initial brainstorming session when the project was started. Recall the initial three interesting, but rather vague goals:

(1) Perform a correlation between unexplained anomalies in the distance learning service and the state of the GigaPoP as a whole, and investigate whether such knowledge could be used to achieve (2) and (3) below.

(2) Be able to answer the question: Can the network accommodate such-and-such new video session.

(3) The ultimate goal is proactive management: Enhance Spectrum so that it can predict when an anomaly is about to happen and possibly prevent it.

The hypothesis is that the ultimate "unexplained anomaly" is reflected in the restart trap. Thus, it is objectively measurable, and lines up with the user's subjective experience.

If the hypothesis is corroborated by empirical means, then we are half way towards working out solutions to (1) – (3). In the next section, we describe some University research that is contributing to the project in that regard.

6.5 University Research in GigaPoP Management

A good approach for commercial vendors who wish to resolve outstanding problems in network management is (i) to state the problems as fully as possible, (ii) hand over the problems to professors and students at universities, and (iii) to support the work on the problems monetarily in the form of scholarships or fellowships.

Everybody wins in that kind of situation: Professors receive grant money and are recognized by their universities, their students gain experience (and write their theses, finish their degrees, and get good jobs), the state-of-the-science in network management is advanced, and the companies that award the fellowships benefit from the work via technology transfer.

Of course, that is not a new idea. Many companies take advantage of it. Aprisma has taken advantage of it by offering fellowships to professors in North Carolina who are interested in advancing the state-of-the–science regarding GigaPoP development and management.

Below we discuss how universities in North Carolina are contributing to the study of GigaPoP management. First, we disclose the announcement of the Aprisma Fellowship Program and then we describe four research programs that show promise for advancing the state-of-the-science in GigaPoP management.

6.5.1 Aprisma Fellowship Announcement

The Aprisma Fellowship Program is looking for projects that further the research and development of next-generation network management techniques, with special focus and co-operation with the Aprisma/NCNI GigaPoP management project. Some items of particular interest are as follows, but proposals are encouraged in all application areas:

- Gather requirements for Internet2 GigaPOP management. Perform an analysis of the requirements. Produce an analysis model that doesn't make reference to available commercial tools. Use the analysis model to evaluate commercial management tools and make recommendations for further research. This fellowship is appropriate for a student who is interested in software engineering methodologies and also has knowledge of network management and the Internet.

- Design and build a suite of management modules within the Spectrum framework that are capable of managing the major devices that support the Internet2 GigaPOP. Establish event correlation requirements and scenarios. Design and develop algorithms for event correlation. Implement the algorithms using Spectrum as a vehicle. This fellowship is intended for a student who is interested in network management, and also is versed in object-oriented design, C++ and Java programming, and web-based application development.

- Researchers in North Carolina have collected a large amount of performance data from the Internet2 GigaPOP test bed. Investigate the use of machine learning methods (e.g. data mining algorithms and neural networks) to analyze the data. Establish goals of data analysis, e.g. symptoms of degradation in application performance metrics or network intrusions. Evaluate existing machine learning algorithms (or develop new algorithms) that infer useful information or knowledge from the data. This fellowship is intended for a student working in the area of Artificial Intelligence (e.g. machine learning and automated knowledge acquisition).

Professors working on research areas of interest to the GigaPoP management program are encouraged to submit a two-page proposal requesting graduate student support. The two-page proposal should include a description of the research project, how the work supports the Aprisma/NCNI GigaPoP management project, and a description of the specific work to be done -- including a list of outcomes or deliverables.

6.5.2 A Synopsis of University Research

Four research programs that show promise for advancing the state-of-the-science in GigaPoP management are described below. There are a number of other university projects that contribute to overall GigaPoP development. The four below, however, are concerned with issues having to do with the management of GigaPoPs.

A Virtual Classroom Model for Distance Education
(North Carolina State University)

This project concerns the development of distance education services in North Carolina and methods to manage the networks and applications that support the service.

NCSU developed a "virtual classroom" model for distance education that began in 1996. The fundamental idea is to develop a service which delivers class sessions and office consultations from the classroom and instructor's office to the student's desktop, thus providing an economical means of delivering interactive distance education to a sparsely distributed student population.

Traditional videoconferencing provides high quality video, but typically involves expensive facilities that require scheduling well in advance. This does not lend itself well to educational workflows, which often require short scheduling, e.g. "I will hold a special help session tonight for those of you who are having difficulty applying Kirchoff's laws," or spontaneous conferences among class participants.

The Virtual Classroom is suitable for lecture delivery and other forms of student/teacher interaction such as office hour consultations, help sessions, one-on-one conferences, and group meetings. It works well because it can be accessed where the people are located (e.g. from homes, faculty offices and student labs) and because it integrates voice, video, and data so that the participants can see and manipulate the concepts being discussed.

The project at NCSU will further develop the distance education service for the North Carolina community, with emphasis on QoS management. It is relevant to the Aprisma/NCNI GigaPoP management program because of the bandwidth demands of real-time audio and video combined with the routing and distribution complexities of the IP multicast protocols. It is relevant to Aprisma Management Technologies in particular because it addresses the need for tools such as Spectrum to monitor and control distance education applications and the networks that support them.

A Quality-of-Service Network for the NanoManipulator
(University of North Carolina at Chapel Hill)

This project is directed towards the provisioning of quality-of-service IP networks for distributed virtual collaborations. UNC's computer scientists are working with physical and biological scientists in order to create a virtual microscopy laboratory for material and biological science research.

UNC's NanoManipulator is a virtual reality interface to a scanned probe microscope constructed by UNC computer scientists. It allows chemists, biologists, and physicists to "see" the surface of a material sample at atomic (nanometer) scale and "feel" the properties of the surface through the use of force-feedback.

Part of the research is to explore the design of a next generation system that will allow remote operation of the NanoManipulator, thereby creating a virtual microscopy laboratory that can be used collaboratively by teams of scientists.

The virtual microscopy laboratory requires (i) audio and video streams for human-to-human interaction, (ii) shared application windows for viewing and interacting with electronic notebooks and data plotting tools, and (iii) remote operation of the NanoManipulator. Thus, the system requires the flexibility to manage multiple data flows, each having different bandwidth, loss, and latency requirements.

In addition, a typical scientific experiment using the system might last for 8-16 hours, creating a relatively constant high demand on the network, and that could disrupt a network that also supports other kinds of applications with QoS constraints.

The research complements the Aprisma/NCNI GigaPoP management program by providing a better understanding of the provisioning of QoS-based networks that will support the complexities of next generation applications. It is relevant to Aprisma in particular because it uncovers the management requirements for QoS-based networks. Aprisma architects, therefore, will be in a better position to build future versions of Spectrum to manage advanced scientific applications.

Proactive Software and Hardware Fault Management in Computer Networks (Duke University)

The project at Duke University focuses on application management, with particular emphasis on predicting software failures and degradations.

Consider that outages in computer networks consist of both hardware and software failures. The management of hardware failures is handled well by the Spectrum management system. However, software failures and corresponding reliability/availability analyses are new areas of study that could contribute to the evolution of Spectrum. Further, the study of software failures is important because computer malfunctions (and sometimes network malfunctions) are due to software faults.

The research is centered around the phenomenon of "software aging," one in which the state of the software degrades with time. Software aging eventually leads to transient failures in software systems. The primary causes of degradation are the exhaustion of operating system resources, data corruption, and numerical error accumulation. These may lead to performance degradation of the software, or ultimately to a crash/hang failure, or both.

The traditional approach to software aging is reactive management on the part of human operators. Software and hardware are occasionally stopped or shut down, the internal state is cleaned, and then the system re-started in a bug-free state.

The goal of the research is to develop mechanisms for monitoring, analyzing, and repairing problems that have to do with software aging. Alarming techniques will notify operators of impending software failures and degradations. Further, it is possible that automated repair mechanisms could be included in the management system. For example, during off-peak hours, Spectrum could remove accumulated error conditions and free up operating system resources before services are disrupted.

Mining Predictive Models for Performance Management
(North Carolina State University)

Detecting and resolving performance problems in distributed systems have become increasingly challenging with the growth in network-based applications and services.

Consider that problem detection is often done by threshold testing, e.g.: Does the response time of an HTTP GET request exceed 1 minute on server X? Once a problem is detected, however, there is often very little time to diagnose the problem and take corrective actions. The root cause of the problem might well propagate and affect other services provided by the network.

Therefore, it would be a useful feature of a management system to be able to predict potential service problems before they happen, thereby enabling system administrators to take the proper corrective actions in advance of widespread service disruption.

The researchers at NCSU aim to find ways to model the behavior of distributed systems and to use the model to anticipate possible future behaviors. The research is similar in concept to the software aging project at Duke. However, it covers the bigger picture of distributed systems in general, including software applications, computer systems, and networks.

The first task is to collect historical performance data, including data that reflects problematic and non-problematic states of the distributed system. The second task is to apply data mining and machine learning algorithms to historical data in order to infer a behavior model. The final task is to combine the behavior model with a reading of system parameters at some time t, thereby predicting possible behaviors beyond t.

Clearly, the goal of the project is quite ambitious. Each task is difficult. However, an apparatus that can make reasonable predictions about impending service problems would be useful for operators charged with managing GigaPoP networks. Further, the incorporation of such an apparatus into the Spectrum management system would be useful for Spectrum customers in general.

6.5.3 Discussion

The university research in North Carolina clearly supports the Aprisma/NCNI GigaPoP management program. It is a good example of collaboration between academia and business for the sake of advancing the state-of-the-science in network management.

Generally, the research falls into two categories:

- Development and study of advanced Internet2 applications, with any eye towards (i) testing existing networking and network management technologies and (ii) understanding new requirements for networking and network management methods.

- Algorithms and techniques for predictive (as opposed to reactive) maintenance and control of Internet2 applications and services.

The distance education and the distributed nanoManipulator research programs fall into the first category. The software aging and the predictive modeling programs fall into the second category.

The first category of research is driven by Internet2 application development, while the second category is driven by techniques in monitoring, analysis, and control of Internet2 applications.

Clearly, these approaches are complementary. For example, discussion is underway to explore the application of predictive modeling methods to years of data collected in the distance learning project. At a high level of description, the task is to look at historical records of distance education sessions, identify normal and problematic sessions, and use machine algorithms to learn the conditions under which problematic sessions recur. The resulting model, then, could be used in Spectrum to proactively manage the distance learning service, including the problem of scheduling impromptu sessions.

But that is a high level of description. The researchers know that there likely will be snags when they get down to details, e.g. what counts as a problematic session? Is the historical data set rich enough to issue useful, non-trivial models?

In sum, we see that GigaPoP management from a network management perspective is fairly traditional. However, from the perspective of applications management, there are several challenges. The university research described in this section is addressing those challenges.

Chapter Summary

In this chapter we studied the issues surrounding Internet2 GigaPoP management. We first described the goals of the Internet2 project, and then described an important component of Internet2 --- the GigaPoP. As a case study, we looked at the North Carolina GigaPoP. We described the topology of the NC GigaPoP, and then described a joint research project between Aprisma and North Carolina scientists that focuses on GigaPoP management. We saw that Internet2 GigaPoP management is quite similar to well-known network management practices, with the exception of managing the new applications and services that depend upon the GigaPoP. In that regard, we described four research programs at universities in North Carolina that contribute to application management, where such applications are complex, resource-intensive, and compete for GigaPoP resources.

Exercises and Discussion Questions

1. What is UCAID?

2. What is the relationship between Internet2 and the Next Generation Internet (NGI)? Internet2 and the Abilene project? Internet2 and vBNS?

3. Describe the terms OC3, OC8, OC12, and OC48. What is OC3Mon? Propose a design that integrates OC3Mon and Spectrum. What benefits would such an integration offer?

4. A research question: Find out the topology of the California Research and Education Network 2 (CalREN-2). How does the topology differ from the NCREN?

5. Another research question: What is the "fish problem" regarding GigaPoP management? What progress has been made towards solving the fish problem?

6. Find an NT workstation on which there is an application that has a MIB. Model the NT workstation in Spectrum and import the MIB.

7. Find a UNIX workstation on which there is an application that has a MIB. Model the workstation in Spectrum and import the MIB.

8. For either #8 or #9, use SpectroWatch to set a threshold on some application MIB variable. Have the watch send you an email when the threshold is overstepped.

9. What are the general goals and methods of data mining? How can data mining methods be used in network management?

10. Visit the web sites of companies other than Aprisma who are involved in networking and network management. Find out which companies sponsor fellowship or scholarship programs. Importantly, find out the kinds of research they wish to sponsor. If appropriate, consider submitting a research proposal.

Further Studies

The best source of information about the next generation Internet activities (including the NC GigaPoP and Internet2 programs) is the World Wide Web. The Internet2 Project site at www.internet2.edu provides information about the various I2 efforts and their current status. The site also maintains historical records, such as an early overview of the Internet2 architecture.

An interesting history of the Internet (starting in 1858!) on the web is Gregory Gromov's paper "The Roads and Crossroads of Internet History" at www.internetvalley.com.

The section in this chapter on the North Carolina GigaPoP was adapted from material at www.ncni.org. A very good paper that describes NCNI's GigaPoP is Collins, Dunn, Emer, and Johnson's paper "Data Express: Gigabit Junction with the Next Generation Internet."

More information on current projects being conducted on the NC GigaPoP can be found at www.ais.unc.edu/I2. Information about the nanoManipulator project, a cornerstone application for NCNI's work on providing differentiated services, can be found at www.cs.unc.edu/Research/nano. Performance analyses of the GigaPOP can be found at www.cnl.ncsu.edu/NC-GNI_flows.

The National Laboratory for Advanced Network Research provides a good deal of information about network monitoring, and OC3mon in particular, at www.moat.nlanr.net.

The history and current projects of the North Carolina Research and Education Network and the North Carolina Network Initiative are to be found at www.ncren.net and www.ncni.org respectively.

At the Aprisma website www.aprisma.com, one can view further installments of the Aprisma/NCNI running report on GigaPoP management, progress and results of the North Carolina university projects, and future announcements of the Aprisma Fellowship program.

References

Collins, J., J. Dunn, P. Emer, and M. Johnson's. "Data Express: Gigabit Junction with the Next Generation Internet." *IEEE Spectrum*. Volume 36, Number 2, February 1999.

Part III
Future Directions of Network Management

Part I of the book consisted of three introductory chapters on network management. Part II consisted of three case studies, wherein we examined the management of three rather diverse kinds of networks.

We wish to round out the book by taking a look at research topics in network management and offering suggestions for further direction. The two chapters in Part III are:

- Combining Research and Practice in Network Management
- Towards a Comprehensive Network Management System

In Chapter 7 we take a look at how network management is practiced in the field in a routine, day-to-day context. That is a bit different from our discussions in the case studies. We will use a method called Contextual Inquiry to uncover the routine operations and glitches at a large networking company in the USA. In addition, we take a look at some research topics in network management and discuss the difficulties of transferring research accomplishments into mainstream network management practices.

Our goal in Chapter 8 is get our arms around a generic architecture that will guide us as we approach increasingly hard management challenges of 2000's type networks. We make a distinction between a "conceptual architecture" for a comprehensive network management system and a "physical embodiment" of the architecture. We argue that a conceptual comprehensive management system is quite possible; however, a physical embodiment of the system is difficult. We discuss some challenges in developing such a physical system and describe directions for further work in network management.

7 Combining Research and Practice in Network Management

In this chapter we discuss the problem of combining research and practice in network management. Our topics are:

- What Do Network Operators Do?
- What Do Network Researchers Do?
- Combining Research and Practice in Network Management

In the first section of the chapter we look at a method for understanding what network operators actually do in the field. As an example, we describe the procedures of an operations staff at a large company in the USA. We will be concerned with (i) uncovering the myriad tasks involved in the operation and (ii) problems that the staff faces.

Next, we take a look at what researchers in network management do. We provide a short review of the sorts of things that researchers in industry labs and universities are working on. Our goal is to understand how researchers identify topics for applied research that is relevant to operators in the field.

Finally, we discuss the general problem of combining research and practice in network management. We look at the sorts of problems that hinder the incorporation of new, advanced ideas into production management systems and sketch a few possible solutions.

7.1 What Do Network Operators Do?

At the end of the case study in Chapter 4, we promised to revisit the question "What do network operators do?" That is an important question when designing network management systems.

Designers, researchers, and developers of network management systems often create rather private interpretations of how operators do their jobs and how they use management tools. Accordingly, they construct systems with the goal of building better and more useful management systems based on their interpretations.

However, what sometimes happens is that the initial interpretations become somewhat expanded and modified during the design and development process. And more often than not, the final product is not quite on the mark of what the network operator would like to see. Recall from Chapter 3 that this phenomenon applies to software engineering in general.

Thus, it is advisable to understand in a fair amount of detail what network operators do in the field. That is not an easy task. Most network operators have neither time nor motivation to sit down and articulate their reasoning mechanisms, decision processes, and behaviors as they do their jobs. That is understandable.

As an analogy, an accomplished musician wishes to play good music, but is not inclined to tell one what is going on in her head when composing or performing music. Similarly, an accomplished network operator wishes to get through the day without mishap, but is not inclined to re-live the day when it is over.

Now, there are various formal techniques and methodologies for finding out what operators do in some particular domain X, where X might be composing music, driving automobiles, flying planes, washing clothes, or operating networks. Traditional techniques include formal interviews and questionnaires.

The traditional techniques, however, have limitations. For one, they rely too heavily on users' memories. The act of designing a product requires an understanding of the details of the work. Traditional interviews (normally conducted out of the context of the work itself) and questionnaires cannot get at the level of detail needed to design a product. In addition, people usually summarize in reporting their activities, providing more of an overview instead of a richly detailed account of their work. Such summaries tend to be inaccurate and incomplete and are therefore insufficient for design.

A recent method that has demonstrated some improvement over the traditional methods is called Contextual Inquiry. Contextual Inquiry is an ethnographic method that is part of a more encompassing design methodology called Contextual Design. The primary goal of the methodology is to improve operations in some domain, for example by designing better tools or modifying a work flow process.

Below we describe the basic technique of Contextual Inquiry. Next we discuss an application of the technique at company X and show the structure of the company's network management operations.

7.1.1 What is Contextual Inquiry?

Contextual Inquiry (CI) is a method for bringing out the structure of operations in some particular domain. The key concept of CI is just what the name implies: inquiring within context. Note that with the traditional methods of formal interviews and questionnaires, the actual living context in which work is carried out is missing. With the CI method, however, the living context is an essential part of the methodology.

The basic principle is that the inquisitor observes the user at work, literally looking over the shoulder of the user, watching what he does, and engaging in conversation. The inquisitor is allowed to ask simple questions such as "Why did you do that?" or "Is that what you expected to happen?" or "What would you like to have happened?" In general, the goal of a CI study is to understand the *intents* of users as they work.

A typical CI study is as follows. A CI team spends two days at a business site. The CI team is grouped into several pairs, where one person plays the role of inquisitor and the second person plays the role of note-taker. Each pair spends roughly three hours per operator, and in some cases an operator is observed by two separate pairs at two different times. After a couple of days of collecting data, including copious notes, audio, or video recordings, the CI team goes home to analyze the data, preferably within twenty-four hours after the interview.

The goal of the analysis is to extract data in order to create models that highlight different work aspects that are interesting in terms of informing design. Such models include the physical layout of the workspace, artifacts that the people work with, task sequences and intents, communications and work flow between people, breakdowns that hinder the work, and cultural aspects that influence work. These models are analyzed collectively, and then consolidated models are developed that look at common aspects of the work. Finally, contextual design methodologies are applied in order to redesign the work and the tools supporting the work.

For purposes of this discussion we'll focus on a work flow model. In particular we wish to identify and name (i) logical groups of operators, (ii) the main functions of each group, (iii) clusters of related tasks that comprise each function, (iv) the tools used to accomplish each task, (v) communications among the groups, (vi) points at which the process is disrupted or slowed down. A work flow diagram is a simple picture that shows the relations among the six items above.

A few caveats regarding the CI method are in order. First, note that the technique remains somewhat subjective. That is, the creation of a work flow diagram from observation data is still an interpretation. Nonetheless, the interpretation is presumed to be better than traditional methods of interviewing and questionnaires. Second, it is clear that the CI team should be rather open-minded and non-disruptive as they observe users at work.

7.1.2 A Day in the Life of a Network Operator

For purposes of illustration, we provide a set of excerpts from the transcripts of a CI study at company X. The study was initiated and led by the Interaction Design Group at Aprisma. The team is cross-functional, including software engineers, technical writers, and testers.

Company X is a real telecommunications company in the USA whose network operations staff is responsible for managing roughly 300 IP LANs and 10,000 network devices.

The study produced multiple transcripts representing multiple interviews. The text below is from one of the transcripts, and it demonstrates a glimpse into what operators do in the field. The work flow diagram that was derived from the total collection of transcripts is discussed in the next section.

How long have you been doing this type of job?

Three years.

Wow...Now when we came over you were on the phone with a customer that was having a problem. Do you want to walk us through how you think that is going to continue? Will they be calling back?

Yeah they'll be calling back...definitely they'll be calling back. This problem started last night. There's a premise router, one that we manage but the only ethernet port off the router goes to a private router. Off that private router are private customers. The private customers can't get outside their private router and they want....they're perceiving this as our premise router problem.

I went into the premise router and was able to assure them that the ethernet segment was up and operational, and I was seeing the IP address for their private router but I couldn't ping their private router, which meant that either (i) a link between our router and their router was down or (ii) a misconfiguration was trying to send traffic somewhere else besides their serial port back to our router, or from their ethernet port back to our router.

We had a technician on site and supposedly he was authorized to access their router to check the configuration, and that's where I find...check their configuration and check the wiring in the box between ours and their router.

We have a tier 1 group that usually takes all the customer calls and they will generate a ticket on a device. Our surveillance area looks at the device event log in the management system and determines if indeed we do have problems. If we do see problems, and we don't already have a ticket on the device, then they'll generate a ticket on the device.

Does the tier 1 group try to do any problem resolution or are they just taking calls and creating tickets?

Sometimes they'll try to ping the IP for the customer while he's on the phone. Sometimes they won't. Sometimes they won't even ask for an IP address.

We'd like to choke them sometimes when we get blank tickets over here and its like...like you're trying to find a problem and all you got is "I cant get to the network" and the user's name and number. So you call them up and ask for the IP Address and they say "well I gave that to the last person" and they're really [expletive deleted] because its an hour later and we're just now contacting them.

The customer is probably thinking "They've been on this for an hour to determine, well, maybe its not just me -- maybe there's a network problem here. So now instead of calling me back with a, well we think we've got your problem isolated, they're just now starting to work on the problem."

The tier 1 people will do some basic pings to see if they can get from here to the users but what we'll do is go into the premise router where the users are located and try and replicate exactly what the users are seeing.

Now you said that this started last night. But somebody else took the call and created the ticket, and someone in your department that works the night shift took the ticket and then passed it off to you, or did it wait until you came in this morning?

Someone last night tried to do some primary investigation on this. The users I guess were impacted this morning and so a technician was sent to the site.

They probably didn't know that we could resolve it remotely. They sent the technician to the site to see what they could see locally. And he was actually calling back inquiring about what he could do. But he also has the router administrators there asking about what we changed on our router. But from what I could see our router looked fine.

From their perspective its something you guys did, and from your perspective you're trying to determine if its something that they did?

Its probably hardware between the two.

I heard you tell them to put a laptop in between the two and see if they could talk to each side.

They mentioned they had a hub between the two routers and if I had an IP address from the hub I could at least test it up to the hub, but it was a dumb hub that didn't have an IP address so I couldn't test it that far. But obviously with this Bay router being in an up state on that ethernet port its communication from...[pause]

The router on your end, the premise router, is a Bay router; what is their private router?

I don't know who their manufacturer is.

So your responsibility goes up to their router, or up to that mystery hub in between?

These people tell us that they're our customers. So we tell them that we'll provide support all the way to their desktop, even if we don't have a topology of their network.
   The local LAN provides support all the way to their desktop. Yea, right. [laughter] That makes it real tough. If I don't have access to their router, I can't tell what their router is doing to the traffic. There are some fights going on right now about this very thing. Our research lab has a private router between our premise router and a Cabletron hub. I can see the hub but I don't have authority on their router to do diagnostics to check configurations.
   But on this one I think I may have already closed it down...on this particular situation that you walked in on, I see an ethernet segment for the

connection to their router that only shows an icon for the premise router and its ethernet segment. It didn't show a hub or any hubs on the side of the private router. Sometimes we'll see an icon for their router which gives us a community string to get SNMP and ICMP information from it, but you don't have telnet authority to actually go into the router and change anything. But we're getting SNMP and ICMP from the hub on the other side of the router so we can go in to isolate problems at the port level and the hub level on these.

Now while we're talking about it I got another ticket in here for...[pause]

How do you know you got another ticket; is it email?

No, we use a special tool which we created. Tier 1 will generate tickets; anybody with an ID can access the tickets. We also have tickets that you can get status on...read only authority that you can get off from the Internet. That way customers will go out and get status on their own tickets and will know how we're working on them. This one says that they can't connect to the LAN with this IP Address. But when I do a traceroute to them I can get response back without any problem. There must be something else that's going on.

You're telnetting into their...?

I'm telnetting into the premise router of the last hop that I have, and I'm assuming that they can't connect to the network because they are getting so many drops or so many errors on their LAN segment that they are not establishing a good connection and I just have go in and get a response back.

Your getting the IP address from the trouble ticket?

Um hum.

Ok. So that IP Address is the recorded one. Its not the IP address of the router that...

No that's the reported problem IP. It could also be the IP on the segment. Someone else has actually been using that IP and its been working fine. But this user can't get on. That doesn't look to be the case. And I did take one drop out of a thousand fifteen-hundred bit packets to that user which is not too bad but it indicates that we probably got a little problem there.

NetBios told me that the user name on this was P.O'Brien so that would indicate since the customer's name is Patrick Obrien...probably not a duplicate IP scenario. Ummm.....and what's nice too is...the ability for us to get the results of our tests and copy it into the tickets. That helps us not only track what we did with the tickets over an extended period of time because we're playing tag with users or something like that, but also if there is a difficult problem to isolate it helps us track where we went and what the results were. So we can see if those results have changed, and it keeps from duplicating processes.

Is this just through experience that you come up with things that you check out, e.g. duplicate IP, dropping packets, etc?

Like a procedure or something written up? No. [laughter] Its because we just know. It's because you hit your head against the wall so many times trying to find other resolutions that you just naturally call them up...Now what we want to do here is see what we know about this segment...

Well, that's enough. We'll take liberty to skip the detailed analysis of the collection of transcripts. Let us look at a segment of the work flow diagram, based on this and other similar interview transcripts.

7.1.3 The Work Flow Diagram

Figure 7.1 shows the work flow diagram that was derived from the CI data collected at the company. The figure is self-explanatory. It shows six logical groups, the tasks of each group, the kinds of generic tools upon which some of the tasks depend, and the communications among the groups.

It is clear that the interviewee in the preceding section is a member of the Tier 2 group.

Now, Figure 7.2 is the same as Figure 7.1, where X's indicate the points at which the operations break down. The X's are described of the following page. Importantly, every breakdown is an opportunity to provide a solution. Thus, the CI team studies each breakdown in order to determine which ones represent opportunities that they wish to leverage in a design solution.

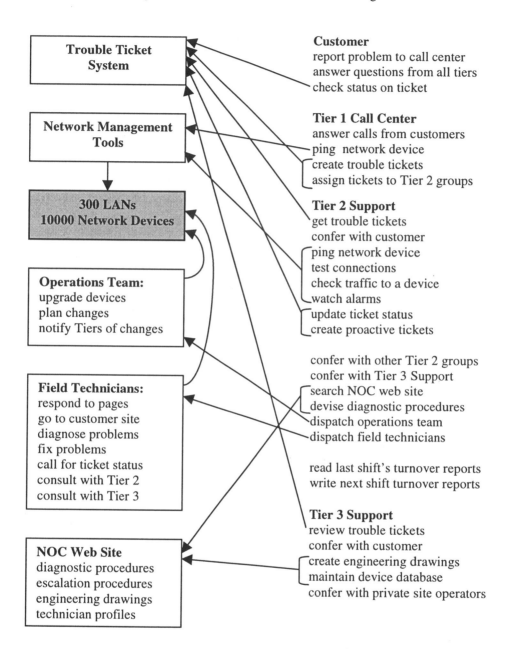

**Trouble Ticket
System**

**Network Management
Tools**

**300 LANs
10000 Network Devices**

Operations Team:
upgrade devices
plan changes
notify Tiers of changes

Field Technicians:
respond to pages
go to customer site
diagnose problems
fix problems
call for ticket status
consult with Tier 2
consult with Tier 3

NOC Web Site
diagnostic procedures
escalation procedures
engineering drawings
technician profiles

Customer
report problem to call center
answer questions from all tiers
check status on ticket

Tier 1 Call Center
answer calls from customers
ping network device
create trouble tickets
assign tickets to Tier 2 groups

Tier 2 Support
get trouble tickets
confer with customer
ping network device
test connections
check traffic to a device
watch alarms
update ticket status
create proactive tickets

confer with other Tier 2 groups
confer with Tier 3 Support
search NOC web site
devise diagnostic procedures
dispatch operations team
dispatch field technicians

read last shift's turnover reports
write next shift turnover reports

Tier 3 Support
review trouble tickets
confer with customer
create engineering drawings
maintain device database
confer with private site operators

Figure 7.1 A Work Flow Diagram

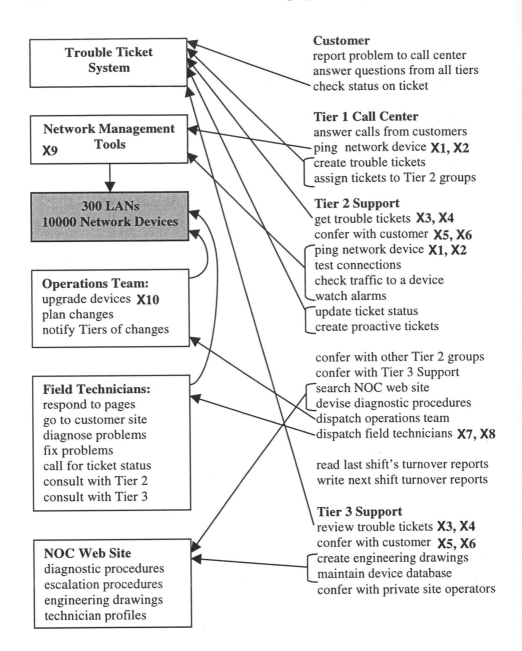

Figure 7.2 The Work Flow Diagram with Break Downs Marked

X1   An IP address is not available for all devices, e.g. a dumb hub.
X2   The device is a private router and therefore inaccessible.
X3   The ticket is sometimes assigned to the wrong group.
X4   The ticket is sometimes incomplete or inaccurate.
X5   A user cannot give information such as IP address or ticket number.
X6   A user is annoyed at giving the same information to multiple people.
X7   Technicians sometimes don't respond to pages.
X8   Technicians are too busy or too far away from a customer site.
X9   Not all devices are modeled in the network management system.
X10   Changes are not always accurate or complete.

There are a few obvious ways in which the process could be improved. For example, consider the problem of X4 in which a trouble ticket is sometimes incomplete or inaccurate. A possible solution is to set up a trouble ticket such that entries in some fields are mandatory. That is, the Tier 1 Call Center would not be able to submit a trouble ticket unless the necessary fields have data in them. Further, one might be able to place constraints on the format of the data so that only certain formats are admissible – e.g. an IP address field would have the format ***.***.***.***.

Of course, that solution won't solve the entire problem; but it helps. In addition, it would help solve the problems of X3, X5, and X6 in a fell swoop.

Next, it would seem that the X7 and X10 problems can be helped only by further training, competency tests, and good management.

The problems of X1 and X2 are interesting, and their solutions are not so obvious. Those problems can be restated thusly: Given the available evidence, what (if anything) can be inferred about the status of a device if it is not directly accessible?

That question leads to a body of research that is addressed by the research community in network management. That is: Can we build an artificial intelligence system that can solve problems at the level of, or better than, seasoned network operators? It would be an accomplishment if we could. Note that this problem is similar to the problem of event correlation that was discussed in Chapter 3.

A promising solution to problem X8 is to investigate the use of scheduling algorithms. And a promising solution to X9 is to investigate the use of management systems that include a dynamic discovery mechanism, whereby the management system adds or deletes devices from the topology map and raises alarms accordingly.

7.2 What Do Network Researchers Do?

Let us now switch gears and take a look at what researchers in network management do.

To start, consider an excerpt from a Call for Participation advertisement for a prestigious network management conference named Integrated Management 2001 (IM01). The IM01 conference is an international conference sponsored by the IEEE Communications Society and co-sponsored by the IFIP Working Group on Network Management.

IM01 Call for Participation

At the dawn of the new millennium, the ubiquitous explosion of the Internet and the fast proliferation of networked devices and business applications create a unique challenge for the network management community. Innovative solutions are required for managing the sheer numbers of devices and the complexity of applications. Further, new ways of strategic thinking must be incorporated in future management products and services to ensure a smooth transition to the new networked society.

Management in this new information era will need to support the integration of data and telecommunications networks, from narrowband to broadband, terrestrial to satellite, fixed to mobile and uni-media to multi-media. The IM 2001 conference provides a forum for discussion of new paradigms and architectures (or new spins on old ones) that can deal with the many management issues related to these next-generation networks.

Authors are invited to submit papers in the following topic areas. Other topics are also welcome and we particularly encourage industrial papers on case studies and experiences that emphasize the lessons learned.

Management Platforms, Standards and Protocols
Emerging Management Technologies and Frameworks (Web, XML, etc.)
Active and Programmable Network Management
Management of Virtual Private Networks
Management of Optical Networks
Management of CATV Networks
Management of Mobile Networks and Services
Management of Voice Networks and Services
Management of IP Networks and Services

Management of Ad-Hoc Networks
Management of Transaction-Oriented Services and Electronic Commerce
Management Aspects of Service Pricing, Accounting and Billing
Management of Service Level Agreements and Bandwidth Brokerage
Data Warehousing, Mining, and Statistical Methods in Management
Mobile and Intelligent Agents in Management
Interoperability and Cooperative Control
Quality of Service Management
Network and Systems Monitoring
Fault and Performance Management
Security Management
Information Modeling
Policy-Driven Management
Applications, Case Studies and Experiences
User Interfaces and Virtual Reality in Management
Open-Source Management Software

Now, what would the interviewee in the CI study think about an opportunity to attend this conference? Probably not much -- unless it were in Hawaii or some other exotic location. The interviewee might be intrigued by the topics "Management of IP Networks and Services" and "Fault and Performance Management." But remember that a network operator simply wants to get through the day without mishap and is not inclined to re-live the day when it is over.

We don't want to commit the fallacy of over-generalization. Indeed, there is a class of individuals who study both what network operators do and what researchers do, with an eye towards transferring research results into practice. Usually, such individuals have titles such as Chief Architect, Chief Technology Officer, or Technology Transfer Officer.

Let us consider an example of the flow from the general statement of a network management problem, to research studies that are motivated by the problem, to the possible incorporation of the research results into everyday network management practices.

First, let us look back at the general problem of resolving network faults from Chapter 2. While reading the transcript in Section 7.1.2, the reader may have been reminded of that discussion.

The General Problem of Resolving Network Faults

All networks experience faults during network operation. Faults may include a failure of hardware portions of the network such as workstations and peripheral devices or a failure of software portions of the network such as software application programs and data management programs.

In small stable homogeneous communications networks (i.e., those in which all of the equipment is provided by the same vendor and the network configuration does not change), management and repair of network faults is relatively straightforward. However, as a network becomes increasingly large and heterogeneous (i.e., those in which different types of equipment are connected together over large areas, such as an entire country), fault management becomes more difficult.

One of the ways to improve fault management in large networks is to use a trouble ticketing system. This system provides a number of tools that can be used by network users, administrators, and repair and maintenance personnel. The basic data structure, a "trouble ticket," has a number of fields in which a user can enter data describing the parameters of an observed network fault. A trouble ticket filled out by a user may then be transmitted by, for example, an electronic mail system to maintenance and repair personnel.

A trouble ticket describing a current network fault that needs to be acted on is called an "outstanding trouble ticket". When the network fault has been corrected, the solution to the problem, typically called a "resolution" is entered into an appropriate data field in the trouble ticket. When a network fault has been resolved, the trouble ticket is closed.

The system provides for storage of completed trouble tickets in a database and thus a library of such tickets is created, allowing users, administrators, and maintenance and repair personnel to refer to these stored completed trouble tickets for assistance in determining solutions to new network faults.

The trouble ticketing system thus provides a convenient, structured way of managing fault resolutions and for storing solutions to network faults in a manner that allows this stored body of knowledge to be accessed and applied to outstanding network faults.

A structured trouble-ticketing system, however, does not provide a complete solution to the fault management problem. For time-critical network services, the downtime that elapses from the observation of a network fault, the submission of a trouble ticket, to the completion of the trouble ticket can be expensive.

Downtime can be reduced by providing a communication link between a network fault detection system and a trouble ticketing system. The communication link allows fault information collected by the fault detection system to be transmitted to the trouble-ticketing system in the form of an automatically generated and filled out trouble ticket. The trouble ticketing system then manages maintenance and repair in the normal manner to resolve the outstanding trouble ticket.

We require, then, an integration between a network management system and trouble-ticketing system. The advantage of such an integration is that network faults may be detected, forwarded to the trouble ticket system, and repaired by maintenance personnel before the end-user begins to observe the effects of the fault.

Although this solution allows trouble tickets to reach the fault management system and appropriate maintenance and repair personnel more quickly, it does not reduce the time necessary to resolve an outstanding fault. A maintenance and repair person is still required to research and resolve the outstanding fault. This is not only time-consuming, but expensive as well.

To reduce the time in which faults are resolved, artificial intelligence (AI) systems may be used to assist in resolving the outstanding trouble ticket. Thus, we require an integration between the trouble-ticketing system and an AI system that helps the administrator determine causes and repair procedures for network faults.

Now, there are pockets of researchers around the globe that are addressing the problem disclosed above – e.g. at the Federal University of Minas Gerais (Brazil), Federal University of Rio Grande do Sul (Brazil), the Leibnitz Supercomputing Center (Germany), the TELCOT Institute at California State University (USA), Aprisma Management Technologies (USA), and others.

To see the approach, let us look at the abstract of an important paper by researchers in Brazil in *Integrated Network Management VI*, published by IEEE in 1999.

*An   Automatic   Fault   Diagnosis   and   Correction   System   for
Telecommunications Management*

Abstract. *In heterogeneous telecommunications networks with a variety of
legacy systems of many kinds, the activity of network supervision is a difficult
task and involves a large number of operators with a diversity of skills. In
such environments, the time to diagnose problems and correct faults usually
is high and subject to many errors. This paper discusses these problems and
some techniques and methods for automated fault management. Next, we
present the design and implementation of a system that automatically
corrects faults collected by a fault management system. Its utilization greatly
reduces the mean time to repair faults, therefore increasing the quality of
service perceived by clients. The system also reduces the cost of fault
management, as it reduces the required work for supervision. The main
characteristics of the system enforces its generality: it can correct faults of
any network element type and it is a case-based reasoning system, thereby
enabling the inclusion of new cases to be corrected without interfering with
the cases already being treated.*

The essence of the approach is shown in Figure 7.3. The idea is two-fold.
See the two encircled items at the top left of the figure.

First, we provide a communications link between the network
management system and the trouble ticket system. In that way, the network
management system creates trouble tickets whenever alarms are detected.
Note that this function automates two tasks that belong to the Tier 2 Support
group, viz. "watch alarms" and "create proactive tickets."

Second, we incorporate intelligence into the trouble ticket system. The
method of artificial intelligence in the pockets of research mentioned above
is "case-based reasoning (CBR)." Recall that we described CBR in Chapter 3
when we discussed various artificial intelligence paradigms for handling the
event correlation problem.

To see how the research contributes to the operations at Company X,
look at the clusters of tasks carried out by the Tier 2 Support Group in Figure
7.3. Several of the tasks are labeled "confer with so-and-so." They are
marked with bars at the right of the task. There is a cluster of tasks that starts
with "ping network device." Two other tasks are "search NOC web site" and
finally "devise diagnostic procedures."

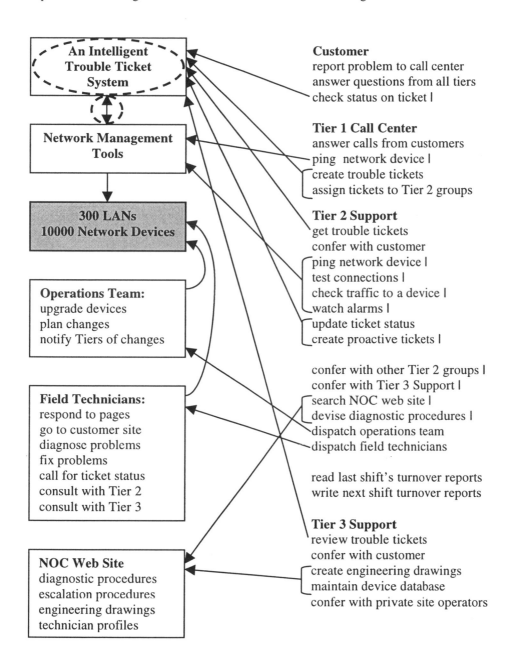

Figure 7.3 An Example of Research Focus

Now combine this with an excerpt from the CI study in Section 7.1.2:

Is this just through experience that you come up with things that you check out, e.g. duplicate IP, dropping packets, etc?

Like a procedure or something written up? No. [laughter] Its because we just know. It's because you hit your head against the wall so many times trying to find other resolutions that you just naturally call them up...

Now, it would be a good thing if a trouble ticket system were intelligent enough to examine past experiences of fault resolutions and propose a solution to an outstanding fault accordingly. It would be a better thing if the trouble ticket system were intelligent enough to carry out tests and, based on the results, propose a solution to an outstanding fault. And finally, it would be yet a better thing if the system could issue instructions to network components to repair the faults automatically.

That is an example of the sort of thing that researchers in network management are trying to make happen. It appears to be a rather obvious advancement in network management that is worthy of pursuit. And it seems to be right on the mark for Company X. However, the approach hasn't quite caught on in the industry. Indeed, there are commercial products available that can fulfill the requirements.

Why is it that such an obvious solution hasn't penetrated the industry? We'll look at some reasons in the next section. Before we proceed, however, the reader should keep in mind that this is an isolated example of applying research results to problems in practical network management. There are numerous other problems that researchers are addressing that have yet to make their way into common practice. Further, the reader should note that in this particular example the time lag between the identification of an outstanding problem and applied research is relatively short. In other cases, the time lag might be ten years or more. For example, research on management by policy, which is rather common today, began around 1990.

7.3 Combining Research and Practice in Network Management

Let us briefly mention five common reasons why advanced research is slow to penetrate the industry:

1. The "More pressing things to be done" problem

2. The "If it works, don't mess with it" problem
3. The "Re-building a boat while it is afloat" problem
4. The "Thinkers vs. Operators" problem
5. The "Research is not ready for prime time yet" problem

These problems are interrelated and rather self-explanatory. One often hears comments in the field such as "That's interesting, but we have more pressing things to worry about right now" and "The management system is working OK for us now, although we know it could be made better."

The third problem suggests that it is difficult to introduce process changes and the introduction of new tools into an existing or legacy management system. It is often compared with the image of trying to overhaul a boat while it is in the water.

Regarding the fourth problem, we certainly don't mean to imply that operators are not thinkers. Indeed, they are very good thinkers. However, the object of their thought is primarily on routine day-to-day management activities and "putting out fires." Often they don't have the time or leisure to contemplate how the management processes could be improved. The so-called thinkers, however, do have time and leisure to study the management processes and suggest ways for improvement. Often, though, they run up against problem 1, 2, and 3.

Finally, it is quite true that not all research and new ideas in network management are good ideas. That is quite OK also. Not all ideas in the history of science turn out to be useful in practice.

Now, what can be done to alleviate the problems of combining research and practice, and to promote good management practices in general?

There are a few obvious approaches that will help out. For example, we saw in the case study on Internet2 GigaPoP management that the new technologies are developed and tested in a research testbed. In general, some businesses are large enough to have a separate test network on which to try out new management technologies before making a decision about incorporating them into the production network.

Next, we saw in the case study on managing service provider networks that network management can be outsourced to a separate vendor who specializes in networking and network management. Businesses are typically specialists in domains other than networking and network management. Thus, it would make sense to depend on the networking specialists to study, evaluate, and possibly incorporate advanced network management practices that are born in research labs.

Finally, a good way to test new ideas is to communicate or visit other people who have tried out the new technologies.

In any case, research and practice in network management continue. Some people argue that it is simply by chance the research ideas get incorporated into practice; but that is a rather extreme view.

Chapter Summary

In this chapter we looked at the problem of combining research and practice in network management. First, we provided a case study at Company X, wherein we used the method of Contextual Inquiry to bring out the structure of the operations. Next, we looked at topics of interest to researchers in network management. As an example, we looked at a research method that shows promise for increasing the efficiency of the operations at Company X. However, we argued that the method, and other research ideas, are slow to make their way into commercial production. Finally, we looked at reasons why that is so and looked at some general approaches for expediting the movement of research results out of the lab and into the commercial sector.

Exercises and Discussion Questions

1. Try to get permission to perform a Contextual Inquiry study for a single network operator. Create an work flow diagram like the one in Figure 7.1. Present it to the operator for corroboration or modification. Discuss the results.

2. Try to get permission to perform a Contextual Inquiry study for a whole network operational staff. Create an work flow diagram like the one in Figure 7.1. Present it to the staff for corroboration or modification. Discuss the results.

3. For either #1 or #2, suggest ways to streamline or improve the operators' work by re-engineering the process.

4. For either #1 or #2, suggest ways to streamline or improve the operators' work by introducing new management tools and/or integrating existing management tools.

5. For either #3 or #4, provide a cost/benefit analysis of the recommendations. Present the analysis to the operational staff and discuss the reaction.

6. Go to www.comsoc.org/confs and examine the upcoming conferences in network management. What are the current topics of interest? If appropriate, submit a paper to one of the upcoming conferences.

7. Pick one of the "Management of X" topics in Section 7.2. Research the status of the topic and report your findings to your peers.

8. A good study of security management is the publication "State of the Practice of Intrusion Detection Technologies" at the web site of the Software Engineering Institute at Carnegie Mellon University (www.sei.cmu.edu/publications). The subsection "What Are the Significant Gaps and Promising Future Directions?" is particularly relevant to the topic of this chapter. Study this publication and suggest ways in which security management could be incorporated into a practical network management system such as Spectrum.

9. Are the ideas of "Automatic Trouble Ticket Generation" and the "Intelligent Trouble Ticket System" in Section 7.2 good ideas? Evaluate and criticize.

10. Discuss the problem of combining research and practice with your peers. What are other promising solutions besides those mentioned in Section 7.3?

Further Studies

The definitive text on Contextual Inquiry is Beyer and Holtzblatt's *Contextual Design: Defining Customer-Centered Systems*. Other good references are the papers by Britton and Reyes, Holzblatt and Reyes, and Holtzblatt and Beyer.

The particular study described in this chapter is based on Cleary's paper "Communicating Customer Information at Cabletron Systems."

A recent book that looks at network management operations in some detail is Ray's *Computer Supported Cooperative Work*.

The reader who is interested in the example of fault management in this chapter should start with the papers by Penido et al and Melchiors and Tarouco. To delve further into the topic, follow the references in those papers.

Finally, a very good way to find out topics of interest to researchers in network management is to examine the Calls for Participation in upcoming conferences and journals. One can see them at www.comsoc.org/confs.

References

Beyer, H., and K. Holtzblatt. *Contextual Design: Defining Customer-Centered Systems*. Morgan Kaufman Publishers, Inc. 1998.

Britton, D. and A. Reyes. Discovering Usability Improvements for Mosaic: Application of the Contextual Inquiry Technique with an Expert User. Electronic Proceedings of the Second World Wide Web Conference '94: Mosaic and the Web. (www.ncsa.uiuc.edu/SDG/IT94/Proceedings)

Cleary, T. Communicating Customer Information at Cabletron Systems. In *Interactions*, 44-49, January-February, 1999.

Holtzblatt, K., and H. Beyer. Customer-centered design work for teams. Communications of the ACM, 36(10), 92-103. 1993.

Holtzblatt, K., and S. Jones, S. Contextual inquiry: A participatory design technique for system design. In Schuler, D., & Namioka, A. (Eds.), Participatory Design: Principles and Practices, Hillsdale, NJ: Lawrence Erlbaum Associates, 177-210. 1992.

Melchiors, C. and L. Tarouco. Troubleshooting Network Faults Using Past Experience. In *IEEE/IFIP Network Operations and Management Symposium* (ed. by J. Hong and R. Weihmayer). IEEE Publishing. 2000.

Penido, G., J. M Nogueira, and C. Machado. An Automatic Fault Diagnosis and Correction System for Telecommunications Management. In *Integrated Network Management VI* (edited by M. Sloman, S. Mazumdar, and E. Lupi). IEEE Publishing. 1999.

Ray, P. *Computer Supported Cooperative Work*. Kluwer Academic/Plenum Publishers. 2000.

8 Towards a Comprehensive Network Management System

In the final chapter of the book we discuss the prospect of a comprehensive network management system that (i) integrates the management of diverse, but connected network technologies, (ii) includes the management of systems and software applications at customer premises, and (iii) allows for the provisioning, billing, and control of services that span across multiple kinds of networks.

There are many individuals who would like nothing better than to see a reasonable approach towards the development of such a system, including services providers, consumers, developers of networking technologies, and developers of management software. However, the development of such a system is hard.

Our topics in this final chapter are:

- A Brief Look at the Space of Networking
- A *Conceptual* Comprehensive Management System is Possible
- A Physical Embodiment is Possible but Hard
- Directions for Further Work

First, we provide a sampling of several varieties of networking technologies, including virtual private networks, optical networks, quality of service networks, and active/programmable networks. We wish to give the reader a sense of the fast pace of development of networking technology and the special management requirements they introduce.

Second, we prescribe a "comprehensive management system" from a conceptual point of view. We develop the conceptual architecture in increments, as it is somewhat complex.

Third, we discuss the challenges involved in the development of a physical embodiment of the conceptual system. We will use the Spectrum management system as an example, although the challenges apply equally to

219

other commercial management systems and prototype systems developed in research laboratories.

Finally, we round off the chapter (and the book) by prescribing some directions for further work in network management, including work towards a common metaphysical framework, a catalogue of integration designs and mechanisms, a catalogue of event correlation scenarios and paradigms, learning and adaptation in network management, automated service provisioning, and ergonomic studies of network management.

8.1 A Brief Look at the Space of Networking

In this section we examine a variety of different kinds of networks. Some of them are on the verge of deployment, while others are in the research stage. Our ultimate goal is to get our arms around a comprehensive network management system – one that can manage today's networks and gracefully accommodate new networking technologies as they enter the market.

As a backdrop for the discussion, let us reproduce a picture that we have seen several times in the book. See Figure 8.1.

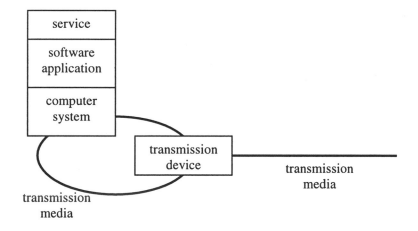

Figure 8.1 The Generic Components of a Network

Different networking technologies can be distinguished with respect to the properties and functionality of transmission devices, the type of transmission media, and the physics and format of data as it travels over the media.

The following sample of network technologies is arranged in order of decreasing commercialization at the writing of this book.

- Virtual Private Networks
- Dense Wavelength Optical Networks
- QoS-based Networks
- Active, Programmable Networks

For example, virtual private networks are fairly common. Single-wave optical networks are also common. However, dense-wave optical networks and QoS-based networks are in the midst of transition to commercial deployment. Active, programmable networks are for the most part in the research stage.

Here we'll describe only the essential characteristics of these kinds of networks. We won't go into much detail regarding network protocols, topology, architecture, and physics. There are good discussions of those topics in the literature. We provide references to them at the end of the chapter.

8.1.1 Virtual Private Networks

A virtual private network (VPN) is a network that is constructed by using both public and private media to connect transmission devices.

For example, in reference to Figure 8.1, we can think of the right-most "transmission media" as including a public network such as the Internet, while the left-most "transmission media" might be a business' private LAN.

There are a number of systems that enable one to create networks using the Internet as the medium for transporting data. These systems use encryption and other security mechanisms to ensure that only authorized users can access the network and that the data cannot be intercepted. A good example is the VPN service offered by Vitts Networks via their *Protected Service Network* (Chapter 5).

One of the underlying technologies that support VPNs is called "IP tunneling." Conceptually, the idea is straightforward. One can think of a private tunnel embedded within the right-most transmission media that connects, for example, business-to-business electronic trading. The tunnel should be virtually impenetrable by unauthorized traffic and hackers with malicious intent.

The tunnel is physically implemented by a combination of several technologies, including encryption, packet monitoring, firewalls, and network address translation (NAT). The latter technology allows businesses to hide their private IP addresses behind a NAT server. Only the IP address of the NAT server is exposed to the public network.

VPN technology raises several management challenges that we have seen in the book already. For example, how does one deal with issues of quality of service and service guarantees? Since public media are not under the control of service providers, it is difficult to insure end-to-end application performance when traffic traverses public media. The current solution to this problem, as we have seen, is to guarantee a certain quality of service only from customer premises to the edge of the public network. But this solution is not entirely acceptable to consumers.

Next, let us consider the situation in which transmission media and networks are actually owned and operated by service providers. In reference to Figure 8.1, if there are a number of right-most transmission media, each owned by separate service providers, then there are likely to be restrictions on traffic that is allowed to traverse the media. This situation is becoming common in the USA, and the Intenet2 community is looking for a solution.

One approach to the problem is "policy-based routing." Simply stated, there would be a policy database that describes admissible flows of traffic among the edge routers of service provider networks, e.g.: Port x on router A is allowed to forward traffic to port y on router B. As policies are modified to reflect business agreements among service providers, a policy enforcer configures the edge routers accordingly.

8.1.2 Optical Networks

Optical networks (a.k.a. photonic networks, or Wavelength Division Multiplexing (WDM) networks) are networks whose transmission devices transmit data in the form of wavelength pulses rather than electronic signals. Optical networks are deployed widely in backbone networks in the USA and Europe in telecommunications.

We can think of a wavelength as a ray of light traversing a (very) long glass or plastic tube, with amplifiers along the way to insure the sustenance of the light from the source to the destination. That should bring to mind the common notion of "speed of light."

Consider a single wavelength. The speed of data transmission over a single wavelength is many orders of magnitude faster than electronic signals over fiber or copper. Thus, with single wavelength optical networks, the volume of traffic that can be carried over an optical network is limited only by the processing power of the transmission devices, where processing includes the translation of electronic signals into pulses and vice-versa.

The 1990s saw the evolution of optical transmission devices that delivered increasingly higher bit rates over optical media. By 2000, however, it was fairly agreed that the physical processing capabilities of transmission devices had reached their peak. Thus, traffic volume came to be limited by the speed of data over a single wavelength.

The next evolution in optical networking is dense wavelength division multiplexing (DWDM). The physics of light is such that one can include forty or more wavelengths in a single fiber and have the transmission devices distinguish among them. The increase in bandwidth by forty or more orders of magnitude is obvious.

The general consensus is that DWDM will be the technology of choice for networking during the 2000s, through which we will enjoy virtually unlimited bandwidth (at least at the backbone level). However, note that now we're back to the situation where the volume of traffic that can be carried over an optical network is limited by the processing power of transmission devices.

Two new kinds of devices that will support future DWDM networks are an optical add/drop mutiplexer and an optical cross-connect. At the writing of this book, scientists at Alcatel research centers are developing and testing prototypes of those devices. In addition, they are developing a prototype agent to manage them, generally called a WDM agent.

To see the management challenges of DWDM optical networks, consider the following introductory quote from a paper in *Integrated Network Management VI* by Alcatel researchers:

The WDM agent has two interfaces. On the one side is the interface between itself and the manager. On the other side is the functional resources (FR) interface between itself and the FR module. The FR module is like a low-level driver. When the agent looks at the FR module through the FR interface it sees the network element as it really is, made of real hardware like space switches and tunable filters. When the manager looks at the agent through the interface it sees the hardware as a generic network element. This generic model is made of mythical standardized parts like Optical Trail/Section Trail Termination Points. The job of the agent is to make the real model look like the mythical model.

And in the conclusion of that paper:

...the agent will inter-operate with other optical network elements and management systems from several vendors. It is our goal to demonstrate that a large-scale high-bandwidth WDM network can operate reliably, and can be administered in a way that is familiar to network operators experienced with SONET/SDH technology.

Thus, in DWDM optical networks, the first challenge is to manage the new devices in the classic style of element management. The first quote above articulates the problem well: to make the physics of the real model look like a mythical model that operators can understand.

For example, the management system should be able to monitor the performance of each wavelength. It should assist operators in troubleshooting the network by isolating questionable wavelengths and the possible locations of degradation.

The second challenge is the inter-operability of the WDM management agent with other network management systems. Inter-operability of management systems is one of the themes of this book; but we have referred to it as "integrated management." We discussed several senses of integrated management in Chapter 1, and we discussed several patterns of integrated management in Chapter 2. We leave it as an exercise to propose an integrated architecture that incorporates the management of optical networks with other kinds of networks.

Finally, there is the challenge of service provisioning. We can imagine a service provider who offers optical bandwidth capacity to consumers. Thus, an apparatus is required to allocate, maintain, and de-allocate optical channels over the network. A single channel might be adequate to accommodate several small customers, while a large customer might require two or more channels.

However, in order to allocate bandwidth intelligently, the service provider needs to know the amount of used and unused capacity per channel. Thus, a management system that can monitor the throughput over a DWDM optical network and infer reasonable measures of used/unused channel capacity is a further requirement.

8.1.3 QoS-Based Networks

A QoS-Based network is generally a traditional network that additionally accommodates multiple qualities of service. The classic example is a multimedia network that carries traffic for diverse kinds of applications, where some traffic can withstand latency but other traffic cannot. If tele-medicine traffic competes with e-mail traffic, clearly the e-mail traffic should stand by until the tele-medicine session is over.

In this section, we look at an example of a QoS-based network under development at Cisco Systems, called a Multiprotocol Label Switching (MPLS) network. MPLS and other QoS-based networks are based on the Resource Reservation Setup Protocol (RSVP).

MPLS networks are networks whose transmission devices make decisions about forwarding traffic based on the following constraints: (i) topology, (ii) bandwidth requirements, (iii) media requirements, and (iv) packet labeling. MPLS-based networks center around the idea of constraint-based routing, in which the path for a traffic flow is the shortest path that meets a set of known constraints.

When packets enter an MPLS-based network, labeling edge routers (LERs) stamp them with a label. The label contains information on the packet source, destination, bandwidth, delay, socket information, and priority.

Once the LER classifies and stamps the packet, it is assigned to a labeled switch path (LSP). As the traffic moves over the assigned LSP, routers place outgoing labels on the packets, again with respect to known constraints.

Some arguments for MPLS-based networks are the following:

- Near-optimal use of backbone bandwidth. Specifically, the best route between a source and destination is determined taking into account the known constraints.

- Reduction in operating costs. With MPLS traffic engineering, an operator does not have to manually configure the network devices to set up explicit routes. The decision-making is automated in the transmission devices.

- Dynamic adaptation and graceful recovery. MPLS-based networks should recover from link or node failures that change the topology of the backbone by adapting to new sets of constraints.

- Regulation of quality of service. From a QoS standpoint, service providers should be able to manage different kinds of data streams based on service priority. For instance, customers who subscribe to a premium service plan should see minimal latency and packet loss, while other customers should expect periodic delays in data transmission.

At the writing of this book, MPLS technology is in the testing stage at Cisco Systems. It is understood that there will be operational challenges when traditional routers are replaced or upgraded to MPLS routers. Thus, Cisco is working on a migration plan to expedite the conversion.

Let us assume that the conversion has been completed. A challenge for managing MPLS-based networks is to verify service levels agreements (SLAs) made with consumers, where consumers have the option of various service levels. But that means that one has to find measurable parameters to include in the agreement.

In our discussion of service provider networks in Chapter 5, we saw that transactional response time is a popular parameter to include in an SLA. However, the guarantee is typically a blanket value, e.g. "a round trip delay of packets sent from the customer site to the edge of the Internet of 50 milliseconds or less."

Response time management will be harder with MPLS-based networks, and with QoS-based networks in general, for obvious reasons. Since there will be multiple grades of services offered to consumers, and assuming that transactional response time will continue to be used in SLAs, then there will be multiple response time guarantees. That observation clearly adds further complexity to service providers' management systems.

8.1.4 Active, Programmable Networks

Let us stop a moment to think about the operations of different kinds of transmission devices.

When a packet or cell reaches a device, the destination of a packet header is read in order to determine the next hop en route to its destination.

Additionally, in MPLS-based networks, a priority parameter is examined to determine the timing and routing of packet transmissions.

The transmission devices on the edge of an optical network translate electrical signals in the form of lightwave pulses, or vice versa. In general, a transmission device may operate upon ingress data in order to transform it into the format required by the egress media and the type of transmission device at the next hop.

Firewall nodes read the packet to determine whether the packet is admissible in the domain it protects.

These and other examples are well-known operations of traditional transmission devices. Let us generalize the notion to the idea that the devices can perform numerous other operations on data that pass through them.

Consider the following rather extreme case. A typical business operation is that a block of data D is selected from a database residing on computer C1 and transferred to a database on computer C2 for further processing. Suppose the processing involves algorithms A1, A2, and A3, all performed sequentially on D once it arrives at C2.

Now suppose that there are intermediate transmission devices X, Y, and Z from the source C1 to destination C2. Conceptually, it is not hard to imagine the block of data D saying to X, Y, and Z upon arrival: "if you have CPU cycles to spare, please expend them to perform A1 on me, and then send me along." Further, it is not hard to imagine that X, Y, and Z have generic resident algorithms A1, A2, A3, or that D carries the algorithms along with it. The end result is that (possibly) data D arrives at destination C2 fully processed.

Active networks, unlike traditional networks, are not passive carriers of bits but instead provide the capability for the user to inject customized programs into the networks. The network nodes would interpret these programs and perform the desired operation on the data flowing through the network.

Researchers involved with active networks argue that the seed of the idea is already with us; what we need to do, they say, is to expose the idea and use it as a research paradigm. Further, they argue that active networks will open many new doors for applications that were unimaginable with traditional networks. For example, there may be a cross-continent video session such that at every intermediate transmission device the video data is modified, thus requiring less processing on the sending and receiving ends, and thereby increasing the quality of the video experience.

Next, researchers argue that the active networks would alleviate the problem of standardization, which is well known to be a slow and sometimes excruciating process. Instead of standardizing translation schemes between different kinds of networks, or standardizing protocols such as IPv6, we would only have to standardize the execution environment and the language by which we program active network nodes.

Finally, they argue that active networks show promise for service provisioning and deployment. If there were a standard execution environment and language that was shared by all transmission devices, then the incorporation of new services would mean downloading customized programs into the network infrastructure.

Now, what are the new management problems that are introduced by the idea of active networks? Is it possible, for example, to download management programs into devices as well as data modification programs? These are open questions that don't have clear answers. To wit, a panel session at a recent conference discussed the following topic: Active and Programmable Networks: Are They Solutions or Problems for Management? We leave that question as an exercise for the motivated reader.

8.1.5 Discussion

Several comments are in order. First, we have looked at a rather small selection of existing, nearly-deployed, or futuristic networks. There are other kinds of networks that should be mentioned.

For example, a "mobile ad hoc" network is a wireless network made up of physically roaming transmission devices. The connectivity of the network is much like an arbitrary graph whose nodes and connectivity change dynamically. And of course there are commonly known network technologies that we haven't discussed – e.g. ATM switched networks, frame relay networks, and cable networks.

Second, note that our discussion has focused on the different types of networking technologies. But if we look back at Figure 8.1, it is easy to see other elements between these components and the end-user, viz. computers, applications, and the services as perceived by the user. Thus, the management of network services, at least from the viewpoint of business and end-users, extends beyond the management of the network.

Now, the general goal of this chapter is to prescribe a comprehensive network management system – one that can manage the complexities of today's networks and also accommodate network technologies on the horizon. As new types of networks are deployed, on the verge of deployment, or being developed in research test beds, and as consumers ask for service guarantees that extend beyond the reach of individual networking technologies, the problem of comprehensive management becomes hard.

8.2 A *Conceptual* Comprehensive Management System is Possible

A conceptual comprehensive management system is by nature complex and multi-dimensional, which means that it cannot be shown in a single picture. Therefore, we will build it up slowly and in increments.

Figure 8.2 is a kind of picture often seen in the literature. It is sometimes called the "divide and conquer" method of network management. A network is partitioned into logical domains where each domain is managed more or less in isolation by low level management systems. However, a higher-level management system presides over the lower-level systems. It is sometimes called a manager of managers (MOM).

Consider different types of networking technologies – the topic of the preceding section. One can imagine a local area network managed by network management system A, an ATM network managed by system B, and an optical network managed by system C, where each network is provided and operated by third parties utilizing their own management platforms and management processes.

Now suppose there is a VPN that spans across all of those networks. Then clearly the management of the VPN depends upon management information collected by A, B, and C. Thus, the picture shows *intra*-domain data from A, B, and C passed to an "*inter*-domain data correlation" box. The latter box is expected to process intra-domain data and forward data back to A, B, or C in the form of operational instructions. Such operational instructions may have to do with faults, configurations, or service provisioning. More often than not, they are carried out by human operators.

Large businesses often have to construct VPNs that span across multiple heterogeneous networks, where some of the networks are privately owned. The result of this, from the network operator's point of view, is management complexity in terms of security management, operations management, problem management, configuration management, policy management, change management… in short, it is close to a management nightmare. That is the problem that we wish to discuss in the remainder of the chapter.

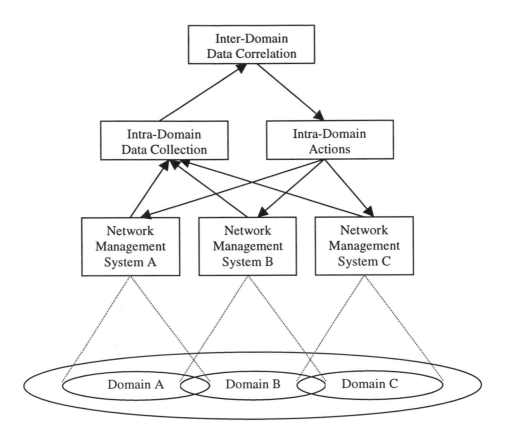

Figure 8.2 First Increment of a Comprehensive Network Management System

Figure 8.2 hides several important features of a comprehensive management system: (i) domain-specific event correlation, (ii) network, systems, and application management, (iii) layered TMN-style management, and (iv) FCAPS-style management.

8.2.1 Domain-Specific Event Correlation

We discussed the topic of event correlation in Chapter 3. To recapitulate, a particular network management system will collect numerous events and statistics as it monitors the elements in its respective domain. The task of event correlation is to map certain collections of events scattered in space and time into *alarms* and possible *actions*. See Figure 8.3.

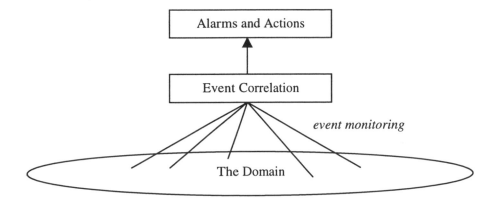

Figure 8.3 Event Correlation per Domain

Our discussion in Chapter 3 revealed several paradigms in the industry for event correlation, including rule-based reasoning, model-based reasoning, state transition graphs, codebooks, and case-based reasoning. Indeed, there are other paradigms that are being investigated in research laboratories, e.g. fuzzy logic and neural networks.

Regardless of the particular paradigm used, domain-specific event correlation is another example of the "divide and conquer" approach to network management. We argued in Chapter 3 that a single event correlation engine for a large heterogeneous networking system will not scale. Thus, it is advisable to employ separate correlation engines for each individual domain, where the output of each engine is passed to a higher-level correlation engine.

The "inter-domain data correlation" box in Figure 8.2 is such a higher-level correlation engine. Its domain, i.e. its input, is the space of intra-domain alarms.

So far, the combination of Figures 8.1 and 8.2 is palatable. We require correlation engines for lower-level intra-domain management systems and higher-level inter-domain systems. The idea is not new. It is similar to the concept of a manager of mangers (MOM) that has been with us since the early 1990s. There are several commercial products in the industry that act as MOMs. Their sole function is to receive input data from lower-level network or element management systems, process the data, and output data in the form of reports and recommended actions.

8.2.2 Network, Systems, and Application Management

We argued in Chapter 1 that there is more to network management than "network management." That is especially true when business executives think of network services in terms of the software applications upon which the operation of the business depends.

When a service provider elects to monitor and control a business's computer systems and software applications in addition to the network, then there are other things to worry about.

Therefore, let us explode the "Network Management System X" boxes in Figure 8.2 into a structure like Figure 8.4. We take the liberty to replace the word "network" with "enterprise" since in the industry the word "enterprise management" has come to connote the management of applications, systems, and networks.

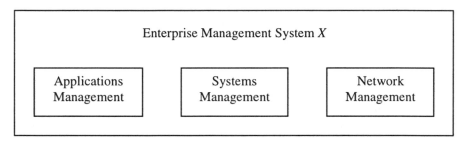

Figure 8.4 Network, Systems, and Application Management

One has to be careful about this enhancement to the conceptual management system. Not all network management systems will have to monitor and control computer systems and applications in addition to the network. For example, the management of an optical network does not include the management of end user systems and applications, although the health of an optical network will affect the health of end user applications.

As an example, recall our case study of the North Carolina GigaPoP Management project in Chapter 6. The NC GigaPoP is an intermediary QoS-based network between an optical backbone and the campus networks at

University of North Carolina, Duke University, and North Carolina State University.

For purposes of research in network management, the target domain for the NC project was carved out to be (i) the GigaPoP network and (ii) the university computer systems and software applications that support a particular service in North Carolina -- distance learning.

The project's target domain does not include the Internet optical backbone or the myriad other networks, computer systems, and software applications that support the business of the three universities. It is quite likely that those networks will bear upon the distance learning service and that they will enter into the project in later phases of the work.

The additional consideration of systems and application management ties in with the discussion of domain-specific event correlation. A common question regarding an end user's complaint is "Is it a network, systems, or application problem?" An RTM system, for example, can raise a problem regarding sluggishness in application transactions, but there is further work to be done to determine whether the cause of the problem has to do with the application, the computer system on which the application resides, or the network.

Often the problem is figured out in the troubleshooter's head; however an event correlation system that covers systems and application events could help in isolating the root cause of the problem. This is the sort of approach underway in the NC distance learning service, in which NT servers and CAMVision applications are monitored along with the GigaPoP network. In addition, it is the sort of work underway in the Camp LeJeune case study in Chapter 4.

8.2.3 Layered Management

An important concept in network management is the five-layer Telecommunications Management Network (TMN) discussed in Chapter 1. As a review of the TMN model, see Figure 8.5.

The TMN model is partitioned into five layers: the element layer, the element management layer, the network management layer, the service management layer, and the business management layer. Each layer, going from bottom to top, represents a transformation of technical detail to more business-oriented information.

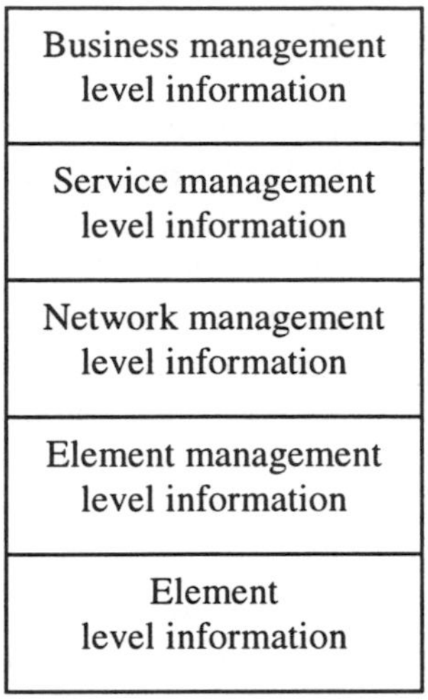

| Business management
level information |
| Service management
level information |
| Network management
level information |
| Element management
level information |
| Element
level information |

Figure 8.5 The TMN Layers of Abstraction

- The business layer is concerned with the overall management of the telecom carrier business. It covers aspects relating to business processes and strategic business planning. Further, it seeks to capture information to determine whether business objectives and policies are being met.

- The service management layer is concerned with the management of services provided by a service provider to a customer or to another service provider. Examples of such services include billing, order processing, and trouble ticket handling.

- The network management layer is concerned with a network with multiple elements. As such it supports network monitoring and remote configuration. In addition, this layer supports issues such as bandwidth control, performance, quality of service, end-to-end flow control, and network congestion control.

- The element management layer is concerned with the management of individual network elements, for example switches, routers, bridges, and transmission facilities.

- The element layer refers to bare elements that are to be managed.

As an example, we saw in Section 8.1.2 that current work in the management of dense-wave optical networks is focused on both the element level and the element management level. Next will come work on combining element level information to produce network level information, and then service level information.

Now, the same idea is applicable to other kinds of networks. The TMN idea has influenced businesses who own their own networks and also businesses who outsource pieces of the network operation to service providers. For the most part, commercial networks are manageable up to (and including) the network layer. The ideas of "services" and "service level agreements" are now on the minds of business executives and service providers. We saw an example of layering service level management applications over the Spectrum management system in Chapter 3, and we saw other examples in our three case studies.

Therefore, let us enhance the picture in Figure 8.4 as shown in Figure 8.6.

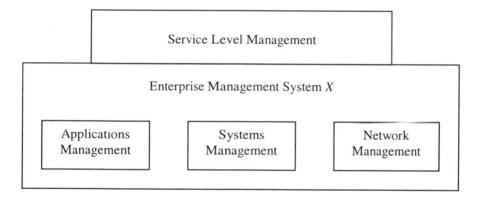

Figure 8.6 Enterprise Management and Service Level Management

Again, though, one should be careful about this simple enhancement. First, the term "service" is slippery. One can think of a service from a user's point of view, from a business' point of view, or from the network's point of view. The service provided by an optical network, for example, is the allocation of bandwidth to a customer. But a service from a business' point of view may be decomposed into the service provided by the optical network plus services provided by its local network, systems, and applications.

That is yet another example of the divide and conquer technique, whereby a higher-level service is composed of several lower-level services. Thus, in reference to our initial picture in Figure 8.2, we can think about end-to-end services at the inter-domain level and local services at the intra-domain level.

8.2.4 FCAPS Management

Finally, let us consider classical FCAPS management (fault, configuration, accounting, performance, and security management). We discussed FCAPS in Chapter 1. Briefly:

- *Fault management* includes trouble management, which looks after corrective actions for service, fault recovery, and proactive maintenance and provides capabilities for self-healing. Trouble management correlates alarms to services and resources, initiates tests, performs diagnostics to isolate faults to a replaceable component, triggers service restoral, and performs activities necessary to repair the diagnosed fault. Proactive maintenance responds to near-fault conditions that degrade system reliability and may eventually result in an impact on services. It performs routine maintenance activities on a scheduled basis and initiates tests to detect or correct problems before service troubles are reported.

- *Configuration management* includes timely deployment of resources to satisfy the expected service demands, and the assignment of services and features to end-users. It identifies, exercises control over, collects data from, and provides data to the network for the purpose of preparing for, initializing, starting, and providing for the operation and termination of services. It deals with logical, service, or custom networks such as the toll network, local public switched telephone network, and private networks.

- *Accounting management* processes and manipulates service and resource utilization records and generates customer billing reports for services rendered. It establishes charges and identifies costs for the use of services and resources in the network.

- *Performance management* addresses processes that ensure the most efficient utilization of network resources and their ability to meet user service-level objectives. It evaluates and reports on the behavior of network resources and ensures the peak performance and delivery of each voice, data, or video service.

- *Security management* controls access to and protects both the network and network management systems against intentional or accidental abuse, unauthorized access, and communication loss. Flexibility methods are built into security mechanisms to accommodate ranges and inquiry privileges that result from the variety of access modes by operations systems, service provider groups, and customers.

A popular way to look at FCAPS management is to consider it along side the TMN model, as shown in Figure 8.7. Each FCAPS area is considered with respect to each layer of the TMN model.

	F	C	A	P	S
Business management level information					
Service management level information					
Network management level information					
Element management level information					
Element level information					

Figure 8.7 Two Dimensions: FCAPS and the TMN Model

Recall that we took liberty to replace the word "network" with "enterprise" in Figure 8.4. We wish to imagine the same replacement in

Figure 8.7, i.e. we wish the network management layer to possibly include the management of computer systems and software applications that reside on the network; and we wish the term "element" to include individual systems and applications in addition to transmission devices.

Now, given a design or a deployment of some particular network management system, one should be able to use Figure 8.7 to demarcate its functionality. For example, how far does it go up the TMN ladder? We have seen that most commercial systems are in fairly good shape at the network management level. Businesses and service providers are now in the midst of designing and deploying a service management system on top of that.

Next, we may ask FCAPS kinds of questions about a particular management system. Given a definition of a service, we may ask: How are service faults defined, identified, and corrected? How are services provisioned? How does one bill for a service? How does one measure the performance of a service? And how does one secure a service? We saw how some management systems are handling these questions in our case studies.

8.3 A Physical Embodiment is Possible but Hard

We have seen physical embodiments of *parts* of our conceptual management system in the body of the book. One should be able to review the case studies and discuss them along the dimensions in Section 8.2.

There are at least five challenges that impede the development of a *physical* comprehensive management system:

1. The Technical Challenge: Management methods generally lag behind new networking technologies.

2. The Standardization Challenge: The standardization of management methods is slow to happen and sometimes does not happen, resulting in proprietary management methods.

3. The Integration Challenge: The integration of different management methods for different networking technologies is not straightforward.

4. The Separation Challenge: Separately owned networks get in the way of comprehensive management.

5.   The Ergonomic Challenge: A single consistent and intuitive interface for managing heterogeneous networks is difficult.

Let us discuss these items in turn.

8.3.1 The Technical Challenge

A good example of a new networking technology at the writing of this book is multi-wave optical networks, which promise to change the face of communications by enabling advanced applications in federal, scientific, and commercial sectors.

The first problem in managing multi-wave optical networks is to understand the physics of optical networks in terms of management concepts. That is sometimes called an "information model" for the new networking technology.

For example, the information model of multi-wave optical networks includes models of optical components (optical-to-electronic terminating equipment, multiplexing equipment, optical amplifiers, etc.) and models of wavelengths (e.g. section trails, multiplex trails, and channel trails). Typically, the information model is used also as a base to develop FCAPS-style and TMN-style management methods for the technology.

Consider what a commercial network management vendor has to worry about in this kind of situation: The vendor is not in the business of developing optical networks. It is in the business of managing them. But in order to understand how to manage them, the vendor's scientists and architects have to keep close watch on the development of the technology, their special management methods, and their commercial viability.

Aprisma Management Technologies is an example of such a vendor. Aprisma's *Spectrum* is commercially popular; it is good at managing existing enterprise networks, service provider networks, ATM and frame relay networks, cable networks, and others. It is also good at multi-vendor device management and event correlation over single- and multi-domain networks.

Aprisma's goal is to provide a comprehensive management solution, and in that regard it competes with vendors such as HP, Tivoli, Computer Associates, Objective Systems, and a number of start-up companies in the network management space.

But now there is a new networking technology on the horizon that is very important (viz. multi-wave optical networks). What are vendors to do?

The encouraging news for Aprisma is that the object-oriented paradigm is more or less a *de facto* paradigm for developing information models for new networking technologies, including multi-wave optical networks. Since Spectrum's information model is based on the object-oriented paradigm, there is a fortunate commensurability between it and the information models of new networking technologies.

The discouraging news, however, is that it is hard to predict how the information models developed by different networking vendors or vendor consortia will stabilize into a standard, even though they are based on the object-oriented paradigm. That observation leads us directly into the standardization challenge.

8.3.2 The Standardization Challenge

We provided a brief guide to standards work in network management in Chapter 1. In sum, today's business and service networks are complex. The current state of any particular network more than likely evolved piecemeal and thus includes heterogeneous kinds of network technologies, equipment from multiple vendors, and various kinds of management methods. To make matters worse, management methods vary over countries and in districts within countries.

In a few cases this state of affairs has resulted in a management nightmare. In other cases the result is piecemeal management, in which narrowly focused management solutions co-exist but do not cooperate. The best case, however, is integrated management, in which these management techniques cooperate in a standardized management framework.

Thus, the ultimate goal of international standards bodies is to provide a uniform framework and methodology in order to correct the current situation. The problem, however, is that the standardization process is often slow and sometimes doesn't mature into a globally accepted standard.

In a sort of arm chair philosophizing style, let us distinguish among four kinds of standards:

1. De Facto standards: ideas that weren't intended to be standards, but more or less took on lives of their own and penetrated the industry (e.g. SNMP-based management).

2. Well-planned, completed standards: ideas that went through the standardization process and matured into a settled, global standard (e.g. SONET/SDH).

3. Incomplete, but Instructive Standards: ideas that have begun the standardization process, but haven't matured into an official standard, but nonetheless serve as useful conceptual guides for designing and implementing comprehensive management systems (e.g. TMN).

4. Laissez-Faire standards: ideas introduced and implemented by large communications companies with a large customer base, such that the "standard" is for the most part imposed upon consumers.

Consider the history of Aprisma's Spectrum. Spectrum started out in 1990 as an SNMP-based system. The slogan in 1990 was "If a device is SNMP-manageable, then Spectrum can model it regardless of the vendor; further the device can be included in the Spectrum model type library and enjoy event-correlation and FCAPS-style management from a single management console."

In the early 1990s, however, CMIP was being developed as a standard protocol for managing devices in the telecommunications space. Thus, by 1995 Aprisma architects began designing and implementing CMIP-based management in Spectrum. But, by the late 1990s, CMIP had for the most part lost momentum. Thus, Aprisma backed away from its CMIP development.

The 1990s also saw the emergence of CORBA and TL1 as protocols for integrating disparate management systems. By 2000 the Aprisma architects developed a CORBA interface for Spectrum. TL1 is under consideration. Fortunately for Aprisma, SNMP and CORBA remain strong as standards for device management and integrated management respectively.

As an aside, we should note that many "incomplete, but instructive standards" from early 1990's research are now being implemented in CORBA. This note complements our discussion of combining research and practice in Chapter 7.

In sum, the introduction and development of standards is under continuous scrutiny by all vendors that develop network management systems. Typically, vendors have to align their plans for future work with the maturity of standards, and sometimes that involves taking chances.

8.3.3 The Integration Challenge

Let us review our discussion of integrated management in Chapter 1. Table 8.1 shows the different senses of integrated network management.

Table 8.1 Dimensions of Integrated Network Management

Generic components	devices, media, computers, applications, services
Functional areas	fault, configuration, accounting, performance, security
Layers of abstraction	element, network, service, business management
Service networks	network 1, network 2, ... , network n
Voice/data networks	network 1, network 2, ... , network n

A comprehensive management system should (i) integrate the management of networks, systems, business applications, and services (ii) integrate the areas of fault, configuration, accounting, performance, and security management, (iii) integrate the element, network, service, and business layers of management information, (iv) integrate the management of diverse networking technologies, and (v) integrate the management methods of both telecommunications and data communications networks.

Clearly, that is a large requirement. Nonetheless, it is the goal of serious enterprise management vendors. Our conceptual comprehensive system in Section 8.2 covered the requirement; but the physical embodiment of the system is rather difficult.

As an example, let us focus on the integration of element and network management. Figure 8.8 illustrates two broad philosophies for doing that.

The left-hand picture illustrates an element-centric management system. With that approach, there are a number of element management systems per element type. Each element management system passes management information to a higher-level network management system. Thus the network management system is once removed from the bare elements.

The right-hand picture illustrates a network-centric management system in which the network management system communicates directly with elements.

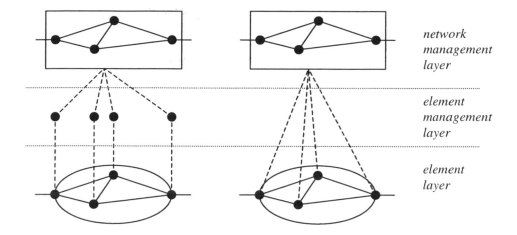

network management layer

element management layer

element layer

Figure 8.8 Two Philosophies of Network Management

One will see both approaches in the industry. The latter approach, for example, is taken by Aprisma's Spectrum.

There are trade-offs between the two approaches. As we have seen, Spectrum is popular in the industry in part because it provides multi-vendor management from a single management station. But that means that Spectrum engineers have to build management modules for new element types as they enter the market, which in turn means that they have to understand the differences between old and new network technologies, their information models, and their specific management methods. That's entirely doable, and Aprisma has done a good job at keeping up with the networking industry during the 1990s. But, plainly put, it's an awful lot of work.

The element-centric approach requires roughly an equal amount of work, but the clear disadvantage is the common problem of the proliferation of point management solutions, each requiring deployment, configuration, and learning curves. A further disadvantage is the lack of a consistent operational interface.

What often happens is that new technologies are developed in research labs with respect to the element-centric philosophy in order to develop appropriate management techniques. When the technology settles, vendors such as Aprisma incorporate the management methods into an existing commercial network management system.

8.3.4 The Separation Challenge

The separation challenge is illustrated in Figure 8.9. Suppose a domain X is managed by provider A, but a service S offered by A (represented by the bold horizontal line) depends upon a domain that is managed by provider B.

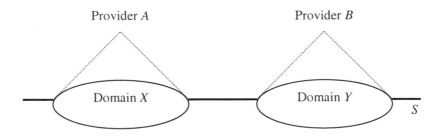

Figure 8.9 The Separation Challenge

The separation challenge is common in the industry. We saw an example of it in Chapter 5, in which A was an ILEC, B was CLEC, X was a telecommunications network, and Y was a data network.

In Chapter 5 we examined four logical approaches to the problem:

1. A limits its service offerings to those that depend upon the networks under its control.

2. A doesn't offer service guarantees in cases where the service depends upon networks not under its control.

3. A and B enter an arrangement whereby network operators collaborate to handle service degradations and faults.

4. B opens its domain to A's management system, or vice versa.

Approaches 1 and 2 sidestep the separation problem altogether, while approaches 3 and 4 tackle it head on. In particular, approach 4 takes us directly back to the problem of integrated management.

Another common manifestation of the separation problem is seen in businesses that control their own local services, where A is a staff dedicated to network management (domain *X*) and *B* is a staff dedicated to systems and applications management (domain *Y*). Often one sees that these people rarely talk to each other, and when they do, it takes the form of finger-pointing. Clearly, an integrated management system would help to alleviate the separation problem.

The reader should begin to appreciate the theme of this section: A *physical* comprehensive management system is possible, but hard. The competition challenge, combined with the technical, standardization, and integration challenges put a lot on one's plate. Unfortunately, we are not through yet. There is one challenge left that is equally important and difficult.

8.3.5 The Ergonomic Challenge

Ergonomics is "an applied science concerned with the characteristics of people that need to be considered in designing and arranging things that they use in order that people and things will interact most effectively and safely."

Our discussion in Chapter 7 focused squarely on ergonomics with respect to network management. We should note however that Chapter 7 looked at a scenario that was concerned with a classic, but very large, IP network. Further, the activity of the network operators was mainly focused on fault management.

Thus, the discussion in Chapter 7 was rather narrowly focused. When we begin to consider ergonomic studies with respect to tasks such as multi-domain management and service provisioning, it gets much harder. The methodology of Contextual Inquiry is a viable approach to building better user-friendly management systems, but clearly there is a lot of work to be done before it happens.

8.4 Directions for Further Work

Our discussion of a conceptual comprehensive management system in Section 8.2, combined with the issues discussed in Section 8.3, offer us direction for further work in network management. Unfortunately (or fortunately, depending how one looks at it), there is certainly plenty of work to be done.

In this final discussion of the book, we use Aprisma's Spectrum as an example, with the understanding that our advice applies equally to other commercial vendors and research projects whose goal is to produce a comprehensive management system.

8.4.1 Improvements in a Common Metaphysical Framework

The first direction is to create a framework, a design, and an implementation strategy for a generic network management system, with an eye towards (i) the graceful incorporation of management methods for networking technologies as they become commercially viable and (ii) the ability to scale with increasingly large and heterogeneous networks.

We discussed the Spectrum framework in Chapter 3. The Spectrum system was originally based on the object-oriented information paradigm in 1990, whereby network components were conceived as objects that represent their real-world counterparts. That basic idea has proved its worth in the industry.

An object-oriented system helps to alleviate the problem of introducing models of multi-vendor elements into an existing system. Further, it expedites the generation of management methods for domains other than networks and network elements. We saw in our case studies how systems, applications, and service management products are incorporated into Spectrum by third-party vendors.

A direction for the industry as a whole is to develop a common language for specifying network technologies and the management of them. Of course, that is not news. It is the main goal of standards bodies. A good start in that direction is the ITU-T Recommendation G.805 – *Generic Network Information Model* (1995). Many of the management concepts for optical networks, for example, are derived from that document. It is advisable that frameworks for network management systems migrate towards an alignment with such information models.

The direction of Aprisma's architects is to continue the study of networking technologies and management methods and to map them into the Spectrum framework. The management of cable networks and virtual private networks (up to the edge of the Internet) are recent additions to the Spectrum portfolio. The management of multi-wave optical networks and QoS-based networks are in the research/design stage at the writing of this book. And a bit beyond the horizon, there is thought about managing homes and apartment complexes whose appliances are networked together.

8.4.2 Useful Integration Designs and Mechanisms

The goal of a generic framework by which to manage diverse networking technologies is certainly a good idea. However, no matter how much a vendor wants to develop a comprehensive, single-console management system, there will be times when an integration with another vendor's management system makes good sense. A good example is the integration of an existing management system with a legacy management system.

Further, consider the argument that no one vendor can provide all the solutions. Vendors are more or less specialists in one domain or another. Some are good at building network management systems, some are good at building network simulation systems, some are good at building trouble ticket and help desk systems, etc.

Thus, a second direction for future work is to catalogue various kinds of integration patterns and mechanisms by which to implement them. Recall that we provided a preliminary discussion on patterns of integrated management in Chapter 2. That is a good start, but there is much room for advancement on the topic.

The direction for Aprisma in particular is to continue to study how special-purpose management systems could integrate with Spectrum in order to satisfy a business requirement. We saw a good example of that in our case study of managing a service provider network (Chapter 5), in which we discussed the business case for integrating Spectrum and a response time management system such as NextPoint's *S3*. In that case, the business justification, the integrated design, and the implementation mechanisms are well understood.

However, an example that is not so well understood is the integration of optical backbone traffic monitoring tools such as *OC3Mon* and Spectrum. In fact, we proposed that as an exercise in our chapter on Internet2 GigaPoP management (Chapter 6). The first question, of course, is whether there is a business reason for entertaining the idea, and then come the engineering considerations.

8.4.3 Better Ways to Program Event Correlation Systems

We saw in Section 8.2 that event correlation plays an important role in comprehensive management. However, event correlation systems in commercial products and research labs are typically problem-specific and/or domain specific. That is understandable because the concept of a "fault" and the detection of events caused by a fault are likely to vary from domain to domain. For example, a fault and ensuing events in the domain of optical networks is quite different than a fault and ensuing events in the domain of business applications.

Thus, a third general direction is to understand commonalities among scenarios that require event correlation. It would be useful to have a catalogue of generic event correlation methods and ways to program them with a user interface.

The Spectrum management system is well known in the industry for its strengths in event correlation. For example, we saw in Chapter 3 that Spectrum uses three methods: model-based reasoning, rule-based reasoning, and case-based reasoning. However, the first method is more or less hard coded into the system, and thus the addition of event handling for new types of problems has to be coded using Spectrum C++ APIs. The latter two methods, however, are more like shells into which one can place new knowledge with a user interface.

Thus, a particular direction for Aprisma architects is to render the model-based reasoning component programmable through a user interface. A second direction is to continue to study alternative correlation systems and the classes of problems to which they are applicable. For example, neural networks or fuzzy logic systems might be more applicable to certain types of problems than the three methods currently used in Spectrum.

8.4.4 Employing Machine Learning Methods in Network Management

A programmable event correlation system is an achievement. However, a better, but harder achievement is to build a system that learns how to handle events by itself. That idea takes us into the areas of machine learning and artificial intelligence.

Consider that current management systems are very good monitoring systems. They log events and statistics in a database. However, often the database simply accumulates data, and at times it is flushed to make room for more data.

Historical data often holds implicit knowledge that could be used to detect and resolve certain classes of network problems. The challenge is to discover it. Let us consider two examples.

Suppose a response time management system measures the transaction delay between a client/server application, where the client resides at customer premises in one geographical domain, the server resides in a second geographical domain, and between the two domains there are various core networks. Now assume that a multi-domain integrated management system is in place such that each domain-specific management system stores performance data for its domain in a historical database.

Now, given a case in which we have sporadic episodes of unacceptable response time measurements, the problem is to find out what causes it. That can be done by sifting through the total collection of performance data with an eye towards noticing certain performance parameters that appear to coincide with the response time parameter. Clearly, that is hard for a human to do, although it is done routinely for much smaller problems on much smaller sets of data. An alternative approach is to apply machine learning algorithms (a.k.a. data mining algorithms, or knowledge discovery algorithms) to do it for us.

As a second example where historical data might be useful, consider the problem of malicious network attacks in which a transmission device is flooded with dummy traffic. Suppose we have performance data for a period of time during which there were sporadic denial-of-service (DoS) attacks. An interesting question is whether there are certain events that seem to always appear before the DoS attack.

For example, one can imagine a hacker who has installed a number of programs on various computers in a networked domain. Periodically, the hacker sends messages instructing the programs to execute themselves, where the function of each program is to forward large dummy packets to a device for 20 minutes and then stop, thus causing network overload and DoS responses.

We can imagine two kinds of events that could be precursors of DoS attacks: a certain class of packets entering the domain (i.e. the hacker's message to start the programs) and (ii) a particular kind of process that begins running on the host computers. It is possible that a knowledge discovery application could identify such precursors of DoS attacks. Clearly, that would be quite useful knowledge.

Thus, a fourth direction for network management vendors, and Aprisma in particular, is to understand the classes of problems to which machine learning methods are applicable.

For example, Aprisma researchers are working on both problems mentioned above. The first problem was discussed in Chapter 6. The second problem – network intrusion detection -- is the topic of a project funded by the US Air Force. Aprisma, Scientific Systems Corporation, and the University of Texas are collaborating to understand how to incorporate network intrusion detection and prevention techniques into the Spectrum system.

8.4.5 Automated Service Provisioning and Billing

The fifth direction is to build a network management system that not only performs traditional management functions such as fault and configuration management, but also provides automated service provisioning and billing.

Consider optical networks as an example. The service offered by an optical network is the allocation of bandwidth to consumers. But that means that an operator has to set up, maintain, and release optical channels between terminal devices with respect to consumer demands. The management system would know the theoretical capacity of the optical core, know the consumers who have contracted portions of bandwidth, be able to configure optical devices in order to accommodate changes in consumer demands, and produce bills for consumers.

Of course, the idea itself is not new. Traditional telephony networks have been doing it for a very long time. But as network services begin to depend on different kinds of network technologies, the challenge becomes much harder.

For example, Aprisma's Spectrum has entered the service provider market for purposes of fault management and configuration management over multi-domain networks. Currently, service provisioning is typically done manually by network operators, and billing is often a flat monthly fee. Service providers, however, are beginning to look for ways to automate the process, and they are naturally looking towards Spectrum as a way to do it.

Thus, Aprisma architects are charged with the task of figuring out how to incorporate a service provisioning/billing apparatus into the existing Spectrum system.

8.4.6 More Ergonomic Studies

Finally, all our technical improvements in network management – multi-domain heterogeneous management, programmable event correlation, learning capabilities, and service provisioning/billing -- might well be moot if operators in the field can't make the system work.

Thus, a sixth important direction for further work is the application of ergonomic methods to the practice of network management.

We have seen two approaches to the design and usability of management systems in the body of the book. In Chapter 2 we described the object-oriented software engineering (OOSE) methodology for software development. An essential step in OOSE methodology is the very first step: the development of a *use case model* from the user's point of view.

And in Chapter 7 we described the method of Contextual Inquiry. The goal there is to uncover the structure of operations, communications, and management systems used by an existing network management staff. Then, the structure is studied with an eye towards improving operations by designing better management tools, modifying the workflow, or simply re-arranging the physical artifacts in a network operations center.

Aprisma's Interactive Design Group has been trained in both Contextual Inquiry and the broader methodology of which it is a part – Contextual Design. The results of the studies are applied to Spectrum in order to improve the usability of Spectrum and to insure that new versions of Spectrum are both technically and ergonomically sound. Further, Aprisma's design engineers undergo training to make sure that the OOSE methodology is properly carried out.

The direction for Aprisma in this regard, then, is to continue to study and practice these methods.

Chapter Summary

In this final chapter we discussed the prospect of a comprehensive network management system. The themes of the chapter were that (i) a conceptual comprehensive system is possible but that (ii) a physical embodiment of it is difficult. First we looked at a sampling of innovative networking technologies. Next we discussed a comprehensive management system from a conceptual point of view. Then, we looked at a number of challenges that impede the development of such a system. Finally, we proposed some direction for further work in network management, including a common metaphysical framework for network management, a catalogue of event correlation scenarios and paradigms, a catalogue of integration designs and mechanisms, off-line knowledge discovery, methods for service provisioning and billing, and ergonomic studies.

Exercises and Discussion Questions

1. What is network address translation (NAT)? What is RFC-1631?

2. What is an RFC? Find a complete list of RFCs. Extract those RFCs that are clearly related to network management. Discuss them with your peers.

3. We discussed several senses of integrated management in Chapter 1, and we discussed several patterns of integrated management in Chapter 2. Which sense of integrated management, and which pattern of integrated management, is applicable to the challenge of the inter-operability of optical network management systems and the management systems discussed in Section 8.1.2?

4. Active and programmable networks: Are they solutions or problems for management? Discuss.

5. In our discussion of QoS-based networks, we discussed MPLS as an example. What other examples of QoS-based network exist? How close are they to practical deployment? How do they differ from the MPLS architecture?

6. Pick one of the case studies in Part II and describe the management system with respect to the topics in Section 8.2.

7. Find a business network or a service network, study it, and describe its management system with respect to the topics in Section 8.2.

8. The management of optical networks is a hot topic. Study the papers on optical networks in the References section below. Also study the references at the end of those papers. After your study is complete,

develop a slide presentation entitled "The Challenges of Managing Optical Networks."

9. A "wireless network" is an important topic in the space of networking. What is a 3G wireless network? What is a 4G wireless network? What are the special challenges (if any) for managing wireless networks? Write a short synopsis similar to those in Section 8.1. Include your references.

10. Evaluate and criticize the discussions in Sections 8.2, 8.3, and 8.4. What is missing from the conceptual comprehensive system? What other challenges impede a physical embodiment of the system? What other directions for further work would you recommend?

Further Studies

The collection of literature for further study is comprised of select papers in the proceedings of two important network management conferences that took place as this book was written: *Integrated Management VI* (IEEE Publishing, 1999) and *Network Operations and Management Symposium* (IEEE Publishing, 2000).

Of course, there is other important literature that is relevant to the topics in this chapter. The motivated reader is advised to circumscribe a particular topic by starting with the papers below and doing a sort of "iterative reference-following" thereafter (e.g. see questions 8 and 9 above).

References

Virtual Private Networks

Gruschke, B., S. Heilbronner, and N. Wienold. Managing Groups in Dynamic Networks. In *Integrated Management VI* (ed. by M. Sloman, S. Mazumdar, and E. Lupu). IEEE. Publishing. 1999.

Kim, E., C. Hong, and J. Song. The Multi-Layer VPN Management Architecture. In *Integrated Management VI* (ed. by M. Sloman, S. Mazumdar, and E. Lupu). IEEE. Publishing. 1999.

Optical Networks

Badt, H., L. Jousset, X. Letellier, V. Vhit, and C. Drion. A Case Study of a WDM Agent. In *Integrated Management VI* (ed. by M. Sloman, S. Mazumdar, and E. Lupu). IEEE. Publishing. 1999.

Lehr, G., R. Braun, H. Dassow, G. Carls, U. Hartmer, A. Gladisch, H. Schmid, M. Dollinger. WDM Network Management: Experiences Gained in a European Field Trial. In *Integrated Management VI* (ed. by M. Sloman, S. Mazumdar, and E. Lupu). IEEE. Publishing. 1999.

QoS-Based Networks

Jiang, Y., C. Tham, and C. Ko. Providing Quality of Service Monitoring: Challenges and Approaches. In *IEEE/IFIP Network Operations and Management Symposium* (ed. by J. Hong and R. Weihmayer). IEEE Publishing. 2000.

Tse-Au, E., and P. Morreale.. End-to-End QoS Measurement: Analytic Methodology of Application Response Time v. Tunable Latency in IP Networks. In *IEEE/IFIP Network Operations and Management Symposium* (ed. by J. Hong and R. Weihmayer). IEEE Publishing. 2000.

Wang, P., Y. Yemini, D. Florissi, and J. Zinky. A Distributed Resource Controller for QoS Applications. In *IEEE/IFIP Network Operations and Management Symposium* (ed. by J. Hong and R. Weihmayer). IEEE Publishing. 2000.

Active, Programmable Networks

Brunner, M. and R. Stadler. The Impact of Active Networking Technology on Service Management in a Telecom Environment. In *IEEE/IFIP Network Operations and Management Symposium* (ed. by J. Hong and R. Weihmayer). IEEE Publishing. 2000.

Brunner, M. A Service Management Toolkit for Active Networks. In *IEEE/IFIP Network Operations and Management Symposium* (ed. by J. Hong and R. Weihmayer). IEEE Publishing. 2000.

Egashira, T., Y. Kiriha. Management Middleware for Application Front-end on Active Networks. In *IEEE/IFIP Network Operations and Management Symposium* (ed. by J. Hong and R. Weihmayer). IEEE Publishing. 2000.

Kawamura, R. and R. Stadler. A Middleware Architecture for Active Distributed Management of IP Networks. In *IEEE/IFIP Network Operations and Management Symposium* (ed. by J. Hong and R. Weihmayer). IEEE Publishing. 2000.

Issues in Comprehensive Network Management

Aizman, A. Multi-Management: An Application-Centric Approach. In *Integrated Management VI* (ed. by M. Sloman, S. Mazumdar, and E. Lupu). IEEE. Publishing. 1999.

Anerousis, N. A Distributed Computing Environment for Building Scalable Management Services. In *Integrated Management VI* (ed. by M. Sloman, S. Mazumdar, and E. Lupu). IEEE. Publishing. 1999.

Chen, G. and Q. Kong. Integrated Management Solution Architecture. In *IEEE/IFIP Network Operations and Management Symposium* (ed. by J. Hong and R. Weihmayer). IEEE Publishing. 2000.

Hariri, S. and Y. Kim. Design and Analysis of a Proactive Application Management system. In *IEEE/IFIP Network Operations and Management Symposium* (ed. by J. Hong and R. Weihmayer). IEEE Publishing. 2000.

Hasan, M., B. Sugla, R. Viswanathan. A Conceptual Framework for Network Management Event Correlation and Filtering Systems. In *Integrated Management VI* (ed. by M. Sloman, S. Mazumdar, and E. Lupu). IEEE. Publishing. 1999.

Jakobson, G., M. Weissman, L. Brenner, C. Lafond, and C. Matheus.. GRACE: Buiding Next Generation Event Correlation Services. In *IEEE/IFIP Network Operations and Management Symposium* (ed. by J. Hong and R. Weihmayer). IEEE Publishing. 2000.

Kar, G., A. Keller, and S. Calo. Managing Application Services over Service Provider Networks: Architecture and Dependency Analysis. In *IEEE/IFIP Network Operations and Management Symposium* (ed. by J. Hong and R. Weihmayer). IEEE Publishing. 2000.

Knobbe, A., D. van der Wallen, L. Lewis. Experiments with Data Mining in Enterprise Management. In *Integrated Management VI* (ed. by M. Sloman, S. Mazumdar, and E. Lupu). IEEE. Publishing. 1999.

Lewis, D., V. Wade, and R. Bracht. The Development of Integrated Inter and Intra Domain Management Services. In *Integrated Management VI* (ed. by M. Sloman, S. Mazumdar, and E. Lupu). IEEE. Publishing. 1999.

Senan, S., J. Gish, and J. Tremlett. Building a Service Provisioning System using the Enterprise Java Bean Framework. In *IEEE/IFIP Network Operations and Management Symposium* (ed. by J. Hong and R. Weihmayer). IEEE Publishing. 2000.

Epilogue

I mentioned my motivations for writing a book on network management in the preface: (i) the enormous advancements in networking technology as we transition from the 20th century to the 21st century, (ii) the increasing dependence of human activities on networking technology, and (iii) the commercialization of services that depend on networking technology (e.g., email and electronic commerce).

Personally, I get excited about new advancements in networking technology and the problems they introduce. Further, I get excited about ways to automate the management and operation of networks so that there is less dependence on humans. That's probably because my choice of study in my early years was logic, philosophy of science, and artificial intelligence.

I'm quite happy with my career of applying concepts in logic, philosophy, and AI to a domain that makes a difference to the state of human society. I don't think I would be happy studying logic or AI for the sake of logic and AI only. It is the application of them to real-world problems that motivates me.

Finally, if the reader will pardon my rambling on about myself, I should like to say that I have a foot in both camps of industry and academia. While I like to see existing management methods work in practice, I also like to experiment with new ideas that show promise for advancing the state of network management.

The reader is invited to get in touch with me regarding concerns in networking and network management -- commercial, academic, or otherwise.

Lundy Lewis
Nashua, New Hampshire USA
July 10, 2000

Spectrum Patents

In Chapter 3 (Introduction to the Spectrum Management System) we promised to provide a list of abstracts of important Spectrum patents. Of course, there are other patents on methods and apparatus for network management held by other businesses and universities. The ones below, however, complement our discussion of Spectrum in Chapter 3.

The reader can visit the web site of the US Patent and Trademark Office at www.uspto.gov to examine the full bodies of these patents and others.

Method and apparatus for determining frame relay connections

US Patent 6,115,362
September 5, 2000

A system determines that a frame relay connection exists between an interface on a first interface device and an interface on a second interface device, for example by comparing addresses resident in routing tables of the interface devices. The system then queries each of the first and second interface devices, to determine the amount of traffic that is communicated by each channel of each of the two interfaces. This data is then correlated to determine the relative amount of data by each channel on each of the two interfaces, and the pair of channels having the best correlation are determined to represent an actual connection.

Inventors: Patrick Bosa, Gregory Mayo, Christopher Crowell

Method and apparatus for surveillance in communications networks

US Patent 6,026,442
February 15, 2000

Control of network surveillance in communications networks is accomplished by dividing the surveillance task into two sub-tasks. The first sub-task automatically identifies communications within the network which are to be monitored. Such identification is accomplished by the application of a reasoning system to data received from the network. The identification of the data to be monitored is received by the second sub-task along with network topology information. The second sub-task also applies a reasoning system to this data in order to configure probes and switches within the network so that the identified data can be captured.

Inventors: Lundy Lewis, Glenn Spargo, Utpal Datta

Method and apparatus for automatically populating a network simulator tool

US Patent 6,014,697
January 11, 2000

Method and apparatus for automatically populating a network simulation tool database with network topology and/or traffic information. A topology extraction tool is provided for reading the topology and traffic information in a network management system database, and translating this information into a matching data format required by the simulation tool database before writing the information to the simulation tool database. This automatic method avoids the time-consuming and error-prone prior art manual method of constructing a network model.

Inventors: Lundy Lewis, David St. Onge, Michael Soper

System for determining network connection availability between source and destination devices for specified time period

US Patent 6,003,090
December 14, 1999

Availability of a computer network is determined by analyzing specific pairs of source/destination devices in the network and alternative paths between them. The topology of the network is analyzed so as to determine all paths between the devices and the availability of devices on each path is determined. If any one alternative path is available, this is included in the determination of network availability. Further, a relative weight may be assigned to various devices/paths on the network depending on usage or other parameters. The availability information is then presented in the format of a report card where specific source/destination pairs and the paths therebetween are chosen as indicia of the network's availability.

Inventors: Vineeta Puranik, Utpal Datta, Rachael Barlow

Method and apparatus for learning network behavior trends and predicting future behavior of communications networks

US Patent 5,987,442
November 16, 1999

Apparatus and method for learning current network behavior and predicting future behavior which utilizes a state transition graph. The graph includes nodes which represent network states, and arcs which represent trends in observable network parameters that result in a transition from a current state to another state. For example, a watch service may be instituted on multiple ports of a router, and the observed network traffic on the ports over time may be transformed into a state transition graph that represents network behavior. The network states may be labeled such as "good", or "bad", etc., according to a predetermined performance criteria. Once a state transition graph is constructed, the system may then monitor the current state and current trends of the network parameters in order to predict and display future network states. The system may include an automatic warning signal for alerting a user that the network is headed in the direction of a problematic state. The prediction of future network behavior may be made from the state transition graph, the current state of the network, and the current network trends.

Inventors: Lundy Lewis, Utpal Datta

Network device simulator

US Patent 5,907,696
May 25, 1999

Method and apparatus for creating the appearance of a network device and its communications, and in particular, an SNMP agent and its SNMP communications. A device dataset contains a plurality of counter variables having instance values which change over time and describe the behavior of the device on the network. A characterization file is created from the device dataset based on correlations among the variables and their instance values. The characterization file is used to generate predicted instance values for a simulated device.

Inventors: Larry Stilwell, Vishwae Gokhale

Policy management and conflict resolution in computer networks

US Patent 5,889,953
March 30, 1999

Method and apparatus for determining an enforceable policy applicable to one or more network devices. The method includes attaching one or more rule elements to one or more domain elements to create policies, the domain elements representing network devices and groups of network devices, and the rule elements defining actions, a method for determining whether a conflict exists between the polices, and a method for resolving the conflicts to produce one or more enforceable policies.

Inventors: Suzzanne Thebaut, Walter Scott, Eric Rustici, Prasan Kaikini, Lundy Lewis, Rajiv Malik, Steve Sycamore, Roger Dev, Oliver Ibe, Ajay Aggarwal, Todd Wohlers

Method and apparatus for defining and enforcing policies for configuration management in communications networks

US Patent 5,872,928
February 16, 1999

Apparatus and method for monitoring parameters that govern the operational characteristics of a network device, including the use of templates for generating configuration records of network devices of a selected model type. A database of models is provided, each model representing an associated network device and including attribute values for the parameters of the associated network device. Templates are used to screen a model in order to retrieve values for each of the attributes and create a configuration record. The configuration records may be stored in the configuration manager or other storage device, and/or transferred to the pre-existing model database for use by a network management system in reconfiguring the associated network devices. Additionally, a method and apparatus is provided that defines network groups, defines network policies for groups, determines conflicts, and resolves conflicts among groups and devices. This system for configuration management is less time consuming, expensive, and error prone than prior systems.

Inventors: Lundy Lewis, Rajiv Malik, Steve Sycamore, Suzanne Thebaut, Walter Scott, Eric Rustici, Prasan Kaikini

---

Method and apparatus for configuration management in communications networks

US Patent 5,832,503
November 3, 1998

Apparatus and method for monitoring parameters that govern the operational characteristics of a network device, including the use of templates for generating configuration records of network devices of a selected model type. A database of models is provided, each model representing an associated network device and including attribute values for the parameters of the associated network device. Templates are used to screen a model in order to retrieve values for each of the attributes and create a configuration record. The configuration records may be stored in the configuration manager or other storage device, and/or transferred to the pre-existing model database for use by a network management system in reconfiguring the associated network devices. This system for configuration management is less time consuming, expensive, and error prone than prior systems.

Inventors: Rajiv Malik, Steve Sycamore, Bill Tracy

Port-link configuration tracking method and apparatus

US Patent 5,822,305
October 13, 1998

A logical representation of a communications network topology has links which represent connections within a network, and models of ports representing elements of devices which form the connections of the network. The logical representation is created and maintained in response to reports from the network, such as new neighbor reports and lost neighbor reports. A new neighbor module creates or changes the logical representation in response to new neighbor reports, based upon whether the reporting port is recently attached and whether the new neighbor port is recently attached. A lost neighbor module changes the logical representation in response to lost neighbor reports, by creating pseudo new neighbor reports, and allowing the pseudo new neighbor reports to be processed following a certain amount of time. The operation of the new neighbor module and lost neighbor module allow reports to be processed independent of the order in which the reports are received, and also facilitates monitoring of complex network topologies, such as those including connections of more than two nodes, and those in which reports may be received in any order.

Inventors: Vick Vaishnavi, Wallace Matthews, Patrick Kenny

Configurations tracking system using transition manager to evaluate votes to determine possible connections between ports in a communications network in accordance with transition tables

US Patent 5,793,362
August 11, 1998

A network is monitored for reports indicative of a connection state among ports of a communications network. Certain ports are designated as being in a transition, and a transition table is created for each transition. The transition table includes locations that directly relate the connectivity of a first port with respect to a second port, as well as locations that relate the connectivity of other ports. The contents of the transition table are evaluated to determine the likely configuration of the communications network. State machines may be used to resolve conflicting data within the transition table, by providing a likely connection output based upon different entries within the transition table. A voting scheme is used to evaluate the outputs of the state machines and update the transition table when appropriate, and the updated transition table may also be evaluated.

Inventors: Wallace Matthews, Vick Vaishnavi

Method and apparatus for policy-based alarm notification in a distributed network management environment

US Patent 5,777,549
July 7, 1998

Apparatus and method for receiving alarms from multiple network management servers and applying a plurality of policy-based filters to the alarms. The filters may be named and stored in a database, and application of the policy-based filters may be scheduled for different times. The same policy-based filters may be applied to one or more multiple network management applications. The invention allows greater control over which alarms get reported to network management applications and provides a means to ensure consistency of reported alarms across multiple network management applications.

Inventors: Russell Arrowsmith, Bill Tracy

Method and apparatus for inter-domain alarm correlation

US Patent 5,768,501
June 16, 1998

A multi-domain network manager provides alarm correlation among a plurality of domains included in a communications network. Individual network management systems each monitor a single respective domain of the communications network, and provide intra-domain alarms indicative of status specific to the single respective domain. The multi-domain network manager receives the intra-domain alarms, and correlates them to provide inter-domain alarms as well as responses in the form of corrective actions. The multi-domain network manager thus provides a high level of correlation and response for the entire network while each network management system provides a lower level of correlation and response for an individual domain of the network.

Inventor: Lundy Lewis

Gateway for using legacy telecommunications network element equipment with a common management information protocol

US Patent 5,764,955
June 9, 1998

A gateway that allows a CMIP/CMIS network manager to manage legacy telecommunications network elements by providing a bidirectional mapping between CMIP messages and legacy syntax messages. The gateway has the ability to understand the individual dialects of each vendor specific legacy syntax; therefore, a single CMIP/CMIS network manager can manage a network composed of a variety of network legacy elements from multiple vendors.

Inventors: Paul Doolan

System for determining the status of an entity in a computer network

US Patent 5,751,933
May 12, 1998

A network management system includes a user interface, a virtual network and a device communication manager. The virtual network includes models which represent network entities and model relations which represent relations between network entities. Each model includes network data relating to a corresponding network entity and one or more inference handlers for processing the network data to provide user information. The system can poll or communicate with certain network entities and can infer the status of network connectors and other network entities for which polling is impossible or impractical. The system performs a fault isolation technique wherein the fault status of a network device is suppressed when it is determined that the device is not defective. User displays include hierarchical location views and topological views of the network configuration. Network devices are represented on the displays by multifunction icons which permit the user to select additional displays showing detailed information regarding different aspects of the corresponding network device.

Inventors: Roger Dev, Mark Nelson

Network connection status monitor and display

US Patent 5,751,965
May 12, 1998

A system provides representations of connections or other relationships among entities that make up a communications network. The representations may each have a color or shading to represent different conditions of the relationship. The representations may be graphical and may also include textual information as well as graphical hot-spots selectable by a user to provide even more detailed information regarding the relationship. The condition of each relationship may be determined based upon a combination of the conditions of the interface elements which are coupled together to form the communications relationship.

Inventors: Gregory Mayo, Roger Desroches, David Nedde

Method and apparatus for digital data compression

US Patent 5,748,781
May 5, 1998

Data compression and decompression are performed on a series of data points, by expressing a plurality of data points as an equation or a series of equations. Variable accuracies, and accordingly variable compression ratios, may be provided. Multiple versions of the compressed data, with corresponding multiple accuracy levels, and resulting multiple decompressions may be displayed for comparison. The method and apparatus may be used for storing network statistical data.

Inventors: Utpal Datta, David Carlson

Method and apparatus for network synchronization

US Patent 5,734,642
March 31, 1998

According to several aspects of the present invention, a network is monitored for status information indicative of the status of a manageable device within the network. A network manager receives the status information, and updates or initializes a device model in accordance with the status information. A state machine may be used to determine a new state for the device model, and to enable or disable the device model. The network manager may also take action to inquire as to the status of the manageable device, for example by polling the manageable device or by initiating a discovery process. The device model may be used by the network manager as a basis by which to control the manageable device, and thus control aspects of the communications within the network.

Inventors: Vick Vaishnavi, Patrick Kenny, Michael Rydeen

Apparatus and method for determining network topology

US Patent 5,727,157
March 10, 1998

An apparatus and method for determining the topology of a computer network including data-relay devices and node devices, based on a comparison of source addresses heard by the various data relay-devices. A source address table is compiled for each port of each data-relay device, and for each select pair of ports the addresses in the source tables are compared to determined whether there is an intersection of heard devices. In order to account for directed transmissions which are not heard at every port, further comparison is made of all of the other ports of the device, eliminating the ports for which the intersection is the empty set. From the determined connections, a topology of the network is graphed showing direct and transitive connections. In cases where there is both a direct and transitive connection, the redundant direct connection is eliminated.

Inventors: Timothy Orr, Eric Gray

Apparatus and method for evaluating network traffic performance

US Patent 5,706,436
January 6, 1998

Traffic on a communications network is evaluated based on intra-subnet and inter-subnet traffic volumes. Values indicative of such volumes and of the overall network balance are displayed, along with alternative node topologies which may be evaluated and displayed. The overall network performance is based on equalizing intra-subnet traffic volume and minimizing inter-subnet traffic volume.

Inventors: Lundy Lewis, Utpal Datta

Method and apparatus for policy-based alarm notification in a distributed network management environment

US Patent 5,696,486
December 9, 1997

Apparatus and method for receiving alarms from multiple network management servers and applying a plurality of policy-based filters to the alarms. The filters may be named and stored in a database, and application of the policy-based filters may be scheduled for different times. The same policy-based filters may be applied to one or more multiple network management applications. The invention allows greater control over which alarms get reported to network management applications and provides a means to ensure consistency of reported alarms across multiple network management applications. A telephonic alarm notification method and apparatus incorporates the policy-based filters and the capability to process alarms from multiple network segment servers so that users can be accurately notified of critical alarms generated in large and complex communications networks, via a public communications system.

Inventors: Lynn Poliquin, Russell Arrowsmith, Lundy Lewis, Bill Tracy

Method and apparatus for monitoring and controlling communications networks

US Patent 5,687,290
November 11, 1997

The apparatus includes a network monitor coupled to the communications network and providing numeric data representative of at least one operating parameter of the communications network. A fuzzifier module is coupled to the network monitor and converts the numeric data into fuzzy input data. A fuzzy inference engine is coupled to the fuzzifier module and processes the fuzzy input data according to at least one fuzzy rule to provide fuzzy output data representative of control actions to effect a desired state of the communications network. A defuzzifier module is coupled to the fuzzy inference engine and converts the fuzzy output data into numeric data which may be then used by a network controller to control at least one network parameter in response to the output data. The apparatus may also include a user interface and a display to allow the fuzzy input data, and the fuzzy output data to be displayed to a user. Using the user interface, the user can then modify the fuzzy input data, the fuzzy output data, and the fuzzy rules. A method for monitoring and controlling communications networks is also disclosed. A methodology for designing membership functions and fuzzy rules useful for monitoring and control of communications networks is disclosed. The system provides for reporting of network behavior in common sense terms, providing recommendations to a user regarding network operational parameters, and, in one embodiment, complete automatic monitoring and control network operational parameters.

Inventor: Lundy Lewis

Method and apparatus for determining a communications path between two nodes in an Internet Protocol (IP) network

US Patent 5,675,741
October 7, 1997

Method and apparatus for determining a communications path between a source and a destination in an Internet Protocol (IP) network. The method determines a path list of next-hop routers between the source and destination by selecting between a Simple Network Management Protocol (SNMP) query of a current router on the path, and by sending a User Datagram Protocol (UDP) probe packet having a destination field with a destination IP address and a Time-to-Live (TTL) field with a value of one greater than the number of hops to the current router. The steps are iterated until the next router is determined to be the destination. Preferably, the UDP probe packets are loose-source routed through the source. In addition, a topology information database may be accessed to resolve an unknown router, and/or resolve intrarouter devices on the path.

Inventors: Ajay Aggarwal, Walter Scott, Eric Rustici, David Bucciero, Andrew Haskins, Wallace Matthews

Method and apparatus for resolving faults in communications networks

US Patent 5,666,481
September 9, 1997

An improved method and apparatus of resolving faults in a communications network. The preferred system uses a trouble ticket data structure to describe communications network faults. Completed trouble tickets are stored in a library and when an outstanding trouble ticket is received, the system uses at least one determinator to correlate the outstanding communications network fault to data fields in the set of data fields of the trouble ticket data structure to determine which completed trouble tickets in the library are relevant to the outstanding communications network fault. The system retrieves a set of completed trouble tickets from the library that are similar to the outstanding trouble ticket and uses at least a portion of the resolution from at least one completed trouble ticket to provide a resolution of the outstanding trouble ticket. The determinators may be macros, rules, a decision tree derived from an information theoretic induction algorithm and/or a neural network memory derived from a neural network learning algorithm. The system may adapt the resolution from a retrieved trouble ticket to provide the resolution using null adaptation, parameterized adaptation, abstraction/respecialization adaptation, or critic-based adaptation techniques.

Inventor: Lundy Lewis

Method and apparatus for managing multiple server requests and collating responses

US Patent 5,649,103
July 15, 1997

In a communications network, a request manager simultaneously dispatches a number of requests to servers corresponding to at least one domain of interest that is specified by a client. Multiple responses are received and a single collated response is sent back to the client that initiated the request. A request context table is provided which includes an anchor context and dependent contexts corresponding to each of the servers, and a session count

for tracking receipt of all responses for each server. An internal cache of
server addresses is also maintained.

Inventors: Utpal Datta, Mark Wagner

**Use of multipoint connection services to establish call-tapping points in a
switched network**

US Patent 5,627,819
May 6, 1997

Method and apparatus for providing a call-tapping point in a switched
network with point-to-multipoint functionality. The tapping point is added as
an additional destination for data being sent from a source node to a first
destination node. The tapping point is also added as a destination for data
being sent from the first destination node to the source node. A merge
operation is performed for finding and combining common segments of the
paths between the source and destination, the source and tapping point, and
the destination and tapping point.

Inventors: Roger Dev, Prasan Kaikini, Jason Jeffords, Wallace Matthews

---

Port-link configuration tracking method and apparatus

US Patent 5,590,120
December 31, 1996

A logical representation of a communications network topology has links
which represent connections within a network, and models of ports
representing elements of devices which form the connections of the network.
The logical representation is created and maintained in response to reports
from the network, such as new neighbor reports and lost neighbor reports. A
new neighbor module creates or changes the logical representation in
response to new neighbor reports, based upon whether the reporting port is
recently attached and whether the new neighbor port is recently attached. A
lost neighbor module changes the logical representation in response to lost
neighbor reports, by creating pseudo new neighbor reports, and allowing the
pseudo new neighbor reports to be processed following a certain amount of
time. The operation of the new neighbor module and lost neighbor module

allow reports to be processed independent of the order in which the reports are received, and also facilitates monitoring of complex network topologies, such as those including connections of more than two nodes, and those in which reports may be received in any order.

Inventors: Vick Vaishnavi, Wallace Matthews, Patrick Kenny

Method and apparatus for monitoring the status of non-pollable devices in a computer network

US Patent 5,559,955
September 24, 1996

A network management system includes a user interface, a virtual network and a device communication manager. The virtual network includes models which represent network entities and model relations which represent relations between network entities. Each model includes network data relating to a corresponding network entity and one or more inference handlers for processing the network data to provide user information. The system can poll or communicate with certain network entities and can infer the status of network connectors and other network entities for which polling is impossible or impractical. The system performs a fault isolation technique wherein the fault status of a network device is suppressed when it is determined that the device is not defective. User displays include hierarchical location views and topological views of the network configuration. Network devices are represented on the displays by multifunction icons which permit the user to select additional displays showing detailed information regarding different aspects of the corresponding network device.

Inventors: Roger Dev, Mark Nelson

Method for determining a best path between two nodes

US Patent 5,521,910
May 28, 1996

A method for determining a best path from a source node to a destination node using a breadth first recursive search in parallel. The determination is based upon a plurality of metrics which are set by the system. A path's metrics are compared to respective threshold values and paths are discarded if the metrics values do not each exceed respective thresholds. In addition, if a path has no metric which is better than one of the already completed paths, the path is discarded.

Inventor: Wallace Matthews

Network management system using model-based intelligence

US Patent 5,504,921
April 2, 1996

A network management system includes a user interface, a virtual network and a device communication manager. The virtual network includes models which represent network entities and model relations which represent relations between network entities. Each model includes network data relating to a corresponding network entity and one or more inference handlers for processing the network data to provide user information. The system performs a fault isolation technique wherein the fault status of a network device is suppressed when it is determined that the device is not defective. User displays include hierarchical location views and topological views of the network configuration. Network devices are represented on the displays by multifunction icons which permit the user to select additional displays showing detailed information regarding different aspects of the corresponding network device.

Inventors: Roger Dev, Dale Emery, Eric Rustici, Howard Brown, Dwayne Wiggin, Eric Gray, Walter Scott

---

Network management system using status suppression to isolate network faults

US Patent 5,436,909
July 25, 1995

A network management system includes a user interface, a virtual network and a device communication manager. The virtual network includes models which represent network entities and model relations which represent relations between network entities. Each model includes network data relating to a corresponding network entity and one or more inference handlers for processing the network data to provide user information. The system performs a fault isolation technique wherein the fault status of a network device is suppressed when it is determined that the device is not defective. User displays include hierarchical location views and topological views of the network configuration. Network devices are represented on the displays by multifunction icons which permit the user to select additional displays showing detailed information regarding different aspects of the corresponding network device.

Inventors: Roger Dev, Howard Brown, Eric Rustici

Network management system using interconnected hierarchies to represent different network dimensions in multiple display views

US Patent 5,295,244
March 15, 1994

A network management system includes a user interface, a virtual network and a device communication manager. The virtual network includes models which represent network entities and model relations which represent relations between network entities. Each model includes network data relating to a corresponding network entity and one or more inference handlers for processing the network data to provide user information. The system performs a fault isolation technique wherein the fault status of a network device is suppressed when it is determined that the device is not defective. User displays include hierarchical location views and topological views of the network configuration. Network devices are represented on the displays by multifunction icons which permit the user to select additional displays showing detailed information regarding different aspects of the corresponding network device.

Inventors: Roger Dev, Dale Emery, Eric Rustici, Walter Scott, Dwayne Wiggin

Network management system using multifunction icons for information display

US Patent 5,261,044
November 9, 1993

A network management system includes a user interface, a virtual network and a device communication manager. The virtual network includes models which represent network entities and model relations which represent relations between network entities. Each model includes network data relating to a corresponding network device and one or more inference handlers for processing the network data to provide user information. The system performs a fault isolation technique wherein the fault status of a network device is suppressed when it is determined that the device is not defective. User displays include hierarchical location views and topological views of the network configuration. Network devices are represented on the displays by multifunction icons which permit the user to select additional displays showing detailed information regarding different aspects of the corresponding network device.

Inventors: Roger Dev, Eric Gray, Eric Rustici, Walter Scott

About the Author

Lundy Lewis is Director of Research at Aprisma Management Technologies. He holds some dozen patents in network management and serves on the architectural board for the Spectrum Management System. He worked on the engineering team that built the first version of Spectrum in 1990.

Lundy publishes in the professional literature and frequently gives presentations and tutorials at IEEE/IETF conferences. His first book, *Managing Computer Networks: A Case-Based Reasoning Approach* was published by Artech House in 1995. His second book, *Service Level Management for Enterprise Networks,* was published by Artech House in 1999.

Lundy is an adjunct professor at the University of New Hampshire and New Hampshire College, where he teaches graduate level courses in Artificial Intelligence, Computer Information Systems, Object-Oriented Methodology, and Software Engineering. He received the Ph.D. in Philosophy from the University of Georgia, the MS in Computer Science from Renssalaer Polytechnic Institute, and BS in Mathematics and BA in Philosophy from the University of South Carolina. He is a member of IEEE, ACM, and AAAI.

Acronyms

3G	3rd Generation
AAAI	American Association for Artificial Intelligence
ACM	Association of Computing Machinery
AI	Artificial Intelligence
AN	AlarmNotifier
API	Application Programming Interface
ASCII	American Standard Code for Information Interchange
ATTG	Automatic Trouble Ticket Generation
ATM	Asynchronous Transfer Mode
BP	Business Process
CalREN	California Research and Education Network
CBR	Case-Based Reasoning
CDO	Central Data Office
CI	Contextual Inquiry
CIM	Common Information Model
CIO	Chief Information Officer
CLEC	Competitive Local Exchange Carrier
CLI	Command Line Interface
CMIP	Common Management Information Protocol
CMIS	Common Management Information Services
CNOC	Central Network Operations Center
CORBA	Common Object Request Broker Architecture
CPU	Central Processing Unit
CV	CAMVision
DB	Database
DE	Delivery Equipment
D-LEC	Data Competitive Local Exchange Carrier
DNS	Domain Name Service
DoS	Denial of Service
DWDM	Dense Wavelength Division Multiplexing
EMS	Enterprise Management System (in context)
EMS	Element Management System (in context)
FCAPS	Fault, Configuration, Accounting, Performance, and Security
FCC	Federal Communications Commission
FCP	Fault, Configuration, and Performance
FR	Functional Resources
FSN	Full Service Network

FTDC	Fault Tolerant Data Center
FTP	File Transfer Protocol
GUI	Graphical User Interface
HTTP	Hyper Text Transfer Protocol
IDC	Internet Data Center
IDL	Interface Definition Language
IEEE	Institute of Electrical and Electronics Engineers
IFIP	International Federation for Information Processing
ILEC	Incumbent Local Exchange Carrier
IM	Integrated Management
I/O	Input/Output
IP	Internet Protocol
ISINM	International Symposium on Integrated Network Management
ISP	Internet Service Provider
IT	Information Technology
ITU-T	International Telecommunications Union – Telecommunications
JNSM	Journal of Network and Systems Management
LAN	Local Area Network
LEC	Local Exchange Carrier
LER	Labeling Edge Routers
LSP	Labeled Switch Path
MA	Management Application
MAC	Media Access Control
MAN	Metropolitan Area Network
MBR	Model-Based Reasoning
MCNC	(not an acronym)
MIB	Management Information Base
MIT	Management Information Tree
MOM	Manager of Managers
MPEG	Moving Picture Experts Group
MPLS	Multiprotocol Label Switching
NAT	Network Address Translation
NC	North Carolina
NCNI	North Carolina Network Initiative
NCREN	North Carolina Research and Education Network
NCSU	North Carolina State University
NGI	Next Generation Internet
NOC	Network Operations Center
NOMS	Network Operations and Management Symposium
NT	New Technology
OC	Optical Carrier
OM	Outsource Management

OOP	Object-oriented Paradigm
OOSE	Object-oriented Software Engineering
OSI	Open System Interconnection
PAP	Performance Assurance Plan
PBX	Private Branch Exchange
PC	Personal Computer
PEI	Platform External Interface
PLEC	Packet-based Local Exchange Carrier
PoP	Point of Presence
POP	Post Office Protocol
PSN	Protected Services Network
QoS	Quality of Service
RBOC	Regional Bell Operating Company
RBR	Rule-Based Reasoning
R&D	Research and Development
RDC	Regional Data Center
RFC	Request for Comments
RMON	Remote Monitoring
RNOC	Regional Network Operations Center
RSVP	Resource Reservation Setup Protocol
RTP	Research Triangle Park
RTM	Response Time Management
SAM	Specific Application Management
SDH	Synchronous Digital Hierarchy
SE	Software Engineering
SG	SpectroGRAPH
SLA	Service Level Agreement
SLM	Service Level Management
SLR	Service Level Report
SMARTS	System Management Arts
SMTP	Simple Mail Transfer Protocol
SNMP	Simple Network Management Protocol
SONET	Synchronous Optical Network
SS	SpectroSERVER
SSAPI	SpectroSERVER Application Programming Interface
STG	State Transition Graph
TCP	Transmission Control Protocol
TELCOT	Institute for Telecommunication Technologies
TINA	Telecommunications Information Networking Architecture
TL1	Transaction Language 1
TMN	Telecommunications Management Network
TT	Trouble Ticket

UDP	User Datagram Protocol
UML	Unified Modeling Language
UNC	University of North Carolina
UNE	Unbundled Network Element
UNIX	(not an acronym)
URL	Uniform Resource Locator
US	United States
USA	United States of America
vBNS	Very High-speed Backbone Network Service
VoIP	Voice Over IP
VPN	Virtual Private Network
WAN	Wide Area Network
WDM	Wavelength Division Multiplexing
WWW	World Wide Web
XML	Extended Mark-up Language

Index